Lockheed M
F/A-22 Raptor

Stealth Fighter

Jay Miller

An imprint of
Ian Allan Publishing

Lockheed Martin F/A-22 Raptor:
Stealth Fighter
© 2005 Jay Miller

ISBN 1 85780 158 X

Published by Midland Publishing
4 Watling Drive, Hinckley, LE10 3EY, England
Tel: 01455 254 490   Fax: 01455 254 495
E-mail: midlandbooks@compuserve.com

Midland Publishing and Aerofax are imprints of
Ian Allan Publishing Ltd

Worldwide distribution (except North America):
Midland Counties Publications
4 Watling Drive, Hinckley, LE10 3EY, England
Telephone: 01455 254 450   Fax: 01455 233 737
E-mail: midlandbooks@compuserve.com
www.midlandcountiessuperstore.com

North American trade distribution:
Specialty Press Publishers & Wholesalers Inc.
39966 Grand Avenue, North Branch, MN 55056
Tel: 651 277 1400   Fax: 651 277 1203
Toll free telephone: 800 895 4585
www.specialtypress.com

Design and concept
© 2005 Midland Publishing and
Stephen Thompson Associates
Layout by Jay Miller

Printed in England by Ian Allan Printing Ltd
Riverdene Business Park, Molesey Road,
Hersham, Surrey, KT12 4RG

Contents

Title page: **Flares are dispensed from units
positioned just aft of the main landing gear
wells.** Lockheed Martin

Below: **The second EMD F/A-22A, 91-002,
launches an AIM-9M during a trial over the
Edwards AFB test range.** Lockheed Martin

Facing page top: **F/A-22A, 01-4021, assigned to
Tyndall AFB, over the Gulf of Mexico during
January of 2005.** John Dibbs/*Plane Picture Company*

Facing page bottom: **Three F/A-22As (00-4012,
00-4013, and 00-4015) at Nellis AFB, Nevada,
during March of 2004.** Jay Miller

Introduction

Today's air-to-air and air-to-ground combat environments are the most complex, sophisticated, and technologically challenging in history. They represent a domain fraught with ever-escalating capability requirements, astronomical cost issues, and a realization that pilots have reached the zenith of their physical limits in the cockpit.

Lockheed Martin's F/A-22A Raptor represents arguably the most concerted effort to date to address the entire spectrum of pressing contemporary air combat issues in a single, multi-disciplined platform. It is, quite literally, a "jack of all trades" aircraft designed to tackle and defeat every conceivable aerial combatant operating in the most saturated and complex electronic warfare environment in history.

Concurrently, the F/A-22A is also now being groomed to deliver stealthy air-to-ground weapons that, if they work, will be among the most accurate and – when nuclear tipped – the most lethal the world has ever known.

When all of these disciplines are wrapped in a shell that not only provides high aerodynamic efficiency and strength with the attributes of an all-but-invisible electromagnetic target, the resulting fighter/bomber is – on paper at least – without peer in the world. Such capability places enormous emphasis – and pressure – on the F/A-22A's technological core and the multiple systems, sub-systems, and weapons that must seamlessly interface to make it into the super fighter Lockheed Martin's designers and builders, and the Air Force, hope it will become.

All of this, it is understood, comes at a very high price, not only in real dollar costs, but also in the less tangible values that define reliability, maintainability, and affordability. As a result, the F/A-22A retains an extremely high public profile and is, consequently, a highly contentious budgetary and political target. As these words are written, the congressional battles that will determine its production quantities and production longevity are far from over.

Even by US standards, the F/A-22A is a monumentally expensive aircraft. Unit cost figures vary considerably, depending on bias and source, but even the Air Force and Lockheed Martin readily acknowledge numbers approaching $200 million. Concurrently, dispassionate federal agencies, including several congres-

sional and Department of Defense budget offices, tout figures closer to $250 million.

And not surprisingly, total program costs continue to rise. To date, they have increased by no less than 127 percent since development officially started during 1986...and the total F/A-22A program price tag as these words are written is now approaching $80 billion. It is predicted to grow beyond those numbers long before the F/A-22A is pulled from the operational inventory.

No matter which dollar figures prove definitive, the F/A-22A is a high-priced Air Force asset that has many significant credibility issues needing resolution. No one yet knows for certain whether its costs are justifiable in terms of its many combat capability claims.

As budget pressures mount and other military aircraft programs gather momentum, critical eyes are continuing to assess whether the F/A-22A's cost-to-value ratio is reasonable...and if its significant expense is merited. Concur-

rently, these same analysts are trying to determine whether there is a threat now in the air or on the horizon that warrants all of the F/A-22A's technological wizardry.

Regardless, by all accounts to date, the F/A-22A is arguably the most capable manned air combat platform that has ever been flown. Based on pilot reports and published capability summaries, the F/A-22A far supersedes its very-capable – but rapidly aging – predecessors, the Grumman F-14, the Boeing F-15, the Lockheed Martin F-16, and the Boeing F/A-18. It is claimed particularly superior in the maneuverability, cruise performance, electronic warfare, weaponry, and radar-cross-section arenas.

No airplane in history has ever been designed from scratch to offer the F/A-22A's combination of armament lethality, electronic interfacing, and supersonic cruise performance in such an electromagnetically transparent and stealthy package. It remains to be seen whether such impressive and for-

ward-thinking technology is within the budget constraints of current and forthcoming US administrations...or whether such extraordinary capability is even needed.

This monograph represents a detailed summary of the F/A-22A program to date.

Acknowledgements
During 1992, I was privileged to team with the director of flight test for Lockheed Martin's YF-22A team, Richard "Dick" Abrams, while co-authoring a brief monograph describing that prototype aircraft's development and abbreviated flight test program. Unfortunately, Dick's premature demise not long after the book was published prevented a program update that was expected to follow. Now, some thirteen years later, I have elected to move ahead with the project on my own. Dick's contributions have not been forgotten, however, and I hope that this new F/A-22A history will serve as a respectable follow-on to the work that he and I undertook so long ago.

When the first iteration of this history was published, Jeff Rhodes, then a junior member of the public relations staff at Lockheed Martin

Top: **F/A-22A, 00-4012 at Nellis AFB, Nevada during March 2004. Red intake plugs bear "67th AMXS F/A-22" logo.** Jay Miller

Left: **F/A-22A, 99-4010, is assigned to OT&E unit at Edwards AFB.** AF

Facing Page Top: **An Edwards OT&E F/A-22A.** Katsuhiko Tokunaga

Facing Page Bottom: **Unpainted F/A-22A, 01-4020, on final to Marietta, Georgia.** John Wilhoff

Aeronautical Systems (LMAS) Marietta, Georgia facility, was kind enough to take me under his wing and guide me through the vicissitudes of a burgeoning fighter program that – he and other Lockheed Martin employees hoped – would result in the most effective air combat platform ever to reach the full-scale hardware, production, and operational service stage. Along with Dick Abrams, Jeff was instrumental in bringing that first YF-22A book to fruition.

Much water has passed under the bridge since, but Jeff is still with Lockheed Martin and he remains deeply enmeshed in the F/A-22A program. Most importantly, he's still a good friend. And once again, he has been critical to bringing this current history to press. Jeff's efforts resulted in the release of photos and miscellaneous details that, to all intents and purposes, appear in this book for the first time

Also, Eric Hehs – with Lockheed Martin Tactical Aeronautical Systems (LMTAS) Fort Worth, Texas division and editor-in-chief of the company's truly superb *Code One Magazine* – can take credit for helping create the monograph you now are holding in your hands.

Without Jeff's and Eric's help, cajoling, and friendship, this book quite simply would never have been possible. To the two of them, I owe a special debt of thanks.

Of course there have been many others who made significant and greatly appreciated contributions either directly or indirectly to this F/A-22A history. They include at Lockheed Martin Fort Worth, Texas: Tom Blakeney, Mike Moore, Dave Russell, James Sergeant, and Joe Stout.

And at Lockheed Martin Marietta, Georgia: Terry Beyer, Greg Caires, Mike Delauder, Rob Fuller, John Hickman, Frank Knowles, Jr., John Pieper, Bob Prester, Dick Martin, John Rossino, and Bob Tuttle.

Special thanks also to the Lockheed Martin photographic team including Judson Brohmer (deceased) and his wife Alesandra, Denny Lombard, Kevin Robertson, and Eric Schulzinger.

I would also like to point out the contributions made by David Aronstein, Michael Hirschberg, and Albert Piccirillo...whose book, *Advanced Tactical Fighter to F-22 Raptor, Origins of the 21st Century Air Dominance Fighter* (*American Institute of Aeronautics and Astronautics*, 1998), was an excellent information resource. This book is highly recommended reading for anyone interested in a definitive insight into the early developmental history of the F/A-22.

Other contributors include: Richard Abulafia of Teal Group, Guy Aceto of *Air Force Magazine*, Ted Black, Don Carson of Pratt & Whitney, Buster Cleveland, Tom Copeland, Kevin Coyne, Jim Evans, Susan Ferns of AF Public Affairs, Wright-Patterson AFB, Paul Gladman of *Flight International*, James Goodall, Ed Jobin of Goodrich, Dana Johnson of Texas Instruments, Dianne Knippel of Lockheed Martin Aeronautics Palmdale, Tony Landis (special thanks for F/A-22A drawings), Sherman Mullin (ret. from LMTAS Palmdale [YF-22A and F/A-22A Program Manager from 1986 to 1991 and President of the Lockheed Advanced Development Company]), Terry Panopalis, Ed Phillips, "Chick" Ramey of Boeing, Mick Roth, Erik Simonsen of Boeing, Richard Stadler (ret. from LADC), James Stevenson, Bill Sweetman, Laurie Tardif of Pratt & Whitney, John Wilhoff, and Chris Woodul.

Most importantly, I'd like to say thanks, once again, to my wonderfully patient wife, best friend, and part-time foot-warmer, Susan. Nothing I've done for the past thirty-one years could have happened without her never-ending encouragement and support.

Jay Miller
January, 2005

Acronyms and Abbreviations

AAA	anti-aircraft artillery
ABI	avionics bus interface
ACC	Air Combat Command
ACEMA	Advanced Counterair Engagement Mission Analysis
ACES	Advanced Concept Ejection Seat
AF	Air Force
AFB	Air Force Base
AFE	Advanced Fighter Engine
AFFDL	Air Force Flight Dynamics Laboratory
AFFTC	Air Force Flight Test Center
AFL	Avionics Flying Laboratory
AFOTEC	Air Force Operational Test and Evaluation Center
AFSC	Air Force Systems Command
AFTI	Advanced Fighter Technology Integration
AGIR	avionics ground prototype
AIL	Avionics Integration Laboratory
AIM	air intercept missile
AMRAAM	Advanced Medium-Range Air-to-Air Missile
ANT	accelerated mission testing
AoA	angle of attack
ARDC	Air Research and Development Command
ASD	Aeronautical Systems Division
ATASMA	Advanced Tactical Attack System Mission Analysis
ATF	Advanced Tactical Fighter
ATS	air-to-surface
AVEL	AMRAAM Vertical Eject Launcher
BMI	bismaleimide
BVR	beyond visual range
CAP	Combat Air Patrol
CAS/BI	Close Air Support/Battlefield Integration
CATIA	Computer-Aided Three-Dimensional Interactive Application
CATS	common automatic test systems
CBWFM	constant bandwidth frequency modulation
CDR	Critical Design Review
CFD	computational fluid dynamics
CIP	common integrated processor
CNI	communications, navigation, and identification
CRT	cathode ray tube
CTF	Combined Test Force
DAB	Defense Acquisition Board
Dem/Val	Demonstration/Validation
DIOT&E	Dedicated Initial Operational Test & Evaluation
DLT&E	Dedicated Logistics Testing and Evaluation
DPE	data processing element
DTU	data transfer unit
DU	display unit
ECU	engine control unit
EMD	Engineering and Manufacturing Development
EOA	Early Operational Assessment
ESA	electronically scanned array
FADEC	full-authority digital engine control
FLCC	flight control computer
FNIU	fiber network interface unit
FOBC	fiber optic bus components
FOG	finger on glass
FSD	Full-Scale Development
FTB	Flying Test Bed
FTDC	Flight Test Data Center
GPVI	graphics processor video interface
HOTAS	hands-on throttle and stick
HUD	head-up display
Hz	Hertz
IFDL	Intraflight Datalink
IFF	identification friend or foe
FPC	integrated flight propulsion control
INEWS	integrated electronic warfare systems
INS	inertial navigation system
INT	intermediate thrust
I/O	input/output
IOC	Initial Operational Capability
IOT&E	Initial Operational Test and Evaluation
IPT	Integrated Product Team
IRST	infrared search and track
ISA	instruction set architecture
IVSC	integrated vehicle subsystem control
JAFE	Joint Advanced Fighter Engine
JDAM	Joint Direct Attack Munition
JIAWG	Joint Integrated Avionics Working Group
KEAS	knots equivalent air speed
lb./lbs.	pound/pounds
LCC	life cycle cost
LCD	liquid crystal display
LRIP	Low Rate Initial Production
LRU	line replaceable unit
MASE	Multi-Axis Seat Ejection
MDP	mission display processor
MENS	Mission Element Needs Statement
MFD	multi-function display
MIVIC	metal-matrix composites
MPE	mission planning equipment
MTBAA	Meantime Between Avionics Anomaly
MTBIE	Meantime Between Instability Events
MWS	missile warning system
NATF	Navy Advanced Tactical Fighter
OASMA	Offensive Air Support Mission Analysis
OBIGGS	on-board inert gas generation system
OBOGS	on-board oxygen generation system
OFP	operational flight program
OT&E	Operational Test and Evaluation
PADS	pneumatic air data system
PAV	prototype air vehicle
PCM	pulse code modulation
PFRT	preliminary flight rating tests
PI	parallel interface
PMD	Program Management Directive
PMFD	primary multifunction display
PPV	Pre-Production Verification
PRTV	Production Representative Test Vehicles
RAM	radar absorbent material
RCS	radar cross section
REU	remote electronics unit
RFI	request for information
RFP	request for proposal
RISC	reduced instruction set computer
RMCC	Ridley Mission Control Center
SEAD	Suppression of Enemy air Defenses
SEM	Standard Electronics Model
SFG	standby flight group
SMFD	secondary multifunction display
SMS	Stores Management System
SPO	System Program Office
Sq	Squadron
SRB	Safety Review Board
SRC	spin recovery chute
SSD	subsystem display
SISEE	systems/software engineering environment
STOL	Short Takeoff and Landing
STOVL	Short Takeoff and Vertical Landing
TAC	Tactical Air Command
TAFTA	Tactical Fighter Technology Alternatives
th.	thrust
TIS	Test Information Sheets
TLSS	tactical life support system
TM	telemetry
TM	test maintenance
TRB	Technical Review Board
TV	thrust vectoring
UART	Universal Asynchronous Receiver/Transmitter
UFC	Unit Flyaway Cost
USAF	United States Air Force
VMS	Vehicle Management System

Chapter One

The Most Advanced Fighter in the World

Lockheed Martin's F/A-22A Raptor is scheduled to become the primary US Air Force air superiority fighter of the twenty-first century. It is anticipated that it will retain this role from its planned initial operational capability (IOC) during late 2005 through what is expected to be the end of its operational life cycle during 2025. It has been designed to provide air dominance at any time and in any place...and in any type of conflict and against any adversary.

Additionally, the F/A-22A, in concert with the Northrop Grumman B-2A, the Lockheed Martin F-117A, and other "stealthy" combat aircraft, is scheduled to serve as a key player in a low-observables fighter and bomber package designed to "break through initial access challenges in a warfighting region." Concurrently, the F/A-22A, configured at least in part for an air-to-surface role, will be used to clear the skies of enemy fighters and cruise missiles while disabling or destroying surface-to-air

missile threats to less-capable types such as the Lockheed Martin F-16, the Boeing F-15, the Fairchild A-10, and the Boeing F/A-18.

Such capability and lofty claims are not made lightly by the AF. Confidence lies in the fact these goals are achievable as a result of a synergistic combination of characteristics and capabilities, including low-observables (stealth), the ability to cruise at supersonic speeds (supercruise) over long range and without the use of afterburners, and an integrated and highly sophisticated avionics suite.

Additionally, the F/A-22A has been designed to be more maneuverable, better armed, more reliable, more easily maintained, more readily supportable, and more capable in the air-to-

ground mission than any other comparable aircraft in history.

Brig. Gen. Larry New, a former 325th Fighter Wing commander, in a recent interview noted, "The Raptor brings on the new generation of applying technology to war fighting, putting our aircraft two generations ahead of any threat and removing us from our current status of weapons system parity. Raptor technology combined with realistic training will provide air dominance, under which all other military actions become possible."

The requirement for a new air superiority fighter, simply acronymed ATF (Advanced Tactical Fighter; it was also referred to temporarily as the Advanced Offensive Strike Fighter), first

Facing Page: Three Edwards AFB EMD F/A-22As – '005, '007, and '002 – refueling from Boeing KC-135R, 59-1464, during a test sortie over the base's test range. Lockheed Martin

Top (and inset): **One of numerous tailless configuration ATF wind tunnel studies leading up to the definite F/A-22A configuration.** Lockheed Martin

Right: **Truncated delta ATF tunnel model with unusual vertical tail configuration optimized for reduced radar cross-section.** Lockheed Martin

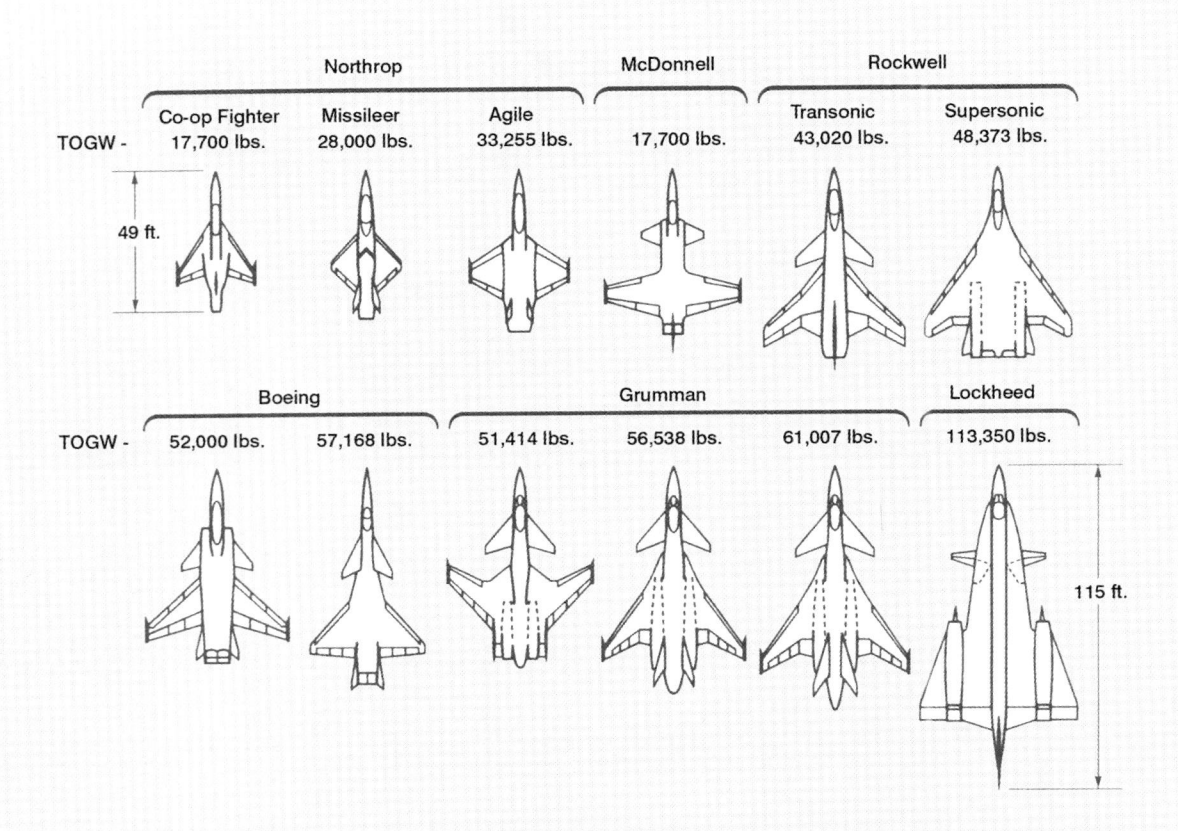

Northrop — Co-op Fighter 17,700 lbs., Missileer 28,000 lbs., Agile 33,255 lbs.
McDonnell — 17,700 lbs.
Rockwell — Transonic 43,020 lbs., Supersonic 48,373 lbs.
TOGW - 49 ft.

Boeing — 52,000 lbs., 57,168 lbs.
Grumman — 51,414 lbs., 56,538 lbs., 61,007 lbs.
Lockheed — 113,350 lbs.
TOGW - 115 ft.

RFI Design Concepts Sized for Air-to-Air Missions

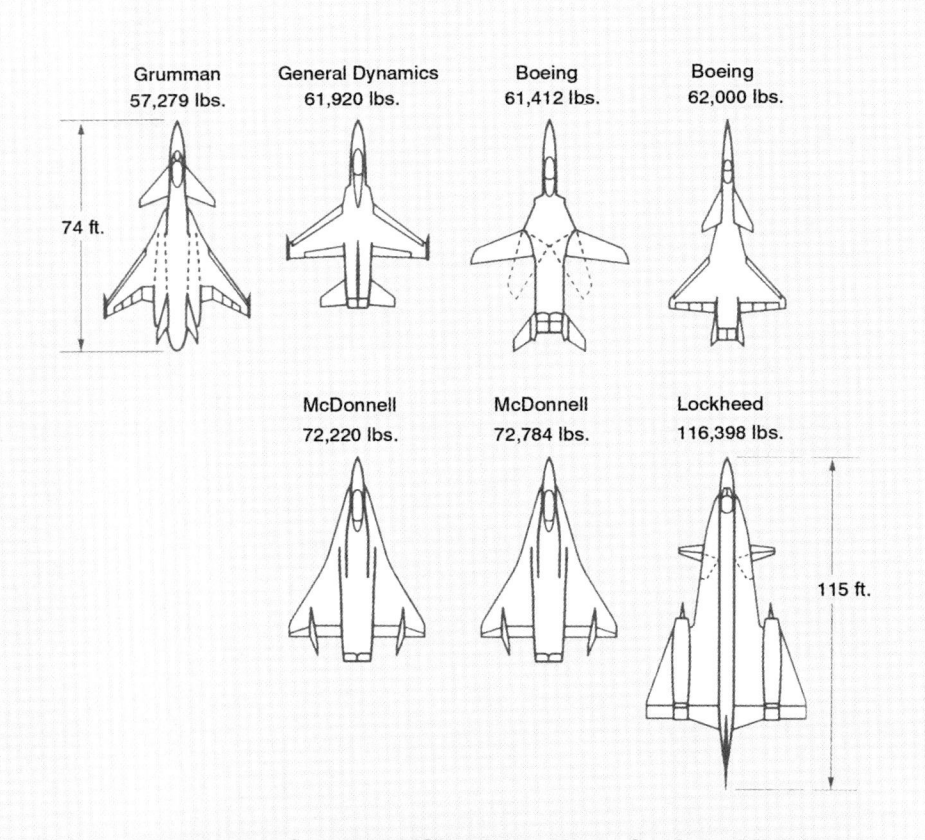

Grumman 57,279 lbs.
General Dynamics 61,920 lbs.
Boeing 61,412 lbs.
Boeing 62,000 lbs.
74 ft.

McDonnell 72,220 lbs.
McDonnell 72,784 lbs.
Lockheed 116,398 lbs.
115 ft.

RFI Design Concepts Sized for Air-to-Surface Missions

via David Aronstein, Michael Hirschberg, and Albert Piccirillo

surfaced under AF auspices during 1969 and 1970 as part of the *US Air Force Tactical Forces 1985 Study* (TAC-85). As conceived, the new fighter's primary mission was air-to-surface strike; air-to-air capability was to be reserved only for self-defense. It was to replace the McDonnell F-4, the Republic F-105, and the General Dynamics F-111.

During April and June of 1971, representatives from the Tactical Air Command (TAC), AF Headquarters, the AF Systems Command (AFSC), the Aeronautical Systems Division (ASD), and Analytic Services, Inc. met to ascertain the ATF's direction.

The AFSC then tasked the ASD with obtaining preliminary design trade-off analysis information and at the same time requested that it solicit input from the US aircraft industry. During November of 1971, eight aircraft companies submitted proposals to perform the study. Eventually, two $200,000 contracts were awarded, one to General Dynamics and one to McDonnell Douglas.

On January 26, 1973, the first formal ATF requirements document, TAC ROC 301-73, was issued in draft form. Calling for a high-subsonic-speed-capable aircraft operating at medium altitudes, it was circulated to ASD, the Air Staff, and other Air Force agencies. The response to the initial draft proved inconclusive.

While the various AF offices continued to review the broad spectrum of ATF options, the AF Flight Dynamics Laboratory, during 1973, initiated the Advanced Fighter Technology Integration (AFTI) program. AFTI resulted in a number of studies, wind tunnel models, and radio control models specifically optimized to explore new technologies applicable to forthcoming "future aircraft". Though not directly tied to the ATF, fall-out from AFTI had considerable influence over the final ATF configuration and flight envelope.

Over the following decade the ATF umbrella was used by the AF to explore a broad spectrum of platforms, configurations, missions, and capabilities. Much of this was accommodated under revisions to the original (ROC) 301-73 document and a series of other studies as follows:

1974 – Air-to-Surface (ATS) Technology Integration and Evaluation Studies

1975 – Close Air Support Mission Analysis

1976 – Close Air Support/Battlefield Interdiction (CAS/BI) Mission Analysis

1976 – Offensive Air Support Mission Analysis (OASMA)

1976/1977 – Strike System Study (S³)

1978 – S³ was absorbed into a two-part effort: Enhanced Tactical Fighter and Advanced Tactical Attack System; together they were referred to as the ITAS (Improved Tactical Attack System).

1979 – Tactical Fighter Technology Alternatives (TAFTA...a follow-on to the ATS noted previously) and the "1995 Fighter Study" (both were actually completed during mid-1981).

Further studies continued under a variety of venues and titles, not the least of which was the Advanced Counterair Engagement Mission Analysis (ACEMA) required to support the Mission Element Need Statement (MENS). Among the questions posed by the latter were:
• What kind of fighter should be developed?
• What will the dominant need be in 1995?
• What can technology support?
• What is affordable?

In turn, ACEMA and MENS were followed by the Advanced Tactical Attack System Mission Analysis (ATASMA) which served to assess TACAIR's air-to-surface deficiencies and to identify and evaluate technology potential, operating concepts, and generic alternatives to meet those deficiencies.

It was not until 1980 that air-to-air was explored for the first time as part of the ATF's mission package. By April of 1980, a new Program Management Directive (PMD) for Combat Aircraft Technology – R-Q 7036(4)/63230F – was issued, reorienting the ATF program and forcing it to focus on the development of core concepts while concurrently proving technology for the next generation tactical fighter. Slowly but surely, "air dominance" was becoming the driving force behind the proposed new fighter.

Options resulting from the various studies had included an air-to-ground strike fighter, an air-superiority fighter, separate aircraft optimized specifically for the ground attack or

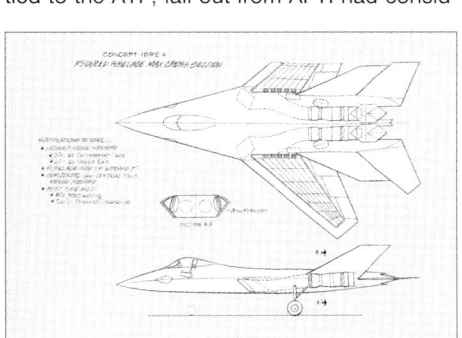
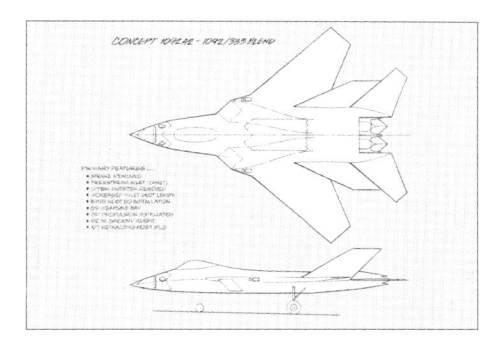
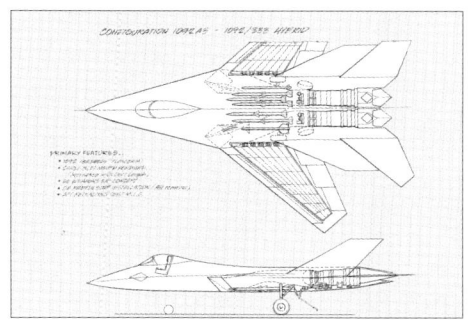

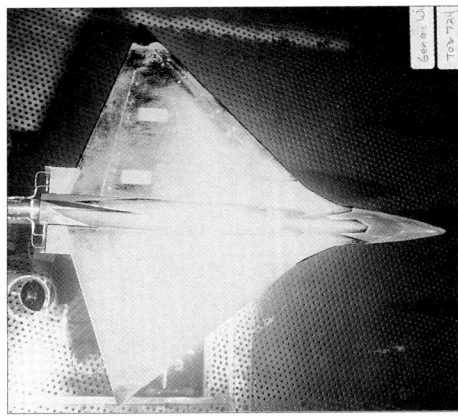

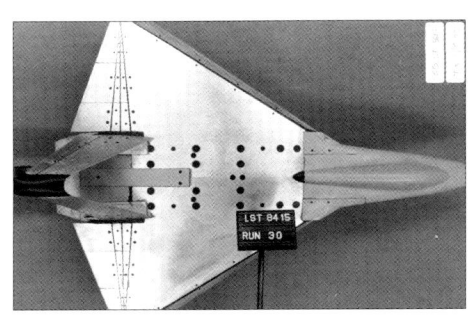

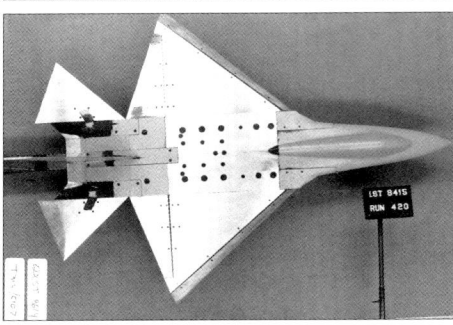

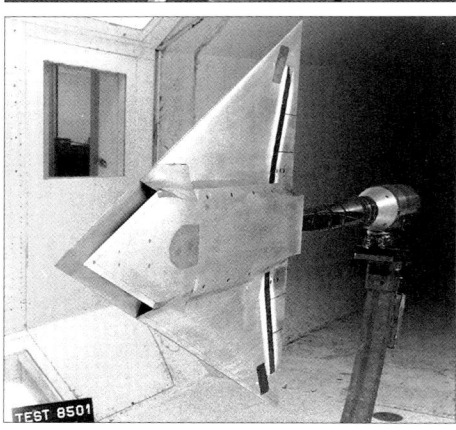

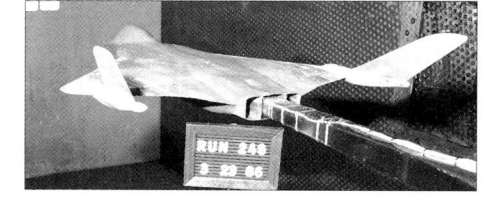

fighter missions, or a single aircraft that could essentially do everything.

On May 21, 1981, a Request for Information (RFI) for the ATF was issued to nine companies: Boeing, Fairchild, General Dynamics, Grumman, Lockheed, McDonnell Douglas, Northrop, Rockwell International, and Vought. They were asked to submit conceptual designs and to prepare position papers on a variety of technical operational issues which would be identified by the government. Technology content was to be consistent with an IOC during the early to mid-1990s. Cost estimates were to be based on possible production runs of 120, 500, or 1,000 aircraft.

The following month, an ATF engine RFI was released. It called for supersonic persistence without afterburner (supercruise), short takeoff and landing (STOL) distances of 1,500 feet, the integration of low-observables technology, a reduced cost of ownership, and a targeted system IOC of 1993.

The RFI process was initially expected to take nine months, with mid-term and final reports to be provided by the aircraft manufacturers. Government review would then be fed back to the companies no later than sixty days following receipt of the reports.

Though the RFI initially gave equal emphasis to the air-to-air and air-to-surface missions, by 1982, the air superiority mission had become the ATF's primary assignment. This shift was the result of a conclusion that an air-to-ground aircraft could not necessarily do what an air-to-air aircraft could do...but an air-to-air aircraft could easily do what an air-to-ground aircraft could do.

Concurrently, and perhaps most importantly, reconnaissance satellites had photographed several new fighter prototypes (the MiG-29 [Mikoyan Product 9-01] and Sukhoi Su-27 [T-10]) at the Ramenskoye flight test center outside of the small city of Zhukovsky (about 40 miles southeast of Moscow). This new generation of Russian fighters represented a significant improvement in capability over anything previously observed by US intelligence services.

It was obvious to all concerned that a new air-to-air combat platform would be required to counter the threat these new Russian aircraft represented. A paradigm shift in the new fighter's mission that had begun in late 1979 now took on a serious air of urgency. From this point forward, the ATF's air-to-air capability would be considered on equal footing with its air-to-surface capability.

This and facing page: **The large number of Lockheed Martin ATF tunnel models and the variations thereof is represented in small part by all the various configurations seen on these two pages. These models were constructed primarily of steel for high-speed work. For a design to have progressed to this point (a very expensive process), indicates it was at one time or another a reasonably serious contender.**
Lockheed Martin

On November 23, 1981, the ATF was given Milestone Zero approval and thus cleared to become a formal weapon system acquisition program (this officially moved the ATF program into "Phase O," or the concept exploration stage). Unfortunately, the following year, funding was temporarily denied – delaying the initiation of concept definition activities – but it was reinstated for FY83.

By now, many new technologies applicable to fighter design had begun to reach appropriate maturity in areas that included composite materials and lightweight alloys, advanced flight control systems and avionics options, propulsion system upgrades, and the low observables (stealth) disciplines.

Concurrently it was projected that by the time the ATF was integrated into the operational service inventory, all front-line Air Force and Navy fighters – including the McDonnell Douglas F-15 Eagle, the General Dynamics F-16 Fighting Falcon, the Grumman F-14 Tomcat, and the McDonnell Douglas F/A-18 Hornet – would be nearing the end of their respective service lives.

Regardless, a detailed requirements definition and operational concept was developed after the November assessment. It was noted:

"...The ATF program is structured to bring air-to-surface and air-to-air aircraft options up to, but short of, engineering development. When threat-driven development decisions are required, the relatively low cost but time consuming (pre-MS II) front end of the acquisition cycle will be complete. This approach...avoids premature commitment to solving one mission area program to the exclusion of another.

"...The program is clearly threat and cost driven. Although uncertainty exists about the future threat, we must be technologically ready when a threat-driven development decision is required. Also, we must be fully aware of the cost trade-offs and we must know what must be given up to purchase each additional increment of capability. The program is structured to answer these questions."

At the same time, a set of milestones was created that would serve as a program evolution template for the future: Full Scale Development (FSD) would start during 1987 and IOC would take place during 1993 or 1994. Additionally, no matter whether the final aircraft was a strike aircraft or an air superiority fighter, both would draw from the same set of emerging technologies and both would operate from the same set of (possibly damaged) bases into a very high threat environment. These issues would, in fact, eventually prove significant drivers when it came time to solidify the ATF's actual design parameters.

Though the primary threat to the US in 1980 was the Warsaw Pact in Europe, it is interesting to note that the ATF was expected to have long range to operate effectively in other global hot spots...most notably the Middle East.

Though many of the responses to the RFI had envisaged multi-role aircraft, the resulting document focused on a clear need for an air

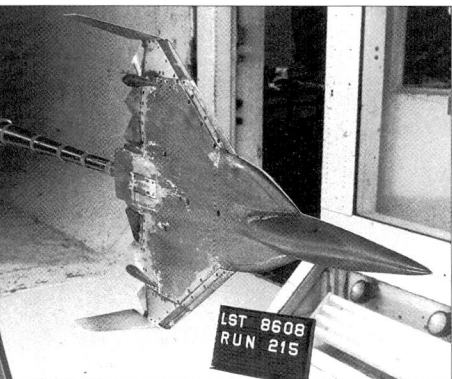

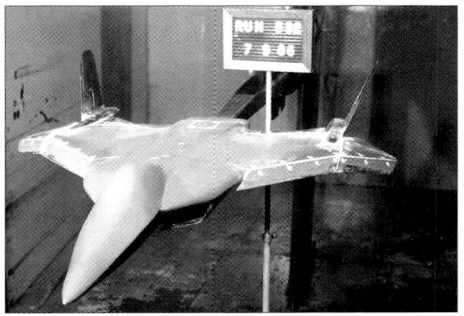

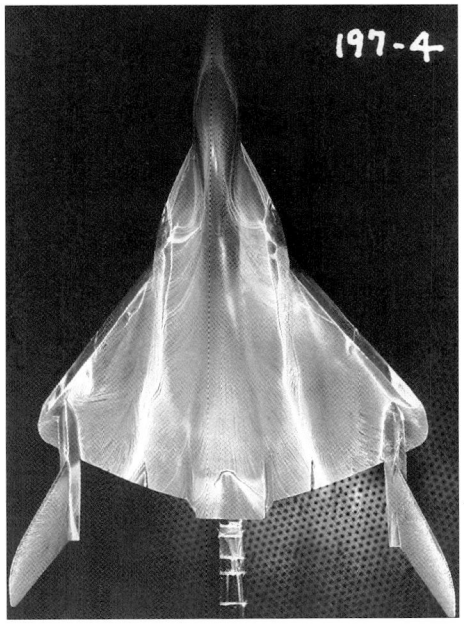

superiority fighter specifically designed to replace the McDonnell Douglas (now Boeing) F-15...and consequently to be capable of countering the sophisticated threats projected to exist during the early years of the next century.

On August 24, 1982, a PMD was released, this changing the name of the program element from Combat Aircraft Technology, to Advanced Tactical Fighter. Concurrently, two sub-projects were established under this banner: the Advanced Tactical Fighter which included concept and technology development (seven airframe companies – Boeing, General Dynamics, Grumman, Lockheed, McDonnell Douglas, Northrop, and Rockwell – each received $1 million Concept Development Investigation contracts); and the Joint Fighter Engine which was an engine technology demonstration program (to be managed jointly with the US Navy; Pratt & Whitney and General Electric each received contracts valued at $202 million during September of 1983; other companies contending for the contract included Allison, Garrett, and Teledyne/CAE).

The seven competing companies submitted some nineteen conceptual designs. These ranged from Northrop's lightweight "cooperative fighter" (smaller than an F-16) to Lockheed's "battle cruiser" (based on the design of their short-lived YF-12A long range interceptor). Additionally, an in-house design – a subsonic low-observable fighter – was submitted by the Air Force's Flight Dynamics Laboratory (AFFDL).

Eventually, of the approximately 19 studies submitted, four were chosen to represent four different mission philosophies: a very light, austere, low-cost design; a supersonic cruise

This and facing page: **A variety of General Dynamics ATF studies in display model form. Features from each of these eventually were blended where appropriate and applied to the definitive General Dynamics configuration...which in turn, when the two companies merged in 1992, was eventually blended with the definitive Lockheed Martin ATF study to create the aircraft that exists today.** Jay Miller x 6

and maneuver design; a subsonic, low-observable design; and a high-Mach, high-altitude design.

From these it was concluded that the ideal air-to-air platform would offer low-observables in combination with super cruise and superior maneuverability. This platform in turn would offer reduced vulnerability to surface-to-air missiles while all but eliminating the aircraft's exposure to AAA and other short-range systems.

In order to achieve the ATF's mission and performance objectives, a variety of technological advances were considered necessary. These included higher engine thrust-to-weight ratios; supercruise capability; size considerations that would be capable of accommodating weapons, fuel, and systems while keeping within the parameters of the low-observables requirements; weapon/aircraft integration; and the development and use of composite materials. Other secondary issues included advanced radars, advanced air-to-air fire control systems; avionics integration, and avionics systems that were compatible with low-observables requirements.

The final report on the RFI, including the AF's analysis of the responses from the various industry competitors, was completed during December of 1982. By then a decision had been reached on the primary mission of the ATF.

By the end of the year, the first funding for the ATF program – $23 million – had been allocated by Congress. A "final" request for proposal (RFP) was released to industry on May 18, 1983. An engine RFP (to Allison, General Electric, and Pratt & Whitney, only) was released that same month.

By the time the RFPs were issued, low-observables...now entering the public domain and commonly known as stealth...technology had surfaced as an important driver in the ATF's design. On May 26, 1983, an amendment to the ATF RFP was issued that placed increased emphasis on low-observables characteristics.

This proved an important windfall for Lockheed and Northrop, as both companies had been exploring the attributes of low-observables in other platforms. Both had concluded it was a viable and – in the case of the ATF – timely technology.

Interestingly, concerns over the integration and application of low-observables technology into the basic ATF design were not without merit during this time. The technology was still in its infancy, and its applicability impacted all aspects of the aircraft, including, perhaps most importantly, the aerodynamic shell and items as apparently mundane as exhaust nozzle design and the configuration of the radar. The former was, in fact, a major concern, as making exhaust nozzles stealthy was a complex and at the time, arcane science. Aircraft performance was directly effected because stealthy exhaust nozzles were, historically, inefficient.

During 1983, an ATF System Program Office (SPO) was formed under the aegis of the Aeronautical Systems Division (ASD) at Wright-Patterson AFB, Ohio. Col. Albert Piccirillo was chosen to become the ATF SPO director.

During September of 1983, concept definition study contracts were awarded to the seven manufacturers capable of producing a fighter to the evolving ATF specification. By the end of 1984, following some four initial drafts, the basic framework for the ATF requirement, calling for a radius of action of approximately 800 miles, supersonic cruise capability of 1.4 to 1.5 Mach, a 2,000 ft. runway requirement, a gross takeoff weight of 50,000 lb., and a unit cost of no more than $40 million in 1985 dollars was released to industry. Importantly, implied in the proposal was a requirement that ATF Life-Cycle Cost (LCC – aircraft unit cost upon delivery plus the cost of all spares, fuel, maintenance, and flying) be at least as good as, if not better than, the McDonnell Douglas F-15.

A plan to produce 750 ATFs at a peak rate of 72 aircraft per year surfaced at this time, as well. As McDonnell Douglas F-15 production had never netted more than 42 aircraft per year,

the numbers touted for the ATF were deemed highly suspect and probably unachievable.

The CDI contracts were completed during May of 1984. Eventually, the number of contractors was reduced in a conventional elimination process and from those remaining, it was proposed that a pair of fly-off prototypes be chosen.

During September of 1985, a formal ATF RFP was released by the AF with the final submission date to be January of 1986. The RFP was approved on October 7, 1985 and copies were delivered to the seven airframe contractors the following day. Differing little from the prototype drafts, it did lower the figure for the maximum unit cost from $40 million to $35 million, based on a buy of 750 aircraft at a total program cost (including full-scale development – or what was soon to be referred to as Engineering and Manufacturing Development [EMD]) of $65 billion. The tight January deadline later was extended to April. Concurrently, the Navy, under severe pressure from Congress, announced it would consider accepting a navalized ATF (NATF) as a Grumman F-14 replacement – by the end of the 1990s decade.

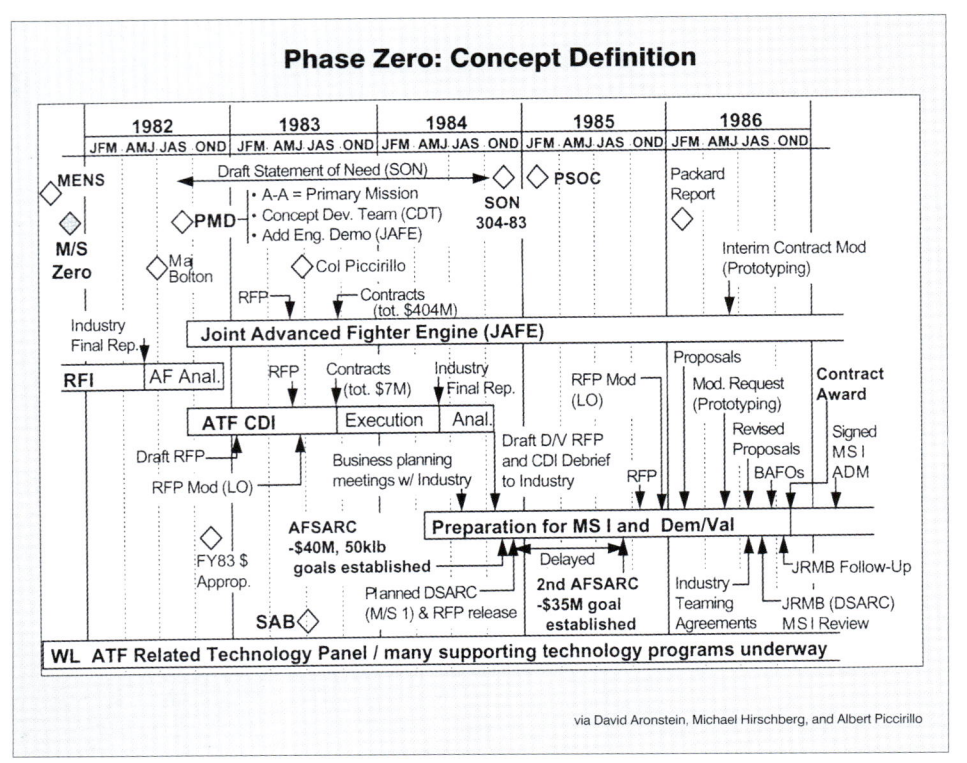

Phase Zero: Concept Definition

	1982	1983	1984	1985	1986
	JFM AMJ JAS OND	JFM AMJ JAS OND	JFM AMJ JAS OND	JFM AMJ JAS OND	JFM AMJ JAS OND

◇ MENS

Draft Statement of Need (SON) ◇ ◇ PSOC Packard Report ◇

◇ PMD • A-A = Primary Mission SON 304-83 ◇

M/S Zero • Concept Dev. Team (CDT) • Add Eng. Demo (JAFE) Interim Contract Mod (Prototyping)

◇ Maj Bolton ◇ Col Piccirillo

Industry Final Rep. RFP → ┌ Contracts (tot. $404M)

Joint Advanced Fighter Engine (JAFE)

| RFI | AF Anal. | RFP Contracts (tot. $7M) Industry Final Rep. | RFP Mod (LO) | Proposals Mod. Request (Prototyping) | Contract Award |

ATF CDI | Execution | Anal. | Revised Proposals BAFOs Signed MS I ADM

Draft RFP Business planning meetings w/ Industry Draft D/V RFP and CDI Debrief to Industry RFP

RFP Mod (LO)

Preparation for MS I and Dem/Val

◇ FY83 $ Approp. **AFSARC** -$40M, 50klb goals established Delayed **2nd AFSARC** -$35M goal established Industry Teaming Agreements JRMB Follow-Up JRMB (DSARC) MS I Review

Planned DSARC (M/S 1) & RFP release

SAB ◇

WL ATF Related Technology Panel / many supporting technology programs underway

via David Aronstein, Michael Hirschberg, and Albert Piccirillo

Integral with the RFP was an initial perspective on what would soon become known as the Demonstration/Validation (Dem/Val) approach to prototyping.

Initial studies leading to actual flightworthy aircraft would be accommodated at relatively modest cost by building full- and reduced-scale models for wind tunnel testing, radar cross section (RCS) computations, avionics development, and miscellaneous sub-systems testing. State-of-the-art capability in such sciences as computational fluid dynamics (CFD – utilized for extremely accurate wind tunnel assessments of analog hardware), radar-cross-section (RCS), and sub-systems test rigs interfaced with advanced computer capability greatly reduced the cost of what otherwise would be an extremely expensive full-scale prototype flight test program.

The concept exploration phase which started during 1983 involved Boeing, General Dynamics, Grumman, Lockheed, McDonnell Douglas, Northrop, and Rockwell International. It ran until the prototype contract awards were announced on October 31, 1986. In the interim, Grumman – known primarily for its Navy products and thus a political long shot – and Rockwell International, preoccupied with its B-1B problems and thus unable to devote the necessary logistical manpower required for a successful bid, dropped out of the competition.

During May of 1986, then-Secretary of the Air Force Edward Aldridge announced a significant and important change in the original RFP. The Air Force had decided not to make its final ATF choice from the paper studies generated under the aegis of the original Demonstration/Validation (Dem/Val) concept, but rather to expand Dem/Val to include a prototype fly-off that would pit the aircraft of the two most promising designs against each other. Each contender would be asked to build two prototypes, each to be powered by examples of the two contending engine manufacturers.

Bidders were now informed that:
• Dem/Val would include best-effort flying prototypes and avionics prototypes
• Only two contractors would be selected for Dem/Val
• Teaming would be encouraged
• Cost proposals would be requested
• They would be asked how they would tailor the remainder of the Dem/Val effort to optimize risk reduction within available funds
• They would be asked for a funding profile

Though considerably more expensive than the paper fly-off, the construction and flight testing of actual hardware – under the revised RFP – would permit a more accurate assessment of capabilities in the critical areas of low-observables technology and basic performance. Though up-front costs would be high, the long-term economics could almost certainly be justified by the resulting hardware revelations.

Facing Page Top: **Phase Zero, Concept Definition chart effectively outlining, step by step, the process leading to the decision to proceed with the ATF, and the resulting prototyping and Dem/Val fly-off.** Lockheed Martin

Facing Page Bottom (together): **Four of Lockheed Martin's final contenders for the ATF Dem/Val competition. The lower right study was the eventual winner.** Lockheed Martin

This Page: **Views of a model of Boeing's ATF Dem/Val design. Many questioned the wisdom of placing the intake in such a prominent position in light of RCS requirements.** Lockheed Martin

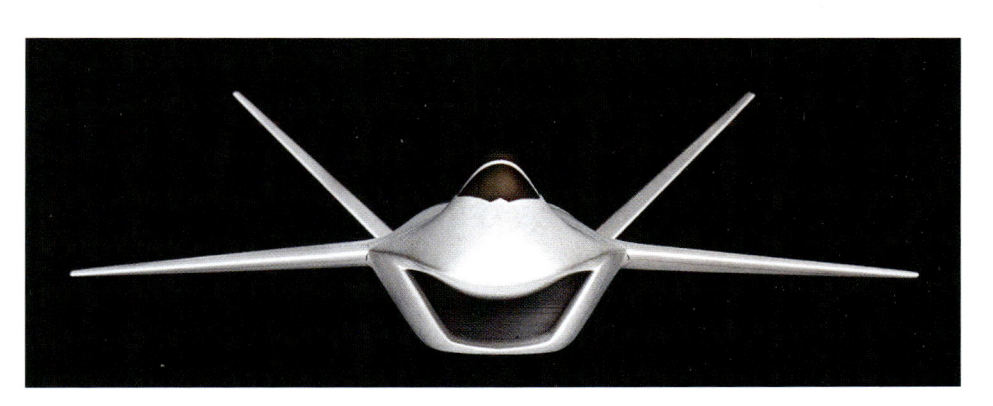

Facing page (all four): **General Dynamics delta wing ATF design continued the company's long association with tailless aircraft configurations.**
Lockheed Martin

Right and below: **Two early configuration studies from the General Dynamics ATF team; neither has a definitive vertical tail design.**
Lockheed Martin

Bottom (two): **Views of a model of Lockheed Martin's ATF Dem/Val design. There was obvious emphasis being placed on the stringent RCS requirements. Many features found on this early configuration later would be seen on the actual YF-22A and later F/A-22A.** Lockheed Martin

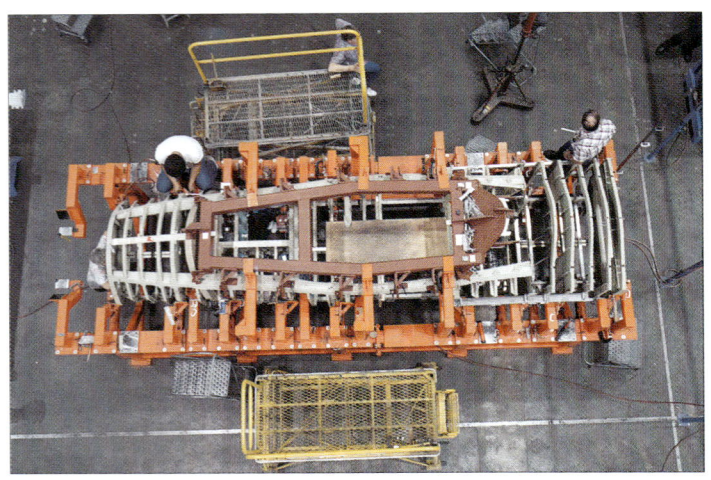

Chapter Two

The Development of Dem/Val

On July 28, 1986, the five remaining contenders submitted their prototype design proposals for analysis. During the following twelve weeks these were reviewed with considerable intensity by ASD. It was concluded the Lockheed and Northrop submissions were superior to those of Boeing, General Dynamics, and McDonnell Douglas. However, it also was concluded the three less desirable designs contained attributes applicable to the two preferred.

Concurrent to this activity, the five contending companies, under the duress of national economic realities and the DoD, now elected to team in order to guarantee themselves at least a small part of the $65 billion pie that might

Facing page top left: **Jigged forward fuselage of first YF-22A, N22YF, at Palmdale.**

Facing page top right: **YF-22A, N22YF, mid-fuselage section being loaded aboard Lockheed C-5B, 87-038, at Lockheed Martin's Fort Worth, Texas facility for delivery to Palmdale, California.**

Facing page middle (two): **First YF-22A, N22YF, following the end of Dem/Val and prior to delivery to the USAF Museum at Wright-Patterson AFB, Ohio.**

Facing page bottom: **YF-22A, N22YF, immediately prior to 1990 roll-out.** Lockheed Martin x 4

Above: **YF-22A high-speed wind tunnel model.**

Right: **YF-22A high-speed wind tunnel model with weapon bays and scale AIM-120s/AIM-9.**

Right inset: **YF-22A 1/12th-scale spin tunnel model.** Lockheed Martin x 3

result from an ATF production contract. Lockheed, whose initial design studies had been considered front runners during the early ATF reviews, had conducted consortium discussions with Boeing and General Dynamics as early as June of 1986 (a public announcement was made on July 2), but did not formalize an agreement with its partners until the following October 13. Consequently, Lockheed assigned Sherman Mullin as General Manager for the ATF Team Program Office. Mullin would direct Lockheed in the "prime contractor" role and consequently take advantage of the unique technical strengths represented by Boeing and General Dynamics. Northrop, some two weeks later, followed suit by serving as lead on a team with McDonnell Douglas.

In response to these teaming decisions, revised proposals from all seven airframe contractors were submitted on July 28, 1986. In effect, this gave the impression of two consortia...albeit representing no less than five major aerospace manufacturers.

Thus, by default, the two consortia were selected on October 31, 1986, to build two prototypes each to compete in the revised Dem/Val phase. Lockheed, under a $691 million contract, would build two of what later would become its Model 1132 (earlier referred to as Configuration 092) aircraft under the official Air Force designation YF-22. Northrop, under a similar $691 million contract, would build two of its N-14 proposal under the official Air Force designation YF-23. The designations were assigned under the auspices of the DoD's revised Aerospace Vehicle Designation System (DoD Directive 4120.15) of September 18, 1962.

Of the $691 million value of each team's Dem/Val contract, approximately $100 million was allocated to radar and electro-optical sensors, $200-million for avionics architecture and integration, and the remainder for airframe and other miscellaneous tasks. The engine companies were funded directly, with each receiving an additional $650-million.

These aircraft, owned and operated by their respective companies, would later be given civil registrations. The Lockheed YF-22As would be registered N22YF (powered by General Electric YF120-GE-100 engines) and N22YX (powered by Pratt & Whitney YF119-PW-100 engines; this aircraft later would be given the military serial 87-701), respectively (the two Lockheed aircraft later were transferred to the Air Force to accommodate tax and operational issues). The Northrop YF-23As would be registered N231YF (powered by Pratt & Whitney YF119-PW-100 engines) and N232YF (powered by General Electric YF120-GE-100 engines), respectively. The Northrop aircraft also were assigned military serial numbers, these being 87-800 for N231YF and 87-801 for N232YF.

The initial plan called for the testbed aircraft to make their first flights during late 1989. FSD proposals would be due in late summer of 1990, and the FSD (i.e., EMD) – source selection decision would be made by the end of 1990.

It is interesting to note for historical purposes that the original ATF designs submitted by Lockheed – in the earliest days of the RFI period – looked like a larger and longer F-117 with a high-mounted wing (instead of the F-117's low-mounted), four tail surfaces, and intakes that were placed below and behind the wing leading edge. Like the F-117, these proposals (some weighing as much as 80,000 lbs.) were highly faceted and essentially representative of second-generation stealth technology.

The propulsion system competition pitted Pratt & Whitney against General Electric. The engine RFP, then referred to simply as the Advanced Fighter Engine (AFE) and later as the Joint Advanced Fighter Engine (JAFE) and initially calling for an engine in the 30,000 lb. thrust range, had been released to the manufacturers during May of 1983. The following September, both were awarded $550 million contracts to build and test static prototypes. General Electric's engine was known in-house as the GE37. Pratt & Whitney's was known in-house as the PW5000. Later they would be designated F120 and F119, respectively, by the Air Force.

Initial preliminary flight rating tests (PFRT) and accelerated mission testing (AMT) runs using the prototype non-flightworthy engines took place during 1986. Two years later, the first flightworthy engines were bench run.

With the advent of the decision to prototype the two contending aircraft, the purpose of the revised Dem/Val phase (for which, proposals had been received on February 18, 1986) was to focus on risk reduction and demonstrate that the advanced technologies required for successful accomplishment of the ATF's mission were feasible and practical and could be moved successfully into EMD.

Under the revised Dem/Val, the winning contenders would be required to deliver two "best effort" proof-of-concept prototypes, each to be powered by the two contending engine submissions. The prototypes would not be intended for a direct competitive fly-off or to show compliance with every performance requirement, but rather to demonstrate that each company's concept was fundamentally viable. Contractors would have maximum flexibility in determining their respective flight test plans.

Above: **YF-22A full-scale pole model at Lockheed Martin's Helendale, California radar cross section test facility.** Lockheed Martin

Left and facing page top and bottom: **YF-22A, N22YF, the GE-powered prototype, immediately prior to official 1990 roll-out ceremony at the company's Palmdale, California facility.** Lockheed Martin

Dem/Val was composed of three major elements:

(1) System specification development, which utilized effectiveness analysis, design trade studies, tests, simulation, technology evaluations, and other efforts to refine the weapon system characteristics and operational requirements.

(2) Avionics prototypes, which were used to demonstrate the achievability of the fully integrated avionics suites, first in a series of ground based demonstrations (Lockheed's first Avionics Ground Prototype [AGP] demonstration took place during October of 1988; Northrop also began to conduct AGP demonstrations around that time; they eventually would demonstrate pilot-controlled real-time fusion of multi-sensor flight data, the integration of 600,000 lines of Ada software code [developed by the US DoD using common software tools], a core processing capability 100 times faster than that of then-current air-superiority fighters, a fully integrated advanced avionics architecture, self-diagnostics/fault isolation, and system reconfiguration) and then, for Lockheed, in the prototype Boeing 757 (N757A; initial tests took place on July 17, 1989), and for Northrop in a modified BAC-111 (N162W; initial tests took place on July 17, 1989) modified as flying avionics laboratories.

Each team completed approximately 100 flight hours with their respective avionics testbeds during 1990. The tests validated the ability to detect a target by multiple sensors and display it reliably and consistently as one symbol on the pilot's display. The Lockheed team's Boeing 757 began flight tests on April 18, 1990 and flew for approximately four months. Sensors tested included the Texas Instruments/Westinghouse active array radar, the TRW CNI system, the Lockheed Sanders/General Electric electronic combat system, and the GE infrared search and track (IRST) system.

The Northrop team demonstrated an active electronically-scanned antenna (ESA), all-aspect threat missile launch and detection and tracking capability, and an imaging IRST system.

With both, the installed performance of each sensor, the integrated avionics suite, and the mission avionics sensor management and sensor track integration functions were thoroughly evaluated. Several tests were conducted against targets of opportunity, including commercial, military, and general aviation aircraft.

As an aside, it should be noted that the ATF avionics prototypes represented one of the largest Ada software developments ever undertaken to that time. The suitability of Ada as the programming language for the avionics suites on a fighter aircraft had been questionable until the advent of this project...which succeeded in removing any doubt that it was suitable for the job.

(3) YF-22A/YF-23A prototypes, which were used to demonstrate the capabilities on which the F-22/F-23 EMD proposals would be based.

With the Lockheed/Boeing/General Dynamics consortia, each company brought substantial, applicable experience to the partnership: Lockheed's experience in F-117A program design and production; Boeing's strength in military avionics development/integration and advanced materials development; and General Dynamics' expertise as designer and builder of the F-16 and its advanced fly-by-wire flight control system.

Northrop and McDonnell Douglas similarly were talented, with Northrop offering expertise in low-observables technology, lightweight fighter design (considerable data had been gained from the company's experience designing and building F-5 Freedom Fighter and F-20 Tigershark aircraft), and advanced materials technology; and McDonnell Douglas having extensive experience in fighter design and fighter production encompassing everything from the XP-67 through F-15 programs.

The overall distribution of work between the team partners was based on the dollar value of work performed, rather than on a man-hours-to-weight equation, etc. In simple terms, the program was divided into thirds for the Lockheed team and halves for the Northrop. This proved no simple task as interfaces required by these arrangements were extremely complex.

Lockheed's responsibilities included weapon system, air vehicle, and avionics system design integration, the forward fuselage (including the cockpit and air intakes), the wing leading edge flaps and tips, the vertical stabilizer leading edges and tips, the horizontal stabilator edges, and final assembly of the complete aircraft.

Boeing's responsibilities included the wing, the aft fuselage, and propulsion system integration. General Dynamics' responsibilities included the mid-fuselage, the empennage, most subsystems, the armament system, the landing gear, and vehicle management system integration (including flight controls).

Primary YF-22A subcontractors totaled at some 650 scattered among 32 states. The most important of these included:

For Lockheed: Hughes Radar Systems Group, Los Angeles, CA (common integrated processor [CIP]); Harris Government Aerospace Systems Division, Melbourne, FL (fiber network interface unit [FNIU]; avionics bus interface [ABI]; fiber optic bus components [FOBC]; Fairchild Defense, Germantown, M D (data transfer unit [DTU] mass memory); GEC Avionics, Atlanta, GA (head-up display [HUD]); Lockheed Sanders Avionics Division, Nashua, NH (controls and displays; graphics processor video interface [GPVII]; Kaiser Electronics, San Jose, CA (unknown); Lockheed Sanders Information Systems Division, Merrimack, NH (mission planning equipment [MPE]); Lockheed Sanders Defense Systems Division, Merrimack, NH (common automatic test systems [CATS] software; and Digital Equipment Corporation, Merrimack, NH (systems/software re engineering environment [S/SEE]).

For Boeing: Westinghouse Electric Corporation, Baltimore, MD and Texas Instruments Defense Systems and Electronics Group, Dallas, TX (radar); and KiddeGraviner Ltd., Slough, UK (fire retardation equipment).

For General Dynamics: Rosemount Aerospace Division (air data probes); Allied-Signal Aerospace Company [Bendix] and AiResearch Los Angeles Division, South Bend, IN (wheels and brakes); Curtiss Wright Flight systems, Fairfield, NJ (leading edge flap driver system, side bay and weapons bay door drive); Dowty Decoto, Yakima, WA (hydraulic actuators); EDO Corporation Government Systems Division, College Point, NY (missile launchers); Lear Astronics Corporation, Santa Monica, CA (vehicle management system modules); National Water Lift Pneumo Corporation, Kalamazoo, MI (flight control actuators); Parker-Hannifin Corporation Parker-Bertea Aerospace Group, Irvine, CA (flight control actuator reservoirs); Simmonds Precision, Vergennes, VT (fuel management system); Sterer Engineering, Los Angeles, CA (nose wheel steering); TRW Avionics & Surveillance Group Military Electronic Avionics Division, San Diego, CA (communications and navigation equipment); XAR, City of Industry, CA (inflight refueling receptacle); Motorola, Scottsdale, AZ (computer security [KOV-5]); United Technologies Corporation Hamilton Standard Division, Windsor Locks, CT (environmental control system [ECS]); Sanders/General Electric Joint Venture Team, Nashua, NH (electronic combat equipment); Texas Instruments Defense Systems & Electronics Group, Dallas, TX (vehicle management system core hardware); and Menasco Aerospace Division, Fort Worth, TX (nose/main landing gear).

Northrop and McDonnell Douglas's responsibilities were considerably different due primarily to the ongoing work loads each company was able to accommodate. As a result, Northrop assimilated most of the design and engineering effort, the total systems integration, final assembly, construction of the aft fuselage and empennage, and defensive avionics and flight control system integration.

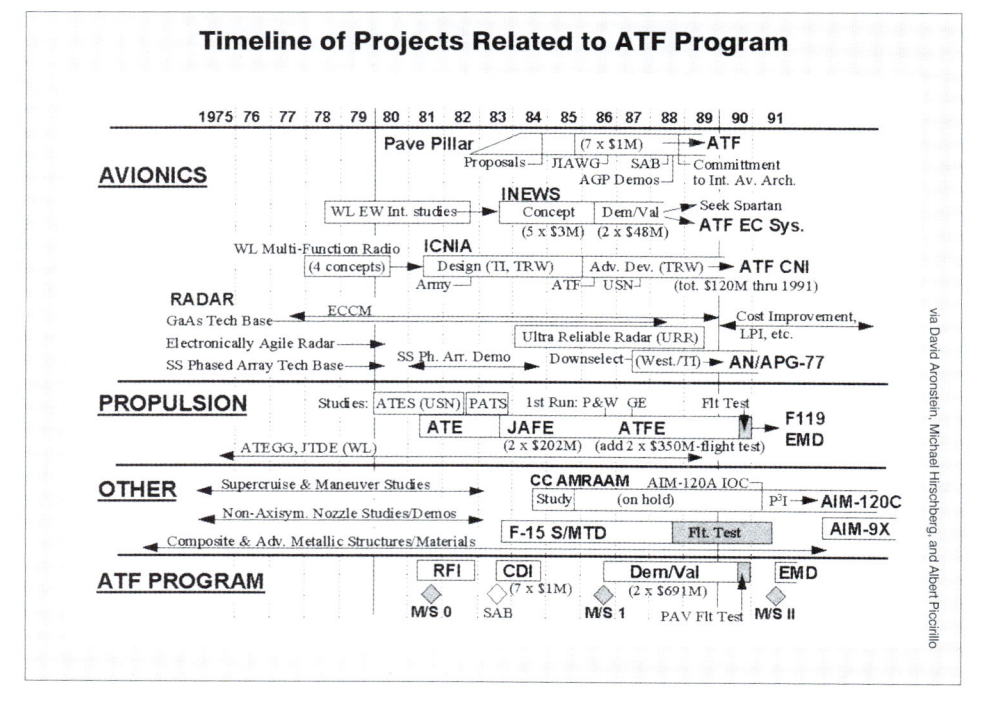

Timeline of Projects Related to ATF Program

via David Aronstein, Michael Hirschberg, and Albert Piccirillo

Top: YF-22A, N22YF, the GE-powered prototype, during the official August 29, 1990 roll-out ceremony at the company's Palmdale, California facility. Mick Roth

McDonnell Douglas assimilated production of the forward and center fuselage, the landing gear and wings, the fuel and armament systems, the offensive avionics, the controls, and the cockpit displays. The crew station and pilot/vehicle interface were a joint responsibility.

By the advent of the roll-outs of the respective Northrop and Lockheed aircraft, the original 50,000 lb. gross weight limitation had been somewhat unwillingly shelved and a more realistic figure of 55,000 lb. had become the design goal. These weight problems had led to a number of design changes that in turn led to delays in scheduling.

For the Lockheed/Boeing/General Dynamics consortium, additional difficulties resulted in a diamond-shaped wing planform (its heritage being the General Dynamics Dem/Val proposal) supplementing an earlier, somewhat less-tapered trapezoidal design. Additionally, the planform area of the forward fuselage was significantly decreased to provide improved high AoA (angle-of-attack) pitching moment forces in the low speed corner of the envelope. Extensive wind tunnel testing was undertaken to optimize the nose and vertical tail configurations in order to meet the AoA objective and generate optimum flying qualities.

Perhaps the most important change imposed on both the Lockheed and Northrop designs at this time was the elimination of engine thrust reversers. Originally an ATF design requirement, they had been studied in great detail by the various consortia members and in fact statically tested, in prototype form, on the McDonnell Douglas F-15 STOL/Maneuver Technology Demonstrator (S/MTD). The consensus was that their attributes would be offset by weight, maintenance, and cost considerations. Most importantly, full-scale testbed research had indicated considerable cooling difficulties and a propensity for the exhaust efflux to adversely affect directional stability when the reversers were used in flight. In addition, and though not widely acknowledged, there was concern that incorporating thrust reversers would considerably complicate the already difficult task of masking the exhaust nozzle assemblies in terms of low-observables requirements.

These anomalies would have necessitated design changes that would have affected the proposed ATF production schedule. Designed to operate throughout the ATF's flight envelope, the reversers would not have been simply an extrapolation of extant reverser technology, but rather a major technology risk – and thus an unknown quantity on an aircraft optimized for dependability and high-performance.

ATF program management had, by now, been placed under the direction of Program Director, Brig. Gen. James Fain. Fain was quick to extend initial security constraints limiting access to the project, and accordingly, it was not until the rollout ceremonies during 1990 that the prototype aircraft were first exposed to public scrutiny. In the interim, development and hardware construction by the two contending consortia centered upon three major groupings: the avionics ground prototypes (AGP) which, as noted previously, served as static testbeds for all avionics, sensors, and cockpit displays; the systems specifications development which accommodated RCS, materials, maintenance requirements, and simulated combat mission studies; and the prototype air vehicles (PAVs) which called for the construction and flight test of the actual aircraft.

The Northrop PAVs would be assembled at the company's Hawthorne, California facility and then transported to Edwards AFB, California for roll-out and initial static tests; and the Lockheed PAVs would be assembled by Lockheed at their Palmdale (Skunk Works), California facility where they, too, would be rolled out and put through initial static testing.

The original Dem/Val schedule called for the ATF prototype designs to be frozen during mid-1987. Lockheed, however, determined in July of 1987 that their "final" design was technically and competitively unacceptable. On July 13, a new design initiative was instated and following a very intense three-month effort, a new configuration (1132) was chosen. The following December, a decision by the AF to ease the runway takeoff length requirement from 2,000 ft. to 3,000 ft. led to deletion of the controversial thrust reverser requirement. This saved weight, lowered nozzle complexity, and improved the aircraft's proposed supercruise performance. In turn, during April of 1988, Configuration 1132

was "unfrozen" in order to attempt a further reduction in supersonic drag. This effort proved successful as a result of a redesign the following month of the forward and aft fuselage sections.

Northrop, in the meantime, had settled on their design even prior to the decision to build two sets of prototypes. No major changes were incorporated even following the selection of the Northrop team as one of two to build the Dem/Val aircraft. The configuration picked during 1987 became the one they would build. The only change, in fact, that took place was the removal of thrust reverser capability. However, rather than redesign the aft sections of the engine nacelles, the Northrop team built their two prototypes with the reverser-accommodating nacelles per the original drawing spec.

It is worth noting that Lockheed's team chose to build their prototypes with a functional thrust vectoring system, while the Northrop team did not. Thrust vectoring – which in the case of the YF-22A added only 30 to 50 lbs. of weight per nozzle – provided the ability to attain and trim at very high angles of attack, and increased pitch rates both in low speed and in supersonic flight. Furthermore, although the nozzles did not vector differentially (an option that may someday be incorporated in the production/operational F/A-22A), the use of thrust vectoring increased the aircraft's roll response and maximum roll rate attainable at high angles of attack. The latter was because the horizontal stabilators provided both pitch and (in concert with the ailerons and flaperons) roll control. Thus the use of thrust vectoring for additional pitch control left more of the stabilator motion available for roll.

The first flightworthy Pratt & Whitney YF119 engines were delivered to Lockheed on June 8 and 17, 1990, respectively. Installation in YF-22A, N22YX, took place shortly after their arrival at the company's Palmdale construction facility.

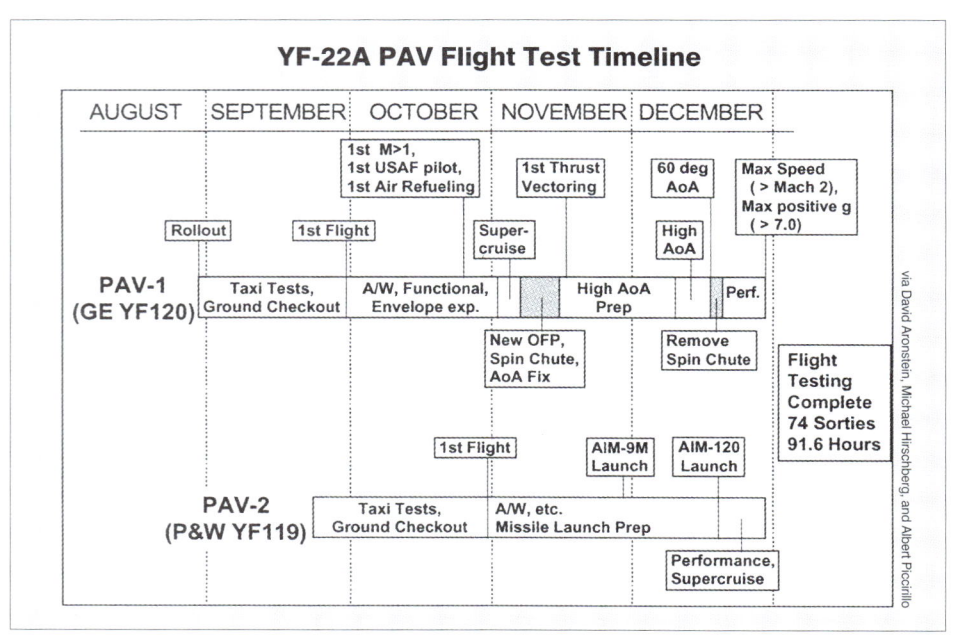

YF-22A PAV Flight Test Timeline

	AUGUST	SEPTEMBER	OCTOBER	NOVEMBER	DECEMBER
			1st M>1, 1st USAF pilot, 1st Air Refueling	1st Thrust Vectoring	60 deg AoA	Max Speed (> Mach 2), Max positive g (> 7.0)
	Rollout	1st Flight	Super-cruise		High AoA
PAV-1 (GE YF120)	Taxi Tests, Ground Checkout	A/W, Functional, Envelope exp.		High AoA Prep	Perf.
			New OFP, Spin Chute, AoA Fix	Remove Spin Chute	Flight Testing Complete 74 Sorties 91.6 Hours
		1st Flight		AIM-9M Launch	AIM-120 Launch	
PAV-2 (P&W YF119)		Taxi Tests, Ground Checkout	A/W, etc. Missile Launch Prep		Performance, Supercruise

via David Aronstein, Michael Hirschberg, and Albert Piccirillo

Noteworthy, too, was the amount of time Lockheed had spent wind tunnel testing the YF-22A configuration. Because supersonic cruise performance was considered critical to winning the contract, particular emphasis was placed on accommodating that requirement handily. A total tunnel-time breakdown is as follows:

- Low Speed Stability and Control – 6,715 hrs.
- Propulsion Aerodynamics – 5,405 hrs.
- High-Speed Drag/Stability/Control – 4,000 hrs.
- Weapons Environment/Separation – 700 hrs.
- Flow Visualization – 695 hrs.
- Air Data – 240 hrs.
- Pressure Model (Air Loads) – 95 hrs.
- Flutter – 80 hrs.

Wind tunnel models consisted of the following:

- 1/20th-scale Stability and Control
- 1/25th-scale Stability and Control
- 1/7th-scale Free Flight
- 1/14th-scale High AoA Rotary Balance Model
- 1/30th-scale Free Spin
- 1/10th-scale Inlet/Forebody Compatibility
- 1/7th-scale Inlet/Forebody Compatibility
- 1/20th-scale Low-Speed Jet-Effects
- 1/5th-scale Air Data System Calibration

The Dem/Val contract required both the Lockheed and Northrop teams to conduct radar cross section (RCS) testing and analysis on parts, computer-based RCS prediction models, and both sub- and full-scale aircraft. The full-scale high-fidelity RCS test models were required to be equipped with all radar reflective features and absorptive materials that would be incorporated into the actual aircraft. RCS was evaluated while they were mounted on a 70-foot-tall low-RCS pole at the Air Force Radar Target Scatter (RATSCAT) facility located at White Sands, New Mexico.

It is germane at this point to provide a brief history of low-observables (stealth) technology and a basic explanation for how it works and why its important. Accordingly, what follows has been excerpted, with permission, from a paper by Alan Brown, the retired Director of Low Observables Technology for Lockheed Aeronautical Systems Co.:

Design for low observability, and specifically for low radar cross section (RCS), began almost as soon as radar was invented. The predominantly wooden de Havilland Mosquito was one of the first aircraft to be designed with this capability in mind.

Against WWII radar systems, that approach was fairly successful, but it would not be appropriate today. First, wood and, by extension, composite materials are not transparent to radar, although they may be less reflective than metal; and second, the degree to which they are transparent merely amplifies the components that are normally hidden by the outer skin. These include engines, fuel, avionics packages, electrical and hydraulic circuits, and people.

In the late 1950s, radar-absorbing materials were incorporated into the design of otherwise conventionally designed aircraft. These materials had two purposes: to reduce the aircraft cross section against specific threats, and to isolate multiple antennas on aircraft to prevent cross-talk. The Lockheed U-2 reconnaissance aircraft is an example in this category.

By the 1960s, sufficient analytical knowledge had disseminated into the design community that the gross effects of different shapes and components could be assessed. It was quickly realized that a flat plate at right angles to an impinging radar wave was a very large radar signal, and a cavity, similarly located, also has a large return.

Thus, the inlet and exhaust systems of a jet aircraft would be expected to be dominant contributors to radar cross section in the nose-on and tail-on viewing directions, and the vertical tail dominates the side-on signature.

Airplanes could now be designed with appropriate shaping and materials to reduce their radar cross sections, but as good numerical design procedures were not available, it was unlikely that a completely balanced design would result. In other words, there was always likely to be a component that dominated the return in a particular direction. This was the era of the Lockheed SR-71 Blackbird.

Ten years later, numerical methods were developed that allowed a quantitative assessment of contributions from different parts of a body. It was thus possible to design an aircraft with a balanced radar cross section and to minimize the return from dominant scatterers. This approach led to the design of the Lockheed F-117A and the Northrop B-2A stealth aircraft.

Over the past 25 years there has been continuous improvement in both analytical and experimental methods, particularly with respect to integration of shaping and materials. At the same time, the counter-stealth faction is developing an increasing understanding of its requirements, forcing the stealth community into another round of improvements. The message is, that with all the dramatic improvements of the last two decades, there is little evidence of leveling off in capability. This article, consequently must be seen only as a snapshot in time.

Radar Cross Section Fundamentals:

There are two basic approaches to passive radar cross section reduction: shaping to minimize backscatter, and coating for energy absorption and cancellation. Both of these approaches have to be used coherently in aircraft design to achieve the required low observable levels over the appropriate frequency range in the electromagnetic spectrum.

Shaping:

There is a tremendous advantage to positioning surfaces so that the radar wave strikes them at close to tangential angles and far from right angles to edges, as will now be illustrated.

To a first approximation, when the diameter of a sphere is significantly larger than the radar wavelength, its radar cross section is equal to its geometric frontal area.

The return of a one-square-meter sphere is compared to that from a one-square-meter plate at different look angles. One case to consider is a rotation of the plate from normal incidence to a shallow angle, with the radar beam at right angles to a pair of edges. The other is with the radar beam at 45° to the edges.

The frequency is selected so that the wavelength is about 1/10th of the length of the plate, in this case very typical of acquisition radars on surface-to-air missile systems.

At normal incidence, the flat plate acts like a mirror, and its return is 30 decibels (dB) above (or 1,000 times) the return from the sphere. If we now rotate the plate about one edge so that the edge is always normal to the incoming wave, we find that the cross section drops by a factor of *1,000*, equal to that of the sphere, when the look angle reaches 30° off normal to the plate.

As the angle is increased, the *locus of maxima* falls by about another factor of 50, for a total change of 50,000 from the normal look angle.

Now if you go back to the normal incidence case and rotate the plate about a diagonal relative to the incoming wave, there is a remark-

able difference. In this case, the cross section drops by 30 dB when the plate is only 8° off normal, and drops another 40dB by the time the plate is at a shallow angle to the incoming radar beam. This is a total change in radar cross section of 10,000,000!

From this, it would seem that it is fairly easy to decrease the radar cross section substantially by merely avoiding obviously high-return shapes and attitude angles.

However, multiple-reflection cases have not yet been looked at, which change the situation considerably. It is fairly obvious that energy aimed into a long, narrow, closed cavity – which is a perfect reflector internally – will bounce back in the general direction of its source. Furthermore, the shape of the cavity downstream of the entrance clearly does not influence this conclusion.

However, the energy reflected from a straight duct will be reflected in one or two bounces, while that from a curved duct will require four or five bounces. It can be imagined that with a little skill, the number of bounces can be increased significantly without sacrificing aerodynamic performance. For example, a cavity might be designed with a high-cross-sectional aspect ratio to maximize the length-to-height ratio. If we can attenuate the signal to some extent with each bounce, then clearly there is a significant advantage to a multi-bounce design. The SR-71 inlet follows these design practices.

However, there is a little more to the story than just the so-called ray tracing approach. When energy strikes a plate that is smooth compared to wavelength, it does not reflect totally in the optical approximation sense, i.e.,

the energy is not confined to a reflected wave at a complementary angle to the incoming wave.

The radiated energy, in fact, takes a pattern like a typical reflected wave structure. The width of the main forward scattered spike is proportional to the ratio of the wavelength to the dimension of the reradiating surface, as are the magnitudes of the secondary and tertiary spikes. The classical optical approximation applies when this ratio approaches zero. Thus, the backscatter – the energy radiated directly back to the transmitter – increases as the wavelength goes up, or the frequency decreases.

When designing a cavity for minimum return, it is important to balance the forward scatter associated with ray tracing with the backscatter from interactions with the first surfaces. Clearly, an accurate calculation of the total energy returned to the transmitter is very complicated, and generally has to be done on a supercomputer.

Coatings and Absorbers:

It is fairly clear that although surface alignment is very important for external surfaces and inlet and exhaust edges, the return from the inside of a cavity is heavily dependent on attenuating materials. It is noted that the radar-frequency range of interest covers between two and three orders of magnitude. Permeability and dielectric constant are two properties that are closely associated with the effectivity of an attenuating material.

They both vary considerably with frequency in different ways for different materials. Also, for a coating to be effective, it should have a thickness that is close to a quarter wavelength at the frequency of interest.

Top: **YF-22A, bearing AF serial number 87-701 instead of the more often seen N22YX, during post Dem/Val testing at Edwards AFB. Noteworthy is rudder borrowed from N22YF.**
Lockheed Martin

Bottom: **Both YF-22As (N22YX l./N22YF r.) set up for a photo session at Edwards AFB.**
Lockheed Martin

High Temperature Coatings:

Reduction of radar cross section of engine nozzles is also very important, and is complicated by high material temperatures. The electromagnetic design requirements for coatings are not different from those for low temperatures, but structural integrity is a much bigger issue.

Jet Wakes:

The driver determining radar return from a jet wake is the ionization present. Return from resistive particles, such as carbon, is seldom a significant factor. It is important in calculating the return from an ionized wake to use non-equilibrium mathematics, particularly for medium- and high-altitude cases.

The very strong ion density dependency on maximum gas temperature quickly leads to the conclusion that the radar return from the jet wake of an engine running in dry power is insignificant, while that from an afterburning wake could be dominant.

Component Design:

When the basic aircraft signature is reduced to a very low level, detail design becomes very important. Access panel and door edges, for example, have the potential to be major contributors to radar cross section unless measures are taken to suppress them.

Based on the discussion of simple flat plates, it is clear that it is generally unsatisfactory to have a door edge at right angles to the direction of flight. This would result in a noticeable signal in a nose-on aspect. Thus, conventional rectangular doors and access panels are unacceptable.

The solution is not only to sweep the panel edges, but to align those edges with other major edges on the aircraft.

The pilot's head, complete with helmet, is a major source of radar return. It is augmented by the bounce-path returns associated with internal bulkheads and frame members. The solution is to design the cockpit so that its external shape conforms to good low radar cross section design rules, and then plate the glass with a film similar to that used for the temperature control in commercial buildings.

Here the requirements are more stringent: it should pass at least 85% of the visible energy and reflect essentially all of the radar energy. At the same time, a pilot would prefer not to have noticeable instrument-panel reflection during night flying.

On an unstable, fly-by-wire aircraft, it is extremely important to have redundant sources of aerodynamic data. These must be very accurate with respect to flow direction, and they must operate ice-free at all times. Static and total pressure probes have been used, but they clearly represent compromises with stealth requirements. Several quite different techniques are in various stages of development.

Onboard antennas and radar systems are a major potential source of high radar visibility for two reasons. One is that it is obviously difficult to hide something that is designed to transmit with very high efficiency, so the so-called in-band radar cross section is liable to be significant. The other is that even if this problem is solved satisfactorily, the energy emitted by these systems can normally be readily detected. The work being done to reduce these signatures cannot be described here.

There are two significant sources of infrared radiation from air-breathing propulsion systems: hot parts and jet wakes. The fundamental variables available for reducing radiation are temperature and emissivity, and the basic tool available is line-of-sight masking.

Recently some interesting progress has been made in directed energy, particularly for multiple bounce situations, but that subject will not be discussed further here.

Emissivity can be a double-edged sword, particularly inside a duct.

While a low emissivity surface will reduce the emitted energy, it will also enhance reflected energy that may be coming from a hotter internal region. Thus, a careful optimization must be made to determine the preferred emissivity pattern inside a jet engine exhaust pipe.

This pattern must be played against the frequency range available to detectors, which typically covers a band from 1 to 12 microns.

The short wavelengths are particularly effective at high temperatures, while the long wavelengths are most effective at typical ambient atmospheric temperatures. The required emissivity pattern as a function of both frequency and spatial dispersion having been determined, the next issue is how to make materials that fit the bill.

The first inclination of the infrared coating designer is to throw some metal flakes into a transparent binder. Coming up with a transparent binder over the frequency range of interest is not easy, and the radar coating man probably won't like the effects of the metal particles on his favorite observable.

The next move is usually to come up with a multi-layer material, where the same cancellation approach that was discussed earlier regarding radar-suppressant coatings is used. The dimensions now are in angstroms rather than millimeters.

The big push at present is in moving from metal in the films to metal oxides for radar cross section compatibility. Getting the required performance as a function of frequency is not easy, and it is a significant feat to get down to an emissivity of 0.1, particularly over a sustained frequency range. Thus, the biggest practical ratio of emissivities is liable to be one order of magnitude.

Everyone can recognize that all of this discussion is meaningless if engines continue to deposit carbon (one of the highest emissivity materials known) on duct walls. For the infrared coating to be effective, it is not sufficient to have a very low particulate ratio in the engine exhaust, but to have one that is essentially zero.

Carbon build-up on hot engine parts is a cumulative situation, and there are very few bright, shiny parts inside exhaust nozzles after a number of hours of operation. For this reason alone, it is likely that emissivity control will predominantly be employed on surfaces other than those exposed to engine exhaust gases, i.e., inlets and aircraft external parts.

The other available variable is temperature. This, in principle, gives a great deal more opportunity for radiation reduction than emissivity, because of the large exponential dependence. The general equation from emitted radiation is that it varies with the product of emissivity and temperature to the fourth power.

However, this is a great simplification, because it does not account for the frequency shift of radiation with temperature. In the frequency range at which most simple detectors work (one to five microns), and at typical hot-metal temperatures, the exponential dependency will be typically near eight rather than four, and so at a particular frequency corresponding to a specific detector, the radiation will be proportional to the product of the emissivity and temperature to the eighth power. It is fairly clear that a small reduction in temperature can have a much greater effect than any reasonably anticipated reduction in emissivity.

The third approach is masking. This is clearly much easier to do when the majority of the power is taken off by the turbine, as in a propjet or helicopter application, than when the jet provides the basic propulsive force.

The former community has been using this approach to infrared suppression for many years, but it is only recently that the jet-propulsion crowd has tackled this problem. The Lockheed F-117A and the Northrop B-2A both use a similar approach of masking to prevent any hot parts being visible in the lower hemisphere.

In summary, infrared radiation should be tackled by a combination of temperature reduction and masking, although there is no point in doing these past the point where the hot parts are no longer the dominant items in the radiation equation.

The main body of the airplane has its own radiation, heavily dependent on speed and altitude, and the jet plume can be a most significant factor, particularly in afterburning operation. Strong cooperation between engine and airframe manufacturers in the early stages of design is extremely important. The choice of engine bypass ratio, for example shouldn't be made solely on the basis of performance, but on a combination of that and survivability for maximum system effectiveness.

The jet-wake radiation follows the same laws as the engine hot parts, a very strong dependency on temperature and a multiplicative factor of emissivity. Air has a very low emissivity, carbon particles have a high broadband emissivity, and water vapor emits in very specific bands.

Infrared seekers have mixed feelings about water vapor wavelengths, because, while they help in locating jet plumes, they hinder in terms of the general attenuation due to moisture content in the atmosphere. There is no reason, however, why smart seekers shouldn't be able to make an instant decision about whether conditions are favorable for using water-vapor bands for detection.

In summary, low signatures achieved by modern special-purpose aircraft are due to a combination of shaping, material, material selection, and careful attention to detail design. Budgeting of component signatures across a wide range of frequencies and attitude angles is mandatory. Just as in a blackout, the game can be given away by one chink of light.

Chapter Three

YF-22A Flight Test Program

Four years after contract signing, the prototype ATFs were ready for flight under the auspices of their respective Combined Test Force (CTF) teams. Each of the latter consisted of personnel from the airframe manufacturers, avionics suppliers and vendors, representatives from the two engine companies, and the Air Force.

Breaking from tradition, Lockheed and Northrop Grumman had overall responsibility for the planning and execution of their respective flight test programs rather than the Air Force Flight Test Center (AFFTC...at Edwards AFB). It was planned that the two contending designs would fly an average of two flights per day, six days per week in order to accommodate the flight test program requirements within the tight, approximately six-month window of opportunity.

Facing page top: **YF-22A, N22YF over Edwards AFB during the course of the flight test program.**

Facing page middle: **YF-22A, N22YF was assigned AF serial 87-701 late in its flight test career.**

Facing page bottom left: **YF-22A test pilots included (l. to r.) Dave Ferguson, Tom Morgenfeld, and Jon Beesley for Lockheed and Mark Shackleford and Willie Nagle for the AF.** Lockheed Martin x 3

Facing page bottom right: **Prototype Boeing 757, N757A, became the avionics testbed (airborne flying laboratory) for the YF-22A and later F/A-22A programs.** Boeing

Above: **YF-22A, N22YX, and YF-23A, N231YF setup for a P&W publicity photo.** Lockheed Martin via Terry Panopalis

Right and inset: **First flight of the first YF-22A completed, N22YF, took place on September 29, 1990.** Lockheed Martin

The first of the ATF prototypes completed, Northrop YF-23A (by now nicknamed – unofficially – *Black Widow* in memory of the company's famous WWII P-61 night fighter; an hourglass shaped marking was temporarily painted on its lower fuselage), N231YF, was rolled out on June 22, 1990. It was followed on August 29, by the roll-out of the first YF-22A (nicknamed – unofficially – *Lightning II* in memory of the company's famous P-38 fighter), N22YF.

The first of the new ATF prototypes to fly was again the Northrop aircraft, this occurring with the first hop of N231YF from Edwards AFB on August 27, 1990, with company pilot Paul Metz at the controls.

Northrop's flight test program progressed rapidly. The first inflight refueling was completed using 87-800 on its fourth mission on September 14; it achieved a supercruise speed of 1.43 Mach on September 18; and its 34th and final flight took place on November 30, 1990. Total flight time logged with 87-800 was 43 hours.

The second YF-23A, 87-801, first was flown on October 26; was supercruised for the first time at 1.6 Mach on November 29; and was flown for the last time on December 18. Total flight time logged by 87-801 was 22 hours during 16 flights. YF-23A maximum speed achieved during flight test was 1.8 Mach and maximum altitude achieved was 50,000 ft. (15,240 m.).

The primary focus of Lockheed's Dem/Val flight test program, under the direction of chief of flight test, Richard Abrams, was on those objectives the CTF felt would provide the Air Force with quantitative data that clearly demonstrated YF-22A performance capabilities directly relatable to the F-22A EMD design. A flight test strategy was developed to use the prototypes to satisfy this objective by demonstrating the following capabilities: super maneuverability/controllability (sometimes referred to as agility); supercruise (i.e., supersonic cruise without the use of afterburner) with both engine options (Pratt & Whitney and General Electric); high AoA flight characteristics; and live missile

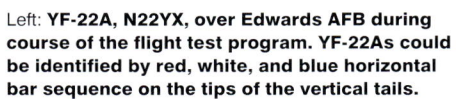

firing of both the AIM-9M Sidewinder and the AIM-120 Advanced Medium Range Air-To-Air Missile (AMRAAM).

In order to accomplish these specific test objectives in the limited time available, it was mandatory that an efficient and aggressive test approach be utilized. This included: ensuring the required resources were available to support a high sortie rate; utilizing inflight refueling to the maximum extent possible; only conducting those envelope expansion tests that were absolutely required to demonstrate the specified performance capabilities; planning for, and utilizing multidiscipline test techniques; and early checkout of both the AFFTC and Air Force Operational Test and Evaluation Center (AFOTEC) pilots and their full participation in the Dem/Val program.

For planning purposes Lockheed assumed that ten productive flights per month per aircraft was a reasonable expectation for the Dem/Val program based on YF-1 6, YF-1 7, and F-117 experience. Based on the probability of nature's cooperation, government holiday and airshow schedules, and aircraft problems, etc., it was recognized there would be weeks when the aircraft would fly many flights, and there would be periods where flights would be infrequent. Manpower and resources, however,

were available to support a minimum of two flights per day, six days a week.

The average flight duration was estimated to be 1.2 hours; 2.8 hours was the expectation with inflight refueling. The flight test strategy was based on early qualification of the YF-22As for inflight refueling, which was planned to be used on 80% of the test missions.

Flight testing of the YF-22A prototypes was conducted at Edwards AFB by a CTF made up of personnel from each of the three consortia contractors along with representatives from the two engine companies, avionics suppliers, vendors, and the Air Force. Air Force representation included personnel from the AFFTC and the AFOTEC. Team composition was as follows: Lockheed Aeronautical Systems Co. – 90 in engineering and administration; Lockheed Advanced Development Co. – 65 in maintenance, quality assurance, material, and piloting; General Dynamics – 45 in engineering, materials, and piloting; Boeing Military Airplanes – 40 in engineering, maintenance, and quality assurance; Air Force (AFFTC and AFOTEC) – 20 in engineering, maintenance, and piloting; General Electric – 20 in engineering and field service; Pratt & Whitney – 20 in engineering and field service. The total personnel committed to the test program thus was 300.

The Lockheed consortium had the overall responsibility for the planning and execution of the YF-22A flight demonstration program.

The overall flight test plan was developed by the contractor team. The engine manufacturers provided inputs to this plan for their propulsion system related test requirements. The only guidelines set forth by the Air Force were that the prototypes should be flown for the purpose of EMD risk reduction. The capabilities to be demonstrated during flight test were left to the discretion of the contractor team. Test planning documentation included the YF-22A Flight Demonstration Program Test Plan and supporting Test Information Sheets (TIS) for the following test disciplines: aircraft performance tests with the General Electric engines; aircraft performance tests with the Pratt & Whitney engines; handling qualities tests; General Electric engine tests; Pratt & Whitney engine tests; structural tests; flight systems tests; weapon systems tests; and crew systems tests.

The test plan review and approval cycle differed significantly from the norm for the Dem/Val program in that the AFFTC did not have approval authority. Therefore, there was no AFFTC test plan Technical Review Board (TRB) coordination, only that of the Safety Review Board (SRB). However, the ATF SPO did have review and approval authority for all of the flight test plans and they frequently looked to the AFFTC for their opinions regarding the plans.

Test mission control and real time telemetry monitoring was accomplished utilizing control rooms located in the AFFTC's Ridley Mission Control Center (RMCC). A telemetry relay van was used at Palmdale to assure good telemetry reception at the RMCC during engine runs, taxi tests, and first flights of both prototypes. In addition to Ridley, a control room with a limited capability to support real-time requirements was located in the YF-22A CTF engineering complex. Because of its limitations, this facility could be used only to control benign test missions. The facility never was used to control a mission during Dem/Val, but it was used extensively to supplement (in a passive mode) the primary control room in the RMCC.

Data processing was accomplished at Lockheed's Palmdale Flight Test Data Center (FTDC) using either tapes from the airborne instrumentation system or telemetry data. Several analysis programs were available at the FTDC that were used to further process the data. Some of these were quite specific with regard to engineering disciplines whereas others were general in nature and used quite widely by all disciplines.

A secure, high-capacity network was used to link the Edwards AFB YF-22A CTF facility to Lockheed's Palmdale FTDC and the Burbank plant, the General Dynamics Fort Worth facility, and Boeing in Seattle. The network was utilized extensively by flight test for many purposes during the Dem/Val program. For example, the flight test data base housed in the Palmdale FTDC could be accessed from many of the other locations for detailed engineering examination and analysis. Flight control system OFPs also could be transmitted directly over the net from Fort Worth to Edwards AFB, completely eliminating the necessity of having to ship discs or cassettes between the various team facilities. The net also was used frequently to transmit various types of flight test documentation such as test plans, reports, etc.

As noted previously, the purpose of the YF-22A Dem/Val flight test program was: to establish readiness for low risk EMD and to generate flight test data required for the EMD proposal and "sealed envelope" comparison. It was not for the purpose of determining the full capabilities of the YF-22A aircraft in the classic sense, nor to determine compliance with design requirements or specifications.

In some respects, therefore, the program had to be structured somewhat differently than a "normal" development flight test program. Both YF-22A prototypes were treated as the first of the type, not only because of the immaturity of the airframe, but because each was powered by different prototype engines (since the first Northrop YF-23A had flown with the Pratt & Whitney YF119 engines, it was assumed that by the first flight date of the No.2 YF-22A, the engine type had effectively already been flown).

Much of the testing intended to be accomplished on the YF-22A first prototype was planned to be repeated on the second in order

to obtain as much comparative data as possible with both engines. The first prototype was tasked with accomplishing the high AoA tests. The second was equipped with a stores management system (SMS) and missile launchers and it would be used for weapons bay environment and armament tests. From the beginning it was intended the AFOTEC would conduct their Early Operational Assessment (EOA) utilizing both aircraft. Each of the aircraft's planned test task assignments were then:

TEST TASK ASSIGNMENT	A/C-1	A/C-2
Initial Airworthiness	Yes	Yes
Limited Envelope Expansion (Flutter/Flying Qual./Loads)	Yes	No
Propulsion System Tests	Yes	Yes
Aerial Refueling Qualification	Yes	No
Supercruise & Performance	Yes	Yes
Maneuverability/Controllability	Yes	Yes
Weapon Bay Vibration & Acoustics	No	Yes
Live Missile Launches	No	Yes
High AoA Tests	Yes	No

Low and medium speed taxi tests were performed on both prototypes prior to their first flights. The primary objectives of these tests were to evaluate ground handling characteristics, braking dynamics, the anti-skid system, longitudinal control capability, FLCC air data accuracy, nose wheel steering characteristics and to ensure there was no landing gear shimmy or adverse interaction between the aircraft's structural bending modes and the flight control system. Secondary objectives were to assure that all onboard systems (including instrumentation) were operating normally in preparation for first flight.

The only anomaly observed during these tests was an apparent bias of approximately 3° between the nose boom and the FLCC air data system AoA indications. FLCC AoA errors of as much as plus or minus 5° had been evaluated in the flying qualities simulator. The consensus

Top: **YF-22A, N22YF over Edwards AFB during course of spin test program. Spin recovery chute canister and support structure are readily visible.** Lockheed Martin

Below: **YF-22A, N22YX, over Edwards during Dem/Val tests. Full-span leading edge flaps are readily discernible.** Lockheed Martin

of the pilots and General Dynamics flight control personnel was that this would not pose any particular flying qualities problem within the intended initial airworthiness flight envelope. The decision was made to fly with the bias and obtain inflight calibration data before attempting to correct it.

The first flight of the number one YF-22A, N22YF (PAV-1), powered by the General Electric YF120-GE-100 engines was made by Lockheed test pilot Dave Ferguson from Lockheed's Palmdale (Plant 10) facility to Edwards AFB on Saturday, September 29, 1990. Flight duration was shorter than originally planned because the takeoff had been delayed while a ground station problem was rectified. The long static time on the ground consumed considerable fuel, and this affected the flight duration.

The landing gear were not retracted during the first flight. It probably would not have retracted anyway, as difficulties with what the F-22 Program Manager termed "Fascist Software" prevented retraction until the fifth flight. As it turned out, the landing gear extension command was hardwired, but the retraction cycle was controlled by the integrated vehicle subsystem control (IVSC). Bypassing the IVSC landing gear retraction control with independent hardwiring solved the problem.

Once the landing gear retraction anomaly was corrected, the pace of the flight test program increased rapidly. The first tasks for N22YF were to complete its initial airworthiness tests in order to establish a reasonable level of confidence with the aircraft's flying qualities, performance, and engine and systems operation. Concurrently with the accomplishment of those objectives, the plan was to expand the flutter envelope clearance up to 1.6 Mach at 40,000 ft. (450 KEAS). This goal was in fact achieved approximately one month into the program on the 14th flight.

The first supersonic flight had taken place on October 25 during the aircraft's 9th flight. This was followed a short while later by KC-135 tanker qualification tests. The first air-to-air refueling took place during the 11th flight on October 26. All refueling trials were flown by the AFFTC YF-22A project pilot, Maj. Mark Shackleford (who, on the aircraft's 10th flight – taking place on October 25 – had become the first Air Force pilot to fly it under the auspices of the 6511 Test Squadron).

A short down time now followed, this permitting incorporation and checkout of a new FLCC operational flight program (OFP) that would enable the use of thrust vectoring. The spin recovery chute (SRC) also was installed and other modifications were made to the aircraft and FLCC software that eliminated the PADS AoA error. The bias was corrected by drooping the air data probes 5° and fine tuning the FLCC local flow angle corrections. Shortly thereafter, high AoA testing was initiated. The objective in this phase was to reach 60° AoA and be able to perform pitch and rolling maneuvers at this flight condition. This was accomplished in one week. The SRC was removed from the aircraft and the majority of test effort for the remainder of the Dem/Val program was devoted to supersonic envelope expansion along with performance, flying qualities, propulsion system and loads testing out to maximum speed.

The first flight of the second YF-22A, N22YX (PAV-2), was made by Lockheed test pilot Tom Morgenfeld on October 30, 1990. Once initial airworthiness testing was completed, the thrust of its flight test program was directed toward the completion of all the prerequisite testing that was required prior to conducting a live AIM-9M Sidewinder missile launch. This task was completed approximately one month after first flight and following the first in-flight weapon bay opening using PAV-2 on November 20 (flight no. 6).

During the 11th flight, with Jon Beesley flying PAV-2, the AIM-9M live launch was accomplished successfully on November 28,1990. This was followed by an AIM-120 AMRAAM live launch just before Christmas, on December 20, 1990. The remainder of the second prototype's flight test program was devoted to supersonic envelope expansion along with performance, flying qualities and propulsion system testing. The YF-22A flight test program was completed on December 28, 1990.

The primary focus of the YF-22A Dem/Val flight test program was to demonstrate the following capabilities:

Dem/Val Prototype Air Vehicle Test Highlights

Jun	(1990)	"Sealed Envelope" predictions provided to SPO.	
22 Jun		YF-23A No. 1 rolled out at Edwards AFB.	
27 Aug		YF-23A No. 1 First Flight (YF119 engines).	
29 Aug	YF-22A No. 1 rolled out at Palmdale.		
18 Sep		YF-23A No. 1 achieves supercruise speed of Mach 1.43 (YF119 engines).	
29 Sep	YF-22A No. 1 First Flight (YF120 engines).		
26 Oct		YF-23A No. 2 First Flight (YF120 engines).	
30 Oct	YF-22A No. 2 First Flight (YF119 engines).		
Nov	EMD RFP issued.		
3 Nov	YF-22A No. 1 achieves supercruise. Highest supercruise speed with this aircraft Mach 1.58 (YF120 engines).		
15 Nov	First thrust vectoring on YF-22A No. 1.		
28 Nov	AIM-9M missile launch from YF-22A No. 2.		
29 Nov		YF-23A No. 2 achieves supercruise speed of Mach 1.6 (YF120 engines).	
30 Nov		34th and final flight of YF-23A No. 1 (43 hrs).	
10 Dec	YF-22A No. 1 begins high AoA testing.		
17 Dec	YF-22A No. 1 completes high AoA testing.		
18 Dec		16th and final flight of YF-23A No. 2 (22 hrs). YF-23A flight testing completed.	
20 Dec	AIM-120 missile launch from YF-22A No. 2.		
27 Dec	YF-22A No. 2 achieves supercruise speed of Mach 1.43 (YF119 engines).		
28 Dec	YF-22A No. 1 achieves max Mach (over 2), max positive g (over 7) (YF120 engines). YF-22A flight testing completed.		
31 Dec	EMD Proposals delivered by both contractor teams.		

via David Aronstein, Michael Hirschberg, and Albert Piccirillo

Top: **YF-22A, N22YX during YF119 static engine run at Lockheed Martin's Palmdale, California facility. Bars on the horizontal stabilator are dynamic load sensors.** Lockheed Martin

Left: **Chart providing comparison details for the YF-22A and YF-23A Dem/Val fly-off.** Lockheed Martin

Right: **YF-22A, N22YX during ground pre-flight check.** Lockheed Martin

Below:**YF-22A, N22YF, equipped with anti-spin chute aseembly. Noteworthy in this photo are the positions of the rudders, ailerons, flaps, and horizontal stabilators.** Lockheed Martin

Below inset: **Top view of YF-22A, N22YX. Visible (red lines) are strip sensors for picking up load and temperature data.** Lockheed Martin

(1) Super maneuverability and controllability with both the Pratt & Whitney and General Electric engines to include specific excess power, turning and rolling performance, and pitch response. Doublets, sideslips, rolls, and wind-up turns were used to evaluate the YF-22A's handling qualities. The resultant data then was compared to wind tunnel and flight simulator results. Qualitative evaluations also were performed for the takeoff, landing, formation, and tracking tasks. Formation flight evaluations included air refueling as well as normal formation tasks. Lastly the effects of thrust vectoring, speed brake operation, and weapons bay door position also were evaluated.

In general there was very good agreement between the predicted and actual results. Handling qualities during takeoff and landing were found to be excellent. The landing evaluations included overhead approaches as well as straight in approaches from normal, high, low, and laterally offset starts. In addition, no problems of any kind were observed during simulated and actual single-engine approaches and landings. The crosswind landing envelope was expanded easily out to 20 kts. within five weeks of first flight.

Sustained load factor and specific excess power test results are classified. However, both of these performance parameters either met, or exceeded predictions. Rolling performance test results were less than predicted. At .90 Mach and 30,000 ft. the predicted full stick deflection roll rate was 200° per second; the flight test value was 180° per second. At 1.5 Mach and 40,000 ft. the predicted value was 185° per second as compared to the demonstrated value of 175°.

Flight test measured roll damping was higher than used in the FLCC control law design, and changing the control law gains to reflect the measured roll damping would increase the roll rate at .90 Mach.

At 1.5 Mach, adverse sideslip induced by the roll maneuver was larger than predicted in part due to the pneumatic air data system measuring AoA 1.5° lower than true. This resulted in incorrect aileron-rudder interconnect scheduling and excessive sideslip.

In the cruise configuration only one small problem was noted, that being a bit of excessive sensitivity to small roll inputs. That was corrected easily by a minor gain change. Formation flying and aerial refueling were accomplished easily, with level one handling qualities being exhibited throughout. As an example, the initial air refueling and subsequent boom envelope expansion were accomplished on the first two flights flown by Air Force test pilot Maj. Mark Shackleford.

The integration of thrust vectoring into the flight control system went very smoothly, beginning with the first thrust vectoring flight (no. 15) on November 15, 1990. This was in spite of the fact two separate sets of control laws were required because of the two different airframe/engine combinations. Thrust vectoring was reported as being transparent to the pilot as far as handling qualities were concerned.

The increased performance gained through thrust vectoring was very evident both at high AoAs and in increased maneuverability at supersonic speeds. In fact, supersonic agility was widely praised by the pilots who likened the YF-22A when supersonic to other fighters when subsonic. In all, the YF-22A was judged by all of the pilots who flew it to be a very pleasant aircraft to fly.

(2) Supersonic cruise performance at intermediate thrust (supercruise) with both engine designs. Supercruise performance was evaluated with both the General Electric (achieved for the first time on November 3, 1990) and Pratt & Whitney engines (achieved for the first time on December 27, 1990), and the method of test was relatively straight forward. Actual temperatures aloft were obtained on the day of the flight from weather balloon data. These data then were used to estimate the predicted supercruise Mach number and altitude for the appropriate prototype aircraft. The aircraft then was accelerated using afterburner to the predicted supercruise flight conditions, the throttles were retarded to intermediate thrust, and the aircraft then was allowed to accelerate or decelerate

Roll control was provided by a combination of ailerons, flaperons, and differential horizontal stabilator, with the rudders being used to coordinate the rolls. The additional pitch control available with thrust vectoring permitted the FLCS roll rate limiter to be increased. This was due to the increased pitch capability required to counter inertially produced pitching moments in low speed rolls. It resulted in the pilot being able to generate significantly higher roll rates with thrust vectoring on as compared with the maximum roll rates with vectoring off.

The YF-22A spin recovery chute system design was similar to that used on the General Dynamics F-16 with the exception of the fact the YF-22A's empennage and exhaust nozzle configuration required the use of a larger quad-mount for the chute canister as compared to the F-16's tri-mount. The chute diameter was 28 ft. and the riser length was 100 ft. to ensure the deployment chute would be well outside the exhaust plume with the exhaust nozzle at its full trailing edge up position. Ground taxi (76 KIAS) and in-flight (165 KIAS @ 25,000 ft.) deployment and jettison tests were conducted prior to initiating the high AoA flight tests. There were no problems encountered during these tests nor was the chute ever used for recovery during the high AoA test program. Additional prerequisite testing included: flying qualities tests (1 g maneuver blocks) up to 20° AoA with thrust vectoring on and off...the maneuver block usually consisted of a trim point, pitch, roll and yaw doublets, sideslips, and bank-to-bank 180° and 360° rolls; engine airstarts; auxiliary power unit/ emergency power unit airstarts; and zero and negative g system tests.

The prerequisite testing was completed on December 10, 1990, just a little over two months after first flight. The actual high AoA test plan consisted of a methodical test matrix which allowed a careful evaluation of aircraft stability and control/handling qualities at progressively higher AoA. A typical high AoA maneuver block consisted of: a 1 g slowdown to the test AoA, trimming at that AoA and then pitch, yaw and roll doublets, rolling maneuvers, throttle transients (up to 40° AoA), and full forward stick pushovers.

All of the maneuvers were accomplished with thrust vectoring on and with the throttles set at intermediate (INT) thrust, except the 1 g pushovers.

The pushovers were accomplished first with vectoring on at INT thrust, and then repeated at idle thrust with vectoring off to determine basic aircraft pitching moment.

Real time comparisons of predicted versus actual maneuver results were used to issue

(if required) in order to stabilize at the test day supercruise flight conditions.

The specific supercruise test results are classified, but, in general terms, the YF-22A proved quite capable of maintaining level flight in supersonic cruise conditions using intermediate thrust for as long as desired. This capability was demonstrated on several occasions during the Dem/Val program at altitudes between 37,000 ft. and 40,000 ft. A cruise in excess of 1.58 Mach was claimed by unofficial sources for the GE-powered aircraft and 1.43 Mach for the Pratt & Whitney. Between the two, a total of more than 4 hours at supersonic speeds was logged. From these test results it was concluded the YF-22A's supersonic installed thrust minus cruise drag (excess thrust) was as predicted.

(3) High AoA flight characteristics. Outstanding low speed agility was considered a hallmark of the YF-22A design. Therefore, early in the development of the Dem/Val flight test plan it was deemed appropriate to devote a relatively significant amount of the flight test effort to demonstrating the aircraft flight characteris-

tics in low speed, high AoA flight conditions. Historically, however, high AoA flight testing has been full of surprises due to the complexities of predicting the results. For this reason, and the inherent hazardous nature of these tests, the test methods to accomplish this testing were thoroughly scrutinized before testing began on December 10, 1990.

As discussed previously, the YF-22A's flight control system was designed to utilize the engine nozzles in the pitch axis. Pitch control, therefore, was provided by a combination of symmetric movement of the horizontal stabilators and thrust vectoring (TV). There were no flight control system AoA limits, and there was sufficient nose-up trim capability to permit trim flight at extreme AoAs. By utilizing thrust vectoring in the pitch axis, it was possible to reduce the area of the horizontal tail. But, it was still large enough to ensure there was adequate nose-down pitching moment capability to preclude the possibility of a deep stall at high AoAs with thrust vectoring off or in the event of a dual engine failure.

Top: **YF-22A, N22YF, over Edwards test range.** Lockheed Martin

Left: **YF-22A, N22YX, launching an AIM-120. Only half of its main weapon bay was actually configured for missile carriage. Chase is a Boeing F-15D, 78-570.** Lockheed Martin

clearance to the next test point. This procedure worked very well and was critical to the aggressive test schedule. All planned Dem/Val high AoA tests were completed in nine flights (14.9 hrs.) over a period of one week with the end of testing on December 17,1990. These were the critical tests used to demonstrate basic aircraft aerodynamics, thrust vectoring, flight control system design, aircraft handling qualities, and to verify correct operation of the air data and inertial navigation systems.

The AoA build-up was accomplished in 2° increments from 20° to 40°, and in 4° increments from 40° to 60° (the change in this increment was due to an extremely small change in aircraft flight condition for a 2° change in AoA above 40°).

The pilots were very pleased with the aircraft's handling qualities at high AoA. Light airframe buffet was noted at 22° and increased slightly at 24°. The buffet intensity or frequency did not change after this point up to 60° and may actually have started to decrease. Of particular note was the precise pitch control at all AoA. Both pitch attitude and AoA could be held to within 1/2° with thrust vectoring on. With thrust vectoring off, control was less precise due to control law changes and the obvious loss of control power, and AoA could be maintained only to within 1° to 2°.

When the doublets had been completed at a given AoA, rolling maneuvers then were accomplished at a slightly lower AoA, usually 4° less. The absence of wing rock made precise and predictable rolling maneuvers possi-

Top: **YF-22A, N22YX, bearing AF serial number 87-701, in landing configuration.** Lockheed Martin

Right: **YF-22A, N22YF, with spin recovery chute canister mounted on steel tripod. Chute was pyrotechically deployed.** Lockheed Martin

Right inset:**YF-22A's thrust-to-weight ratio exceeded 1.4 to 1.** Lockheed Martin

ble. Rolling performance was very impressive. Roll response was immediate up to approximately 30° AoA and then only hinted at the slightest delay at higher AoA.

With aircraft N22YF, the test aircraft, there was a slight asymmetry between the left and right rolls. The left rolls were slightly faster, with less roll coast (rolling after the input was removed) and more AoA. As 30° AoA was approached, lateral trim requirements to maintain wings level began to increase. Above 30° AoA the trend then began to decrease and trim asymmetries at higher AoA flight conditions were negligible. This was observed in the cockpit as a slight increase in roll control activity but was not perceived as a noticeable handling qualities deficiency. As AoA increased from 40° to 44°, roll control became slightly more sensitive and thus appeared to require more attention. Roll angle could be precisely controlled and deviations from wings level flight were less than 1°.

At 50° AoA, a phenomenon that was observed in the flight simulator was confirmed in flight. At that AoA (in the simulator) pilots had noted a slight roll oscillation of plus or minus 5° that could be induced by small lateral stick inputs. This appeared to be caused by inputs that were made faster than the aircraft could respond. This motion would quickly damp out if the stick was held frozen in the lateral axis, and with more careful inputs would not occur at all. Most were skeptical about the simulator's ability to predict this. Amazingly, it turned out to be a very accurate simulation, even at these extreme AoA. Aircraft roll response was always positive, and it was easy to hold the wings level for prolonged periods at these incredibly high AoA. Throughout the testing engine operation was excellent.

The high AoA program was very aggressive. Wind tunnel and simulator predictions were confirmed in a very complex portion of the envelope while demonstrating the aircraft's outstanding high AoA capabilities. The YF-22A's high AoA handling qualities were best summarized by General Dynamics' test pilot Jon Beesley when he said, "It always did what I wanted it to do and never did anything that I didn't want it to do."

(4) Live launch of both an AIM-9M Sidewinder and AIM-120 AMRAAM. Internal weapons carriage was fundamental to the YF-22A's stealth characteristics and design and the team felt it was important to demonstrate live firings of both the AIM-9 and AIM-120 air-to-air missiles. The prototype aircraft were designed to carry air-to-air missiles in three bays; an AIM-9M in each side, or cheek bay (located aft of the engine intakes), and an AIM-120 in a central main weapon bay (located ventrally). Trapeze type launcher mechanisms were used to extend both missile types from the bays prior to launch.

The second YF-22A, N22YX, was utilized for the armament test program. Two of the three bays (left half and main) were fitted with launchers. A stores management system also was incorporated. Contrary to what one might expect to find in a prototype aircraft missile launch system (i.e. a pilot activated toggle switch that is hardwired to the launch mechanism), the YF-22A incorporated an essentially production type software-controlled stores management system (minus sensors).

Weapons bay vibration and acoustics tests were accomplished prior to the live missile firings. In the case of the AIM-120, these included the carriage of an instrumented missile to determine its internal environment prior to carriage and launch.

Both missile firings were accomplished at .70 Mach and 20,000 ft. The AIM-9M test was conducted on November 28, 1990 at the China Lake Naval Weapon Test Center and was successful in all respects. The missile separated as predicted. There was no evidence of rocket exhaust impingement on the aircraft structure, nor engine exhaust plume ingestion.

The AIM-120 firing, which took place on December 20, 1990, also was an unqualified success. This test was accomplished utilizing the Navy's Pacific Missile Test Center range at Pt. Mugu. Missile separation and ignition was as predicted and it flew its intended trajectory.

All of these demonstration objectives were achieved in just over three months of flight testing. The Air Force Operational Test and Evaluation Center (AFOTEC) participated in the YF-22A Dem/Val flight test program and conducted an early operational assessment (EOA) of the YF-22's capabilities with regard to its ultimate operational role.

Eleven flights were devoted to the AFOTEC EOA effort and a total of 13.9 hours were accumulated on both prototypes. All AFOTEC sorties were made up of tests extracted from approved test plans. However, the particular tests chosen for the EOA were more operationally oriented than typical engineering tests. For these evaluations the more tactical (as compared to engineering flight test) types of MFD display formats were utilized by the AFOTEC pilot.

At the conclusion of the Dem/Val program an independent assessment was prepared by the AFOTEC team and briefed by them up through the Tactical Air Command (TAC) chain of command. The YF-22A team's AFOTEC pilot, Lt. Col. Willie Naigle, stated the YF-22A was a "mighty fine machine at this phase of development."

Several unplanned tests also were accomplished during the Dem/Val program. The first of these was a wet runway landing at the end of the first flight. Thunderstorms had moved

Top: YF-22A, N22YF, at altitude over Edwards AFB.
Lockheed Martin

Left: YF-23A, N231YF/87-800, was the first of the two Northrop ATF contenders to fly.
Terry Panopalis collection

through the Antelope Valley area on that day. Rain fell on the Edwards AFB runway a few minutes before the aircraft arrived for landing. Nothing unusual was noted by the pilot with regard to ground handling or operation of the brakes and anti-skid systems.

The first single-engine landing was accomplished on the third flight of N22YF following an inflight uncommanded shutdown of the left General Electric engine. The engine's control system logic had commanded the shutdown immediately after takeoff when an engine hydraulic system seal failed and all engine hydraulic fluid was lost. The aircraft's single engine flying qualities were judged to be excellent, and no special compensation on the part of the pilot was required for the subsequent landing.

To keep the competition between the engine manufacturers even, the first single engine landing on N22YX was made on its fifth flight following a precautionary shutdown of the right Pratt & Whitney engine when it was suspected that an air turbine starter had failed. The landing was uneventful even though it was General Dynamics' Jon Beesley's first flight in the aircraft.

The YF-22A's crosswind limit was raised to 20 kts. much earlier than planned when unforecasted high winds came up after N22YX had taken off on its third flight. The turbulence and crosswind posed no problems for the test pilot, Tom Morgenfeld.

The last unscheduled demonstration occurred on the 11th flight of N22YF. This flight was terminated early due to the loss of fluid from the No. 1 hydraulic system following the failure of a pressure switch. The aircraft reacted to the loss of the hydraulic system as had been observed previously in the flight simulator and the return to the base and landing were accomplished by test pilot Maj. Mark Shackleford without any particular difficulty.

In early 1990, the ATF SPO had requested Lockheed to provide preflight predictions of various YF-22A performance characteristics against which they would be able to compare actual YF-22A test results determined from flight testing. The choice of parameters was left to the company. These preflight predictions were provided the SPO as the YF-22A "sealed envelope" performance during late June. These predictions were to serve as credibility criteria and as a "report card" to verify actual versus predicted performance.

The majority of the "sealed envelope" predictions and actual flight test results are classified, but the following provide general observations:

(1) Supersonic cruise was as predicted.

(2) Subsonic drag numbers agreed at .90 Mach. In addition, the drag data obtained from both aircraft/engine combinations were in agreement with each other.

(3) Supersonic drag numbers agreed at low lift coefficients. However, insufficient data was available at higher lift coefficients to make a valid comparison.

(4) Sustained load factors were as predicted.

(5) Specific excess power was as predicted.

(6) Based on flight demonstrations showing better acceleration performance than predicted, it was concluded the YF-22A drag rise and transonic drag numbers were lower than predicted.

(7) Specific range at all test conditions was within 3% of predictions.

(8) Maximum speed was as predicted (and achieved on December 28, 1990).

(9) Maximum roll rates and time to specific bank angles at subsonic and supersonic cruise were less (and greater) than predicted, but judged to be quite satisfactory.

(10) Flying qualities at AoAs greater than 20° were judged to be excellent with thrust vectoring on, and acceptable with vectoring off. The ability to recover from any AoA was never in question.

(11) Flight measured buffet onset and maximum center of lift were higher than predictions.

(12) Maneuver stability was close to predicted.

(13) Flying qualities were in the desirable and adequate range. However, some tailoring of the FLCC schedules or gains were considered desirable to improve the ratings.

(14) Excellent engine/inlet compatibility was demonstrated with no throttle restrictions. No compressor stalls were experienced during the program.

(15) Engine operation was unaffected by AIM-9M and AIM-120 launches.

(16) Missile trajectories matched predictions.

(17) Weapon bay vibration and acoustic measurements showed good agreement with wind tunnel predictions.

(18) All airstart attempts were successful, with start times equal to or less than predicted.

(19) Measured stability derivatives were in good agreement with predicted values from wind tunnel data.

(20) No flutter was encountered, nor was it predicted to occur within the YF-22A's full flight envelope.

(21) In general, the pneumatic air data system calibrations matched the wind tunnel predictions.

In the course of a three-month flight test program, the YF-22As were able to clear a demonstration flight envelope of over 7 gs, 82 KCAS to over 2.0 Mach, and 50,000 ft. An aggressive flight test plan included the demonstration of supercruise capability with both the Pratt & Whitney and General Electric engines, flight control development (specifically thrust vectoring), demonstration of unequaled maneuverability across the airspeed spectrum from extremely low speed to high supersonic Mach numbers, and weapon separation from internal weapons bays. Despite the limited time available, all of these primary test objectives were accomplished without encountering any major snags.

From first flight of a new aircraft design to a cleared demonstration envelope in 91 days is an unequaled achievement in the modern history of aviation. Additionally, this was accomplished with two new engine designs and with the most advanced cockpit/avionics architecture ever flown in any fighter. Throughout this high intensity testing there was no foreign object damage (FOD) or safety incidents. Upon conclusion of the flight test program, 43 flights and 52.8 hours had been logged on N22YF and 31 flights and 38.8 hours had been logged on N22YX.

After a three-month-long review of the Dem/Val results and the associated EMD proposals from both Northrop and Lockheed (Lockheed's was approximately 20,000 pages in length and weighed approximately 4,500 lb.; it was flown to Wright-Patterson AFB, Ohio aboard a specially chartered Convair 880 transport on December 31, 1990), on April 23, 1991, Secretary of the Air Force Donald Rice announced that the Lockheed, Boeing, and General Dynamics consortium had been selected to proceed with the EMD F-22A. At the same time, the Pratt & Whitney YF119-PW-100 engine was selected as the preferred powerplant. Rice noted the Lockheed and Pratt & Whitney designs clearly offered better capability at lower cost, thereby providing the Air Force with a true best value.

The superiority of the Lockheed and Pratt & Whitney designs was attributed to their higher ratings on their technical proposals and their respectively better program management plans. Additionally, an Air Force assessment of risk led it to believe the Lockheed and Pratt & Whitney designs were more likely to accomplish their proposed objectives and that their management would be more effective. It also was stated that cost differences, though slight, favored the Lockheed and Pratt & Whitney designs.

Lockheed's Dem/Val efforts can be summarized as follows:
- 18,000 hours of wind tunnel time involving at least nine different models
- 3,200 hours of RCS testing
- 10,000,000 hours of design/analysis
- 159 hours of Avionics Flying Laboratory tests
- Five major Avionics Ground Prototype demonstrations
- 1,100 hours of manned simulations
- 400 distinct RM&S demonstrations
- 110,000 hours of P&W component tests
- 3,000 hours of full-up engine tests
- 91.6 hours of YF-22A flight tests

Additionally, the Lockheed consortia invested $675 million in company funds while Northrop invested $650 million. Each of the engine companies also invested $100 million of their own money. Total Dem/Val costs, excluding government costs, were $5.349 billion.

Northrop YF-23A: The first Northrop YF-23A, N231YF, was equipped with two Pratt & Whitney YF119 engines. It was transported by truck from the company's Hawthorne, California

Top and left: **The first YF-23A, N231YF/87-800 as it appeared during temporary storage under the auspices of the NASA at Edwards AFB/Dryden Flight Research Center during 2000.**
Terry Panopalis

facility to Edwards AFB where it was officially rolled out on June 22, 1990. Northrop test pilot Paul Metz, who later would go to work for Lockheed Martin on the F/A-22A program, successfully completed the first YF-23A flight in this aircraft on August 27.

The YF-23A completed its first inflight refueling during its fourth flight on September 14. A supercruise capability of 1.43 Mach was demonstrated on September 18. This aircraft also was used to reach a maximum speed with afterburner for type of 1.80 Mach. Later it served as the weapons bay test aircraft and was used to explore acoustical measurements in the bays, carriage of an inert, instrumented AIM-120, and evaluation of aircraft handling quality with the weapons bay doors open. No actual weapons tests were attempted, though the aircraft was capable of live launches.

The first YF-23A ended its flight test program on November 30 with the demonstration of a "combat surge" sortie generation capability. Six missions were flown on that day in a period of less than ten hours. The shortest turn-around time was 18 minutes and included simulated missile and gun rearming. By the time of its permanent grounding, this aircraft had logged 34 flights and accumulated 43 hours of flight time.

The second YF-23A, N232YF, powered by two General Electric F120 engines was flown for the first time on October 26 with Northrop's Jim Sandburg at the controls. This aircraft, following initial airworthiness and functional checks, was used primarily for supercruise, performance, and maneuverability testing. Upgraded flight control software was installed to perform an automatic optimum deflection of wing leading edge flaps (the first aircraft had only two position options).

The second YF-23A demonstrated a supercruise capability of 1.6 Mach on November 29 and, shortly afterwards, a 25° AoA capability (wind tunnel studies indicated the aircraft would remain controllable to 60°). Flight testing with this aircraft ended on December 18 after logging 16 flights and a total of 22 hours of flying time.

Like the YF-22, the YF-23s also had some minor problems, including one engine shutdown on November 6, when a high-pressure hydraulic line discharge tube developed a leak.

The Northrop YF-23As logged a total of 50 sorties and 65 flight hours over a 104 day period and cruised supersonically at between 1.4 and 1.6 Mach for a total of 7.2 hours. Though Northrop has never publicly acknowledged details of the aircraft's accomplishments during the fly-off with the YF-22A, it is known that demonstrated YF-23A performance figures generally matched the company's "sealed envelope" predictions and met Air Force ATF goals.

Additionally, some sources note the YF-23A outperformed the YF-22A in all arenas with the exception of maneuverability (the YF-23A did exceed the requirement for combat maneuverability). Additionally, the YF-23A was found to have a larger weapons capacity, a lighter wing loading, superior low-observables specifications, and a planform that was more readily adaptable to the proposed deep-strike/interdiction mission.

During July of 2004 it was revealed that the YF-23A was being considered by Northrop Grumman as a possible competitor for the "regional bomber" mission currently envisioned for the proposed Lockheed Martin F/B-22A. The second prototype YF-23A, earlier in the year, was retrieved from the Western Museum of Flight in Hawthorne, California (where it had been displayed as a museum artifact) by Northrop Grumman and moved into a company facility. There it was being restored for display purposes. Sources indicated that new cockpit displays were being installed and external changes in concert with the proposed bomber role were being integrated.

Above and inset: **YF-22A, N22YF, as it is currently displayed at the USAF Museum, Wright-Patterson AFB, Ohio. Markings noting its use as the GE YF120-powered prototype have been removed. Inset depicts YF-22A, N22YX, modified to serve as F/A-22A pole model.** Jay Miller and (inset) Air Force

Right: **Chart summarizing the YF-23A flight test program for Dem/Val.** Air Force

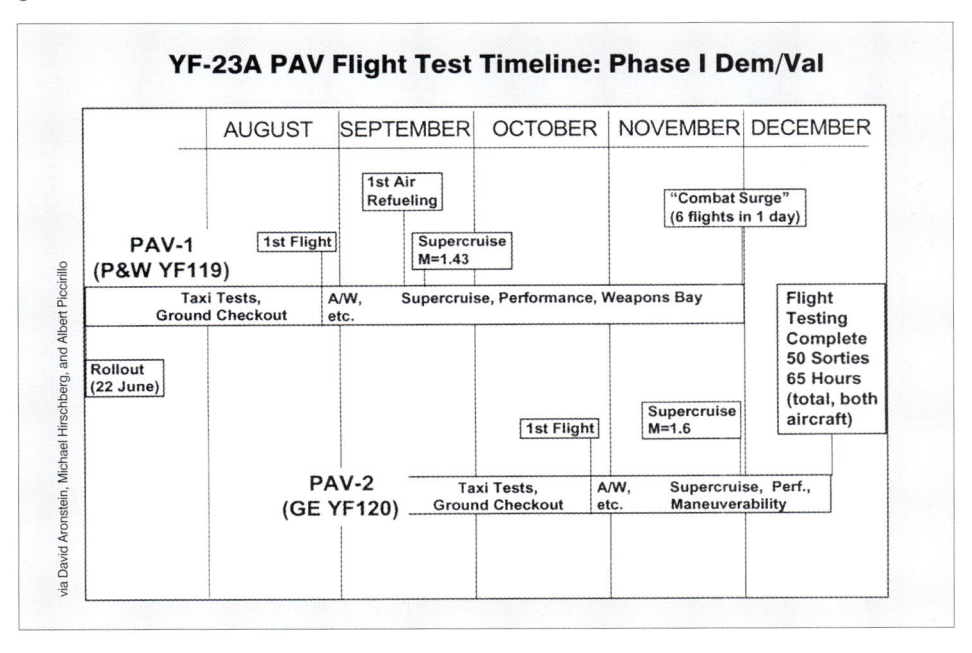

YF-23A PAV Flight Test Timeline: Phase I Dem/Val

via David Aronstein, Michael Hirschberg, and Albert Piccirillo

	AUGUST	SEPTEMBER	OCTOBER	NOVEMBER	DECEMBER
PAV-1 (P&W YF119)		1st Air Refueling		"Combat Surge" (6 flights in 1 day)	Flight Testing Complete 50 Sorties 65 Hours (total, both aircraft)
	1st Flight	Supercruise M=1.43			
	Taxi Tests, Ground Checkout	A/W, etc.	Supercruise, Performance, Weapons Bay		
Rollout (22 June)					
PAV-2 (GE YF120)			1st Flight	Supercruise M=1.6	
		Taxi Tests, Ground Checkout	A/W, etc.	Supercruise, Perf., Maneuverability	

Chapter Four

EMD and Production

Ongoing during Dem/Val was planning for the EMD aircraft and subsequent phases of the proposed production program. The first overall ATF Acquisition Program Baseline was prepared during 1988. This document served as a contract between the program manager and the applicable DoD acquisition authority. The APB was, in fact, approved by Lt. Gen. Thurman (ASD Commander) and forwarded to the Air Force Service Acquisition Executive, Mr. John Welch, for signature during May of 1988.

During early 1989, the Air Force announced that the first FSD F-22 flight would be delayed by one year – from 1992 to 1993 – in order to (1) allow more time to take advantage of maturing technology; (2) to reduce concurrency; and (3) to trim near-term budgets.

Finally, on August 18, 1989, the draft RFP calling for Full Scale Development (FSD...shortly afterwards this acronym was changed to EMD –

Engineering & Manufacturing Development) was released to the weapon system and engineering contractors for response.

Events in the Soviet Union (i.e., its collapse) had a ripple affect throughout the defense community at this time. Virtually all military contracts, not the least of which was that for the ATF, were impacted by the implosion of what, to that point in time, had been viewed as the primary threat to US interests. As a result, the

Facing page top and inset: **First of the EMD F/A-22As, 91-4001, over Edwards AFB.**

Facing page middle left: **F/A-22A radar cross section pole model being tested at Lockheed Martin's Helendale, California facility.**

Facing page middle right: **EMD F/A-22A, 91-4002, equipped with spin recovery chute assembly.** Lockheed Martin x 3

Facing page bottom left/inset and right: **Boeing 757 prototype, N757A, as configured for F/A-22A systems and hardware testing.** Boeing (inset and r.), Jay Miller (l.)

Above: **F/A-22As, 91-4001 and 91-4002 on the Lockheed Martin ramp at Edwards AFB.**

Right: **F/A-22A, 91-4001 in final assembly at Lockheed Martin's Marietta, Georgia facility.** Lockheed Martin x 2

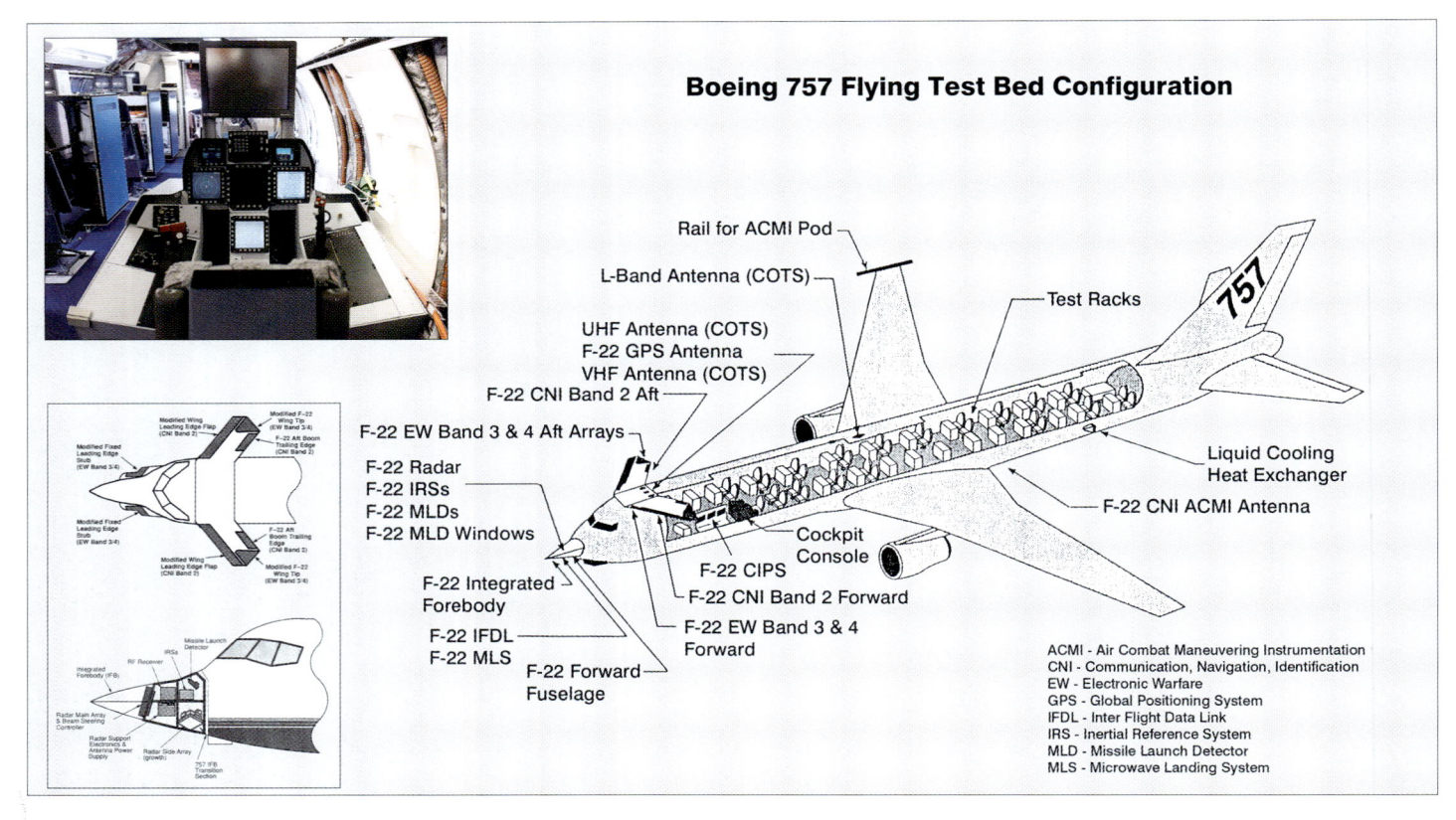

Boeing 757 Flying Test Bed Configuration

Rail for ACMI Pod
L-Band Antenna (COTS)
UHF Antenna (COTS)
F-22 GPS Antenna
VHF Antenna (COTS)
F-22 CNI Band 2 Aft
Test Racks
757
F-22 EW Band 3 & 4 Aft Arrays
F-22 Radar
F-22 IRSs
F-22 MLDs
F-22 MLD Windows
Liquid Cooling Heat Exchanger
F-22 CNI ACMI Antenna
Cockpit Console
F-22 CIPS
F-22 Integrated Forebody
F-22 CNI Band 2 Forward
F-22 IFDL
F-22 MLS
F-22 EW Band 3 & 4 Forward
F-22 Forward Fuselage

Modified Wing Leading Edge Flap (CNI Band 2)
Modified F-22 Wing Tip (EW Band 3/4)
Modified Fixed Leading Edge Stub (EW Band 3/4)
F-22 Aft Boom Trailing Edge (CNI Band 2)
Modified Fixed Leading Edge Stub (EW Band 3/4)
F-22 Aft Boom Trailing Edge (CNI Band 2)
Modified Wing Leading Edge Flap (CNI Band 2)
Modified F-22 Wing Tip (EW Band 3/4)

Missile Launch Detector
RF Receiver
IRSs
Integrated Forebody (IFB)
Radar Main Array & Beam Steering Controller
F-22 Aft Boom Trailing Edge (CNI Band 2)
Radar Support Electronics & Antenna Power Supply
Radar Side Array (glowth)
757 FTB Transition Section

ACMI - Air Combat Maneuvering Instrumentation
CNI - Communication, Navigation, Identification
EW - Electronic Warfare
GPS - Global Positioning System
IFDL - Inter Flight Data Link
IRS - Inertial Reference System
MLD - Missile Launch Detector
MLS - Microwave Landing System

planned mid-1991 EMD start date was maintained, but a Low Rate Initial Production (LRIP) decision was deferred by no less than four years (to 1996). It was expected that, if that schedule were maintained, production would continue through 2014. Peak production was now reduced from 72 to 48 aircraft per year and estimated unit flyaway cost (UFC) was increased – as a result – from $41.2 million to $51.2 million.

During late July of 1991, the Defense Acquisition Board (DAB) announced the Milestone II decision calling for EMD to start. At the same time, the planned production quantity was officially reduced from 750 to 648 and production was now scheduled to end during 2012. System requirements were changed to increase the level of avionics integration, and to add a two-seat trainer variant (designated F-22B) to the program. These changes were estimated to add significantly to the F-22's UFC (i.e., raising it to $56.9 million per aircraft).

EMD contracts were awarded on August 3, 1991. Total initial value was roughly $11 billion with $9.55 billion going to Lockheed and $1.375 billion going to Pratt & Whitney. Original

Top and inset: **Boeing 757 Flying Test Bed aircraft played an integral role in F/A-22A systems development. Inset depicts FTB interior and F/A-22 primary instrument panel.** Boeing

Middle: **First EMD F/A-22A, 91-4001, bore distinctive markings.** Lockheed Martin

Left: **Second EMD F/A-22A, 91-4002, immediately prior to official roll-out on February 10, 1998.** Lockheed Martin

Right: **F/A-22A, 91-4001 during roll maneuver over Edwards AFB.** Lockheed Martin

Middle: **Distinctive vertical fin markings on F/A-22A, 91-4002, during course of flight test work at Edwards AFB were short-lived.** Lockheed Martin

Bottom: **F/A-22A, 91-4001 during the course of its first flight on September 7, 1997. Chase was F-16B, 78-0088.** Lockheed Martin

EMD plans called for 13 F-22 airframes to be delivered (9 single-seat and 2 two-seat) plus one static test and one fatigue test airframe. During 1993, these figures were subsequently, reduced to 9 aircraft (7 single-seat and 2 two-seat; during 1998, it was announced that all were to be single-seaters).

The F-22 outer mold line was frozen during October of 1991. On December 16, external design was declared frozen sufficiently to permit wind tunnel and radar cross section models to be built, the internal design to be completed, and tooling preparations to begin. Fabrication of the first EMD aircraft was slated to begin during December of the following year. The initial aircraft batch was to be followed by four "pre-production verification" F-22s (i.e., Initial Operational Test & Evaluation [IOT&E] aircraft).

Lockheed, during January of 1991, now moved its F-22 team headquarters from Burbank, California to Marietta, Georgia. By 1992, a 190,000 sq. ft. automated production line for the F-22 was under construction in the southwest corner of the company's 3,500,000 sq. ft. primary production building (B-1). Located alongside the long-standing C-130 production line that had dominated the Marietta facility for over four decades, it later would be converted back to a more conventional (240,000 sq. ft.) non-automated line when difficulties with the former proved too expensive and time con-

suming to overcome. Concurrent to this, a 138,000 sq. ft. adhesive bonding plant also was built by the company at its Charleston, South Carolina location.

During the late summer of 1991, Lockheed revealed plans to resume flight testing of the second YF-22A, N22YX (the Pratt & Whitney-powered prototype). This aircraft took to the air – for the first time since the end of the fly-off – on October 30, 1991, piloted by Tom Morgenfeld.

Follow-on work using this aircraft took place at Edwards AFB. It was to consist of an additional 100 hours of flying time (approximately 25 flights) to expand the YF-22A's flight envelope and explore select envelope segments in greater detail. Approximately ten flights were scheduled to explore additional air loads data at high-g with the weapons bay doors open and closed. Additional flights were to explore the low altitude/high-speed envelope, flutter testing, high AoA in maneuvering flight, and load measurement work. Missile launch trials also were to be undertaken.

Unfortunately, a landing accident on April 25, 1992, with Morgenfeld at the controls, ended the follow-on flight test program after over 60 hours of EMD-related testing had been completed. The accident followed a series of pitch oscillations that had started at roughly 40 feet above the runway during landing approach. The aircraft hit the runway with the landing gear up, slid approximately 8,000 feet, and caught fire. Morgenfeld departed the aircraft unhurt,

but the YF-22A was severely impact and fire damaged. Restoring it to flightworthy condition proved both mpractical and economically unjustifiable. Fortunately, by the time of the accident, most of the post-Dem/Val flight objectives had been met. Total flight time logged on this airframe was 100.4 hours.

The aircraft was rebuilt, but was not made flightworthy. It was reconfigured instead to be representative of the EMD configuration and later was used as an antenna testbed at the Rome Air Development Center at Griffiss AFB, NY.

Key F/A-22A EMD and Follow-On Program Dates are as follows:

1992:

•On April 25 the number two (Pratt & Whitney F119 powered) YF-22A crash-landed at Edwards AFB.

•On June 4 design review update of the F-22 was officially completed.

•On June 30 Critical Design Review (CDR) for the F119 EMD test engine was completed.

•On October 22 the Air Force released is investigative report on the YF-22A accident.

•On December 17, the first EMD F119 engine was tested for the first time.

1993:

•During January a decision was made to rephase the EMD program in consideration of a FY1993 funding shortfall. Key deadlines were set back between six and eighteen months. Total development aircraft and engine quantities were again reduced (EMD aircraft were reduced to 9 and F119s to 27). A year later, the rephasing process was instigated again, further setting back production scheduling and the introduction of the aircraft into the operational inventory.

The accident led to a detailed examination of the YF-22A's flight control system algorhythmic control laws and control law design methodology. Morgenfeld's piloting technique was not at fault. Changes to the aircraft's control system were instituted and later applied to the production aircraft.

The first YF-22A, N22YF (the General Electric powered prototype), following the conclusion of testing at Edwards AFB, was partially dismantled and on June 23, 1991 loaded aboard a Lockheed C-5A for transport to Lockheed Martin's Marietta, Georgia facility where it was used as a full-scale mock-up for EMD systems and hardware integration. It later was repainted and given the markings seen originally on N22YX (Pratt & Whitney logo on the intake cheeks, etc). Additionally, the General Electric engines were removed and replaced with P&W engines. Following completion of the EMD integration mule program, the aircraft was transferred to the US Air Force Museum at Wright-Patterson AFB, Ohio, where it currently resides as a key exhibit artifact.

• On March 1 Lockheed officially purchased General Dynamics Fort Worth Division. The $1.5 billion purchase increased Lockheed's majority share of the F-22 program from 35% to 67.5%. Boeing's share was 32.5%.

•On April 26 occupancy of the L-22 building at Marietta begins.

•On April 30 the air vehicle Preliminary Design Review was completed and was followed by detailed design final development.

•On May 25 under a $6.5 million contract, the F-22's main weapon bay and avionics systems were adapted for delivery of the forthcoming AIM-9X and standard 1,000 lb./GBU-32 Joint Direct Attack Munition (JDAM).

•During May a decision was made to formally integrate a dedicated ground attack capability into the aircraft's mission profile.

•On December 8 fabrication of the first EMD F-22A ('4001) began at Boeing's Kent, Washington facility. Albert Ferara, a milling machine operator at Boeing's Kent, WA facility, started machining the titanium forward boom keelson panel (one of eight).

All four: **Second EMD F/A-22A, 91-4002, during the course of spin testing. A spin recovery chute was mounted in a canister and mortar deployed upon pilot command. The chute was 28 ft. in diameter with a 125 ft. riser/suspension lines distance to the base of canopy.** Lockheed Martin

1994:

• On February 10 F-22 procurement was formally reduced from 648 aircraft to 442. The two F-22Bs in the EMD batch were cancelled and changed to single-seat F-22As.

• On March 4 it was announced that the F-22 AF/industry design team had identified some shortfalls in the aircraft RCS. The shortfalls, which were identified through a new computer modeling technique, were mitigated by late spring through an intensive in-house effort that included reducing the number of drain holes in the bottom of the aircraft and combining select maintenance panels.

• During November, acquisition of F119 flight test engine long-lead time hardware was initiated.

• On December 9 Secretary of Defense William Perry announced $8 billion in budget changes to seven DoD modernization programs. This necessitated a third rephasing of the F-22 program.

1995:

• On February 24 the Critical Design Review was officially completed. Some 231 reviews of software and systems were undertaken. Lockheed Martin's Model 645 became the official identifier of the production configuration (this superseding the earlier Model 639).

• On March 15 Lockheed and Martin Marietta were formally merged. The new company, which also included General Dynamics Fort Worth division, became Lockheed Martin Aeronautical Systems Company.

• On April 20 Lockheed Martin received a $9.5 million, two-year AF contract calling for the study of F-22 derivatives, including a "suppression of enemy air defenses" (SEAD) variant, a non-lethal suppression of enemy defenses variant, a reconnaissance variant, an attack/interdiction variant, and a surveillance variant.

• On June 2 assembly of the first F-22 midbody began at the Fort Worth plant.

• On June 27 assembly of the first flightworthy EMD (as opposed to static test article) was officially started at Lockheed Martin's Marietta, Georgia facility.

• By mid-1995, Lockheed Martin had accumulated 16,930 hours of wind tunnel time fine-tuning the basic design that had led up to the YF-22A. Some 23 modes were tested in 14 facilities across the US. This resulted in the company's "Configuration 645"...which effectively was the final design for the F-22 in its proposed production form. Six major categories had been explored during the tunnel tests: aerodynamic loads and weapons bay acoustics; inlet and engine compatibility; mission/maneu-ver performance; inlet icing; stability and control and flying qualities; and weapons and stores separation. An additional 900 hours of tunnel work, mostly on weapons and stores separation issues, remained to be completed during 1995 thru 1997.

• During July Pratt & Whitney's F119 turbine demonstrated improved fuel efficiency and elimination of turbine blade vibratory stress problems.

• On October 4 assembly of the first F-22 aft fuselage section and wings began at Boeing.

• On November 2 assembly of the first F-22 integrated forebody began at Lockheed Martin's Marietta, Georgia facility.

1996:

• On January 17 Boeing began assembly of the first wings shipset.

• During February the F-22's flight control system control laws software was tested in flight using the Lockheed Martin VISTA NF-16D testbed. The flight control laws were explored over the course of 21 sorties totaling 26.8 hours of flight time divided into two sessions.

• On May 6 Pratt & Whitney began assembly of the first flight test F119-PW-100 engine.

• On July 9 Pratt & Whitney conducts a "Last Bolt" ceremony at Middletown, CT to recognize the completion of the first flight test F119 engine.

- On July 10 the airframe team received formal notification from the Air Force that the requirement for design and development of the two-seat F-22B was being deferred. The two planned EMD F-22Bs were replaced by two single-seat F-22As, thus making all nine EMD F-22s single-seaters.
- On August 29 Lockheed Martin Tactical Aircraft Systems (LMTAS) commemorated completion of the first mid-fuselage.
- On September 6 the mid-fuselage for the first flyable F-22A (Ship 1) arrived in Marietta after a four-day truck trip from Fort Worth.
- On September 24 Pratt & Whitney announced that the first flight test F119-PW-100 engine had been delivered to the AF. It was first taken to Arnold AFB, TN for testing and then delivered to Marietta.
- On October 1 Northrop Grumman (formerly Westinghouse) announced that the first developmental AN/APG-77 electronically steered, active element, phased-array radar had begun system level integration and testing.
- On October 8 the first two flight test Pratt & Whitney F119 engines were delivered by truck to Marietta.
- On October 16 the aft fuselage for the first F-22A arrived at Lockheed Martin's Marietta, Georgia facility from Boeing as cargo aboard a Lockheed C-5. On the same day, fuselage mating started on the first F-22A ('4001).
- On October 27 the completed fuselage of the first F-22A was lifted from the body mate tool and moved to the wing mate tool.
- On November 9 the wings for the first F-22A arrived at Marietta from Boeing. Mating was completed two days later.
- On December 20 electrical power was applied to the F-22A ('4001) for the first time.

1997:
- On January 21 the first F-22A's left vertical stabilizer was installed.
- On January 24 the first F119 engine fitcheck was performed on the first F-22A.
- Early in 1997 the four PPV (preproduction verification) aircraft program was cancelled. These were to follow the single static and single fatigue test airframes, the two YF-22As, and the nine EMD aircraft.
- On February 6 the first F-22A's right vertical stabilizer was installed.
- On February 17 the F119 engine endurance testing was completed.
- During February the F-22 Sled Test Integrated Product Team (IPT) successfully completed the safety-of-flight test program at the Air Force's ejection seat proving grounds at Holloman AFB, NM. The six-month program, for-

Top: **Third EMD F/A-22A, 91-4003, firing an AIM-9L while executing a rolling maneuver.**

Middle and left: **Second EMD F/A-22A, 91-4002, during flight trials over the Edwards AFB test range. Only the first three EMD aircraft, '01, '02, and '03 were equipped with flight test nose booms.** Lockheed Martin x 3

Right: **Icing trials that had started with wind tunnel tests in the early 1990s was completed during 2004 using production-standard F/A-22A, 01-4022 (shown).** Lockheed Martin

Bottom: **External fuel tanks for the F/A-22A are optimized for ferry and ultra-long-range missions. Tank separation was qualified using EMD F/A-22A, 91-4003.** Lockheed Martin

mally known as the Vehicle Compatibility Sled Test Program, consisted of a series of escape system tests using the McDonnell Douglas-built ACES II ejection seat, instrumented test mannequins simulating small (130 lb.) and large (208 lb.) human occupants, and the Dynamic Engineering Inc.-built simulated F-22 forward fuselage mated to the Air Force's Multi-Axis Seat Ejection (MASE) rocket sled. Tests included a canopy jettison, a zero-speed, zero-altitude (zero/zero) ejection; a 275 KEAS ejection; a 325 KEAS ejection; a 450 KEAS ejection, and a 600 KEAS (maximum speed) ejection.

• On March 6 the first F-22A ('4001) was moved to the "Hush House" (Building B-22 engine noise attenuation facility) where it underwent fueling operations and engine runs.

• On March 31 the F119-PW-100 was granted Initial Flight Release.

• On April 9 the first EMD F-22A ('4001), officially named Raptor (an earlier attempt to name the aircraft *SuperStar* failed in 1991), was rolled out in a public ceremony at Lockheed Martin's Marietta, Georgia facility for the first time.

• During May of 1997 the Quadrennial Defense Review report resulted in planned F-22A production being reduced to 339 aircraft (including 8 PRTV aircraft). Some figures at this time called for production of as few as 180 aircraft.

• On June 10 the AF officially granted Pratt & Whitney Initial Flight Release certification for the F119-PW-100 engine.

• On August 16 the first low-speed taxi test was completed using the first aircraft ('4001).

• On September 5 the high-speed taxi tests were completed.

• On September 7, the first EMD F-22A aircraft ('4001) successfully completed its first flight following delays of several weeks caused by fuel leaks and hardware anomalies. Lockheed

Top: **F/A-22A has been cleared for external carriage of AIM-9 and AIM-120.** Lockheed Martin

Middle top: **An AIM-9 launch from 91-4002.** Lockheed Martin

Middle bottom: **An AIM-120 launch from main weapon bay of 91-4002.** Lockheed Martin

Bottom: **Ejection seat test sled with F/A-22A forebody at Holloman AFB, New Mexico.** Lockheed Martin

pilot Paul Metz was at the controls. The flight, lasting 58 minutes, took place from Lockheed Martin's Marietta, Georgia facility. Maximum speed during the first flight was 288 mph; handling assessment and a simulated powered approach were accomplished. No significant anomalies were discovered and the flight was declared an unreserved success.

•On September 14 the second F-22A flight, lasting 35 minutes, was successfully completed. The pilot was Jon Beesley. Following this flight, the aircraft went through some minor structural modifications and was then placed in a structural test fixture for static testing and calibration of strain gauges.

•On November 11 the magazine, *Popular Science* declared the F-22A to be one of the 100 "Best of What's New for 1997".

•During November avionics tests began. Included was the AN/APG-77 radar for the F-22A on the Boeing FTB. Block 1 software was also tested giving the radar basic capability in search and track mode.

1998:

•On February 5 the first F-22A was transported by Lockheed C-5B to Edwards AFB for continuation of its flight test program under the auspices of the Air Force Flight Test Center.

•On February 10 the second F-22A was rolled out at Marietta.

•On March 31 the first YF-22A (N22YF) was officially placed on display at the US Air Force Museum in Dayton, Ohio.

•On May 17 formal F-22A flight testing got under way at Edwards AFB using '4001. It was the aircraft's third flight.

• On June 29, the first flight of the second F-22A, '4002, was successfully completed at Marietta.

• On July 30 the first inflight refueling was successfully undertaken by '4001 at Edwards AFB.

• On August 26 the second F-22A, '4002, was flown nonstop from Marietta, Georgia to Edwards AFB, California. The pilot was Lt. Col. Steve Rainey.

• On October 10, '4001 made the first F-22A supersonic flight.

• On November 12 the avionics software manager final Block 2 CDR was completed.

• On November 23 the first Block 1 integrated production software was released to the Flying Test Bed (FTB) Boeing 757. On the same day, Lockheed Martin achieved the congressionally mandated 183-flight-hour mark.

• The achievement of the 183-flight-hour mark allowed the release of $195.5 million during late December for advanced procurement of six Lot 1 LRIP aircraft as well as long lead items. The LRIP aircraft were later reclassified as PRTV (Production Representative Test Vehicles) 2 aircraft following a funding resolution by Congress during mid-1999.

• On December 7 Block 2 avionics software was delivered to Boeing for testing on the FTB.

• During December, a contract for $503 million for two PRTVs and associated F-22A program support was approved by Congress.

Top: **OT&E F/A-22As on Lockheed Martin ramp at Palmdale, California.** Lockheed Martin

Middle top: **EMD F/A-22A, 91-4003 dropping an inert 1,000 lb. Joint Direct Attack Munition (JDAM) from its main weapon bay. The F/A-22A can carry two JDAMs**. Lockheed Martin

Middle bottom and bottom: **EMD F/A-22A, 91-4004 at roll-out and during a transient stop at Fort Worth JRB during 2004.** Lockheed Martin and (bottom) Andy Wolfe

Left, middle, bottom: **Three views of EMD F/A-22A, 91-4005, all probably taken during a transient stopover at Boeing Field, Seattle, Washington during 2004.** Lockheed Martin

• Communications/navigation/identification (CNI) and electronic warfare system testing – using a pole-mounted full-scale F-22A model – was initiated during 1998 at Lockheed Martin's Fort Worth facility using the company's roof-mounted system. Tests were completed during 1999. The CNI and EW systems later were tested in a real-world environment aboard the FTB. The latter included a set of three common integrated processors (CIP) to accommodate the F-22A's 1,400 hour software flight test program.

• A wing, in the form of a canard surface, was mounted on the FTB during late 1998 for the testing of conformal antennas.

1999:

• On February 15 Sanders delivered the first AN/ALR-94 EW system to the Avionics Integration Laboratory in Seattle, Washington.

• On March 11 Boeing began testing the first conformal antenna avionics package aboard the FTB Boeing 757.

• On April 5 Tom Burbage left the F-22A Team Program Office to become President of Lockheed Martin Aeronautical Systems.

• On April 26 Bob Reardon became the Lockheed Martin Aeronautical Systems Vice President and F-22A Team Program Office General Manager

• On April 29 '4002 flew for the first time with both main and side weapons bay doors open.

• On May 4 '4002 recorded the program's 100th flight test sortie.

• On July 13 the House Appropriations Committee proposed to cut $1.8 billion from the $3 billion F-22A fiscal year 2000 development budget. The Committee noted the massive increases in F-22A unit costs as justification. The cut was approved, then later rescinded less$500 million and contingent upon the F-22A achieving certain milestones.

• On July 21 '4001 demonstrated supercruise for the first time (1.5 Mach or approximately 1,000 mph) for three minutes without the use of afterburners.

• On August 25 '4002 conducted a 60° high angle-of-attack test.

• On September 25 design limit load testing of article '3999 – a non-flightworthy static loads test airframe (it was manufactured between '4002 and '4003) – was completed. There was also a fatigue test airframe, '4000, which was built between '4003 and '4004. Final assembly

Top: **OT&E F/A-22A departing Edwards AFB during the course of the 2004 base airshow. View shows the outward retraction sequence of the main landing gear.** Katsuhiko Tokunaga

Right: **EMD F/A-22A, 91-4006, during the course of anechoic chamber tests exploring the aircraft's radar cross section and other electromagnetic characteristics.** Lockheed Martin

Below: **EMD F/A-22A, 91-4006 and X-35B (X-35A in STOVL configuration), "301", on the ramp at Edwards AFB.** Lockheed Martin

Above: **EMD F/A-22A, 91-4007 observes F-16A, 83-1082 take fuel from KC-10A, 84-0185 during a test sortie over Edwards AFB test range.** Lockheed Martin

Left: **EMD F/A-22A, 91-4002 over Edwards AFB with main weapon bay doors in full open position.** Lockheed Martin

Below: **EMD F/A-22A, 91-4007 launches an AIM-120 from its main weapon bay. The F/A-22A is capable of carrying up to six AIM-120s internally.** Lockheed Martin

of '3999 took place during July of 1998. Following completion the following January, it was transferred to the structural test facility in Marietta where load testing began during March. All planned static tests were completed by May of 2002 including "first service-life" fatigue testing which ended on May 17. A second cycle of full lifetime testing was initiated immediately following the first. Tests using '4000 were designed to simulate a 20-year airframe service life, equivalent to 8,000 simulated flight hours. Each lifetime testing equivalent involved more than 1.2 million stress events simulating aircraft maneuvers up to 9 gs. '4000 was scheduled to undertake fatigue testing equivalent to two lifetimes or 16,000 flight hours before program termination.

• On November 23 KC-10 refueling qualification tests were completed.

• On December 21 the 500th flight test hour was logged.

• During December the FTB had accumulated 641.9 hours of F-22A related flight test time during 126 sorties. Other FTB/F-22A flight test aircraft included a Rockwell T-39 (target aircraft) and a Lockheed T-33 (calibrated airborne trials). Some of the latter tests started during 1998.

2000:

• On March 6 the first flight of the third F-22A, '4003, was undertaken at Marietta. The pilot was Chuck Killberg.

Left: **F/A-22As, 99-4011, 91-4008, 91-4007, and 91-4005, in formation over the Edwards Test range. 4011 bears OT tail code. Other three aircraft bear ED tail code.** Lockheed Martin

Below: **Chart depicts evolution of ATF from air-to-ground origins to today's ATF program.** Lockheed Martin

• On March 15 '4003 was flown non-stop from Marietta to Edwards AFB. The pilot was Bill Craig.

• On April 24 Sanders Block 3S software began testing on the FTB. The 3S was an early version of the Block 3.0 software which was in fact, delivered to Boeing on August 11. Tests of Block 3 software began in mid-September.

• During May, hairline cracks in the canopy of '4001 and '4002 caused temporary cessation of the F-22A flight test program; flight testing resumed, with restrictions, on June 5 using '4002.

• On July 25 the first AIM-9 launch from '4002 was successfully undertaken. The F-22A was flying at 0.7 Mach and 20,000 ft. over China Lake NAS, California. The missile was launched from the F-22A's left weapons bay. The pilot was Chuck Killberg.

• On August 19 the AF approved converting some of its F-15 training missions at Tyndall AFB to the F-22A. The F-22A conversion, which will gradually replace 60 F-15s over a five year period beginning in 2003, included construc-

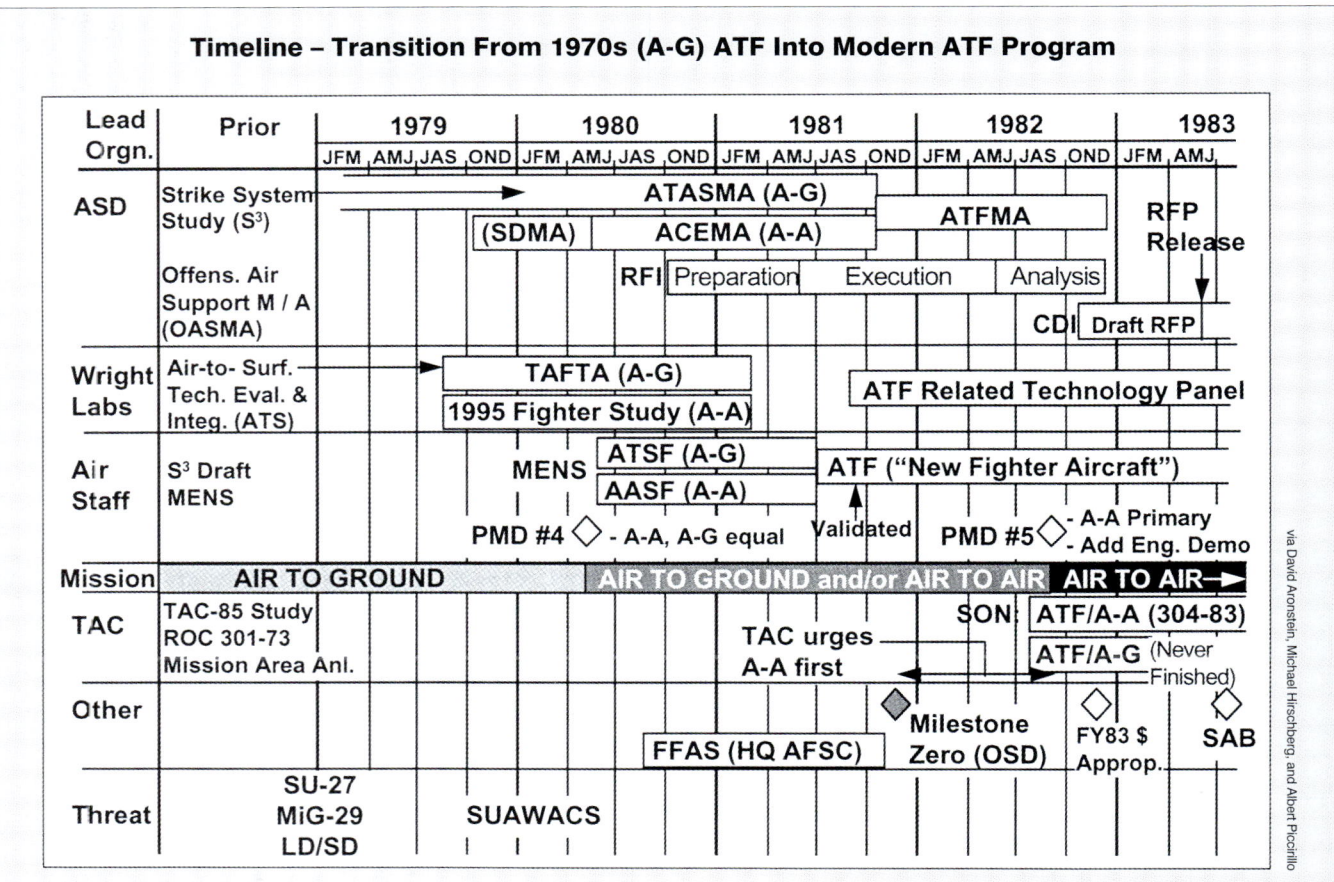

Timeline – Transition From 1970s (A-G) ATF Into Modern ATF Program

Lead Orgn.	Prior	1979	1980	1981	1982	1983
ASD	Strike System Study (S³)	→ ATASMA (A-G)	(SDMA) / ACEMA (A-A)		ATFMA	RFP Release
	Offens. Air Support M/A (OASMA)		RFI Preparation	Execution Analysis	CDI Draft RFP	
Wright Labs	Air-to-Surf. Tech. Eval. & Integ. (ATS)	→ TAFTA (A-G) / 1995 Fighter Study (A-A)		ATF Related Technology Panel		
Air Staff	S³ Draft MENS	MENS / ATSF (A-G) / AASF (A-A)		ATF ("New Fighter Aircraft")		
		PMD #4 ◇ - A-A, A-G equal	Validated	PMD #5 ◇ - A-A Primary / - Add Eng. Demo		
Mission	AIR TO GROUND		AIR TO GROUND and/or AIR TO AIR	AIR TO AIR →		
TAC	TAC-85 Study ROC 301-73 Mission Area Anl.		TAC urges A-A first	SON ATF/A-A (304-83) / ATF/A-G (Never Finished)		
Other			FFAS (HQ AFSC)	Milestone Zero (OSD)	FY83 $ Approp.	SAB
Threat	SU-27 MiG-29 LD/SD	SUAWACS				

via David Aronstein, Michael Hirschberg, and Albert Piccirillo

tion of facilities and an increase of about 400 personnel to support training and maintenance.

• On August 22, tests of flight characteristics at high angles-of-attack with the weapons bay doors open were successfully completed using '4002. The pilot was Jon Beesley.

• On September 30 the design review of the avionics software version 3.1, for which Boeing was responsible, was completed.

• On October 24 the first AMRAAM was launched from '4002 over China Lake, California. The pilot was Lt. Col. David "Doc" Nelson. Launch speed was 0.9 Mach at 15,000 ft. A total of 60 similar launches were planned.

Top: **F/A-22A, 99-4010, bearing OT tail code during Edwards AFB 2004 Open House.** Katsuhiko Tokunaga

Right (both): **F/A-22A, 99-4010, during transient stop at Boeing Field, Seattle, Washington (middle top), in 2004, and landing at Edwards AFB during 2004 Open House.** Lockheed Martin and Katsuhiko Tokunaga

Below: **F/A-22A, 99-4010, refueling during cross-country flight.** Lockheed Martin

Below left: **F/A-22A, departing on its first flight at Marietta, Georgia. The aircraft is unpainted. Visible panels are, in part, made up of radar absorbent materials. OT tailcode is noteworthy in that it was painted on vertical tails before the whole aircraft was painted.** Lockheed Martin

• On October 31 Pratt & Whitney successfully completed 2,150 TACx, 1/2 full hot section life tests on the F119. 2,168 total accumulated cycles (approximately five years of operational service) were accomplished during the course of these tests

• On November 2 '4001 was ferried from Edwards AFB to Wright-Patterson AFB, Ohio to undergo live-fire tests wherein it would be used as a target for survivability studies.

• On November 7 the Air Vehicle Final Production Readiness Review was successfully completed.

• On November 11 '4008 received its wings and empennage.

• On November 15 the first flight of '4004, the avionics testbed aircraft, was successfully completed. The pilot was Bret Luedke. '4004 had been rolled out in June but flight testing was delayed as a result of avionics cooling problems.

• On December 21 Defense Acquisition Board review culminating in the contract award for an initial batch of LRIP aircraft was delayed until January 3. On this same date, the static testing of '3999 was completed in order to accommodate prototype flight envelope expansion. This had been delayed by test stand damage that occurred in November. Also on this date, fatigue testing of '4000 got underway in Marietta.

• On December 30 Lockheed Martin was awarded a contract for approximately $1.3 billion covering procurement of six PRTV 2 aircraft, augmenting an earlier contract for $195.5 million for long-lead-time items. Another contract for $277.1 million covered long-lead-time items for ten Lot 1 LRIP aircraft. On the same date, Pratt & Whitney was given a separate $180 million contract to produce twelve F119 engines. At this time the total program funding cap was set by Congress at $38 billion.

• Of the 590 hours of flight testing planned for the F-22A during the year, only 324 were completed as a result of ongoing structural, system, and software anomalies.

2001:

• On January 3 a Defense Acquisition Board review culminating in the contract award for an initial batch of LRIP aircraft was delayed a second time due to inclement weather preventing completion of 3 of 11 critical test objectives. During the course of the month, bridge contracts amounting to a total of $353 million were awarded to Lockheed to keep the program viable thru March.

• On January 5 the first flight of '4005 was successfully completed following several days of weather delays. The pilot was Randy Neville. This was the first flight of an F-22A equipped with a combat-capable avionics system. The Block 3.0 software provided functions such as radar processing and sensor fusion, electronic warfare and countermeasures, and communication, navigation, and identification.

• On January 30 '4004 was ferried to Edwards AFB.

• On February 5 '4006 was flown for the first time. The pilot was Al Norman. By this date, the F-22A had been subject to and had passed its RCS testing program.

• On March 11 '4005 was ferried to Edwards AFB.

• During March the General Accounting office released a report indicating the F-22A was not far enough along in flight testing to offer confirmation of the DoD's estimates of weapon systems performance. It also noted a lack of stability in both design and fabrication and recommended capping F-22A production at no more than ten aircraft per year until IOT&E was successfully completed.

• On March 19 assembly of the first LRIP aircraft ('4018) was started at Lockheed Martin's Fort Worth, Texas plant

• During late spring, a vertical fin "buffet" problem surfaced with no ready solution in sight. A shortened fatigue life was projected. The buffet problem was first detected during July of 1999. The cause was a vortex originating at the inboard junction of the intake and the fuselage. A second vortex originating at the wing root leading edge/fuselage intersection forced the first vortex to impinge upon the vertical tails. The turbulent flow caused higher than expected vertical fin structural stress levels. A series of flight tests incorporating a "Zorch" maneuver helped identify the problem...which tended to become most apparent at an AoA above 18° and at very specific altitudes and Mach numbers. A fix consisting of software changes and structural strengthening (by changing the rear spar from composite to titanium) was later developed. All 23 aircraft slated for purchase during fiscal 2003 were completed with the fix in place.

• On April 17 an F-22A successfully launched an AIM-9 while rolling at 60° per second.

• On April 18 the F-22A program reached its 1,000th flight test hour.

• On May 17 '4003 successfully flew at the F-22A's maximum Mach number.

• On May 18 '4006 was ferried to Edwards AFB; full afterburner was used for the first time on takeoff.

• On June 13 the F-22A became the first tactical fighter to successfully launch an AIM-9 missile while rolling at 100° per second.

Top and top right: **F/A-22A, 99-4011, was the second PRTV-I aircraft and was assigned to Edwards AFB.** Katsuhiko Tokunaga x 2

Middle left and right: **F/A-22A, 91-4003 (left) and 91-4007, as of 2004 are both wearing nose art depicting various missile launches.** Katsuhiko Tokunaga x 2

Right: **F/A-22A, 00-4015, at Nellis AFB during early 2004.** Tim Cullum

•On August 15 the Defense Acquisition Board (DAB) unanimously recommended to proceed with F-22A LRIP. An initial batch of ten aircraft were approved for production with FY'01 funding. Thirteen more aircraft were to follow in FY'02 and twenty-three more in FY'03. Concurrent to this it was revealed that LRIP would continue until FY'05, with full-rate production starting in FY'06 and continuing until at least FY'13. A funding cap of $45 billion was placed on the entire program and the total buy was to settle at between 295 and 331 aircraft depending on production-generated savings.

•On August 22 a live-fire test using '4001 was conducted at Wright-Patterson AFB. The aircraft had been flown to Wright-Patterson AFB, stripped of all usable equipment, and set up as a target for potential enemy weapons.

•On August 23 wing live fire testing was completed.

•On September 19 the Lot 1 contract, for $2.1 billion was awarded.

•On September 21 the first guided AIM-120C AMRAAM launch was successfully completed.

•On September 26 the first fit check of JDAM with a 600-gallon external fuel tank on pylon took place.

•On October 15 the first flight of '4007 was successfully completed.

•On October 24 the DAE authorized the Lot 2 contract.

•On November 14 avionics software 3.0FT2.3 was loaded for the first time.

•On November 30 the last PRTVII mid-fuselage section was shipped to Marietta.

2002:

•During the spring and summer, '4009, while still in Marietta, was subjected to a series of tests conducted by the AF to validate how easily the F-22A could be maintained and repaired. Known as Dedicated Logistics Testing and Evaluation (DLT&E) the program was successful and verified Lockheed's claims.

• A 49-day-long strike at the Lockheed Martin's Marietta plant significantly impacted the F-22A production program.

•On January 5 '4007 was ferried to Edwards AFB.

•On January 31 the Lot 2 production contract was authorized.

Top: **F/A-22A, 00-4013, at Marietta prior to first flight and delivery to Nellis AFB.** Jay Miller

Left (both): **Two views of F/A-22A, 00-4013, following flight to Palmdale for update program and prior to being delivered to Nellis AFB, Nevada.** Lcokheed Martin x 2

- On February 1 an F-22A pulled 9 gs for the first time.
- On February 5 the Block 3.1 software package was delivered; it was flown for the first time on '4006 on April 25.
- On February 8 '4008 made its first flight.
- On March 14 a successful AIM-9 launch was conducted at 5,000 ft. and 0.9 Mach.
- During the first quarter of the year, radar-cross-section testing of '4002 was successfully completed.
- On March 27 the EMD EAC was submitted to the SPO.
- On April 5 the DD250 was completed on the last EMD aircraft ('4009).
- On May 10 Brig. Gen. Shackleford replaced Brig. Gen. Jabour as F-22A SPO director.
- On March 17 the first F-22A lifetime fatigue test objectives were completed.
- On May 21 the F-22A's arresting gear system was successfully tested.
- On May 28 '4004 was ferried from Edwards AFB to Langley AFB, Virginia and then, on the next day, on to Eglin AFB, Florida for initiation of climate testing. After arrival, the aircraft was prepared for testing and installed in the lab's 252 ft. wide by 201 ft. deep by 70 ft. tall main test chamber (temperature extremes of -65° to +165° F. are possible in this facility).
- On May 30 '4004 – the first F-22A with a complete avionics system – began climate testing one day ahead of schedule in the McKinley test chamber at Eglin AFB, Florida.
- On May 31 '4009 was delivered to Edwards AFB.

Top: **F/A-22A, 00-4012, at Nellis AFB during early 2004.** Erik Simonsen

Middle: **F/A-22A, 00-4016, a PRTV-II aircraft, dropping a 1,000 lb. JDAM bomb. The aircraft is seen following delivery to Nellis AFB. It has yet to be painted.** Lockheed Martin

Right: **F/A-22A, 00-4016, over Nellis test range.** Lockheed Martin

- On June 7 F-22A flight testing reached 2,000 hours.
- On June 11 '4009 completed the F-22A's dedicated logistics testing and evaluation.
- On July 26 air combat simulation flight test readiness was completed. Also on this date Lockheed Martin announced the development of a new F-22A horizontal stabilator design. The new stabilator, to be built under contract by Vought Aircraft Industries of Grand Prairie, Texas, through Alliant TechSystems of Clearfield, Utah would save approx. $1 million per aircraft shipset of two. The new design involved mechanically fastening composite materials around a control shaft rather than bonding the materials under high-pressure and heat in an autoclave. The new design also had removable edges and was about 30 lb. lighter than the older surfaces.

- On August 2 the first F-22A launch of an AIM-9 at supersonic speed (1.1 Mach) was successfully accomplished.

- On August 16 Block 3.1.1.0 software for the F-22A was successfully certified.
- On August 21 the first supersonic separation of an AMRAAM (at 1.19 Mach) was successfully accomplished.
- On August 27, Gens. Pearson and Shackleford approved the avionics replan.
- As of September 9 the F-22A had finished 600 sorties totaling 1,300 hours of flight science testing, leaving 400 hours remaining in the EMD program.

Facing page top: **F/A-22A, 00-4017, at Edwards AFB.** Katsuhiko Tokunaga

Facing page bottom: **F/A-22A, 01-4018, in a newly constructed F/A-22A hangar at Tyndall AFB, Florida.** Eric Hehs

Top: **Two F/A-22As , 01-4018 and 01-4019, at Tyndall AFB.** Eric Hehs

Right: **A contrast in generations. F/A-22A, 01-4021, awaiting departure next to a Boeing F-15C at Tyndall AFB, in build-up to William Tell competition during late 2004.** Eric Hehs

Bottom: **F/A-22A, 01-4021 embarks on mission from Tyndall AFB during late 2004. This aircraft was officially delivered during 2003.** Eric Hehs

Left: **F/A-22A, 01-4018, over Tyndall AFB. This aircraft was officially accepted by the AF during 2003. Tyndall AFB is the home of the 325th Fighter Wing and 43rd Fighter Squadron.** Lockheed Martin

Below: **Unidentified F/A-22A moves in for inflight refueling session behind a Boeing KC-135R. Noteworthy is open refueling receptacle which is normally covered by two mechanically actuated and low-observables optimized doors.** Lockheed Martin

• On September 16 the first F-22A production representative test vehicle (PRTV), '4011, was flown from Marietta for the first time.

• On September 17 AF Chief of Staff Gen. Jumper announced that the F-22A's designation was formally changed to F/A-22A...thus emphasizing the aircraft's multi-mission capability that had been highlighted as early as May of 1993. The mission encompasses the requirement that the aircraft be capable of carrying the JDAM and SDB. In fact, during an August of 2002 interview with Elaine Grossman, Maj. Gen. Dan Leaf was quoted as saying, "The F/A-22A has been in [development] for decades...and the world has changed...and our view of how we are going to employ it has changed. It is, in essence, a recast airplane. It was envisioned as a pure air superiority fighter to shoot down other airplanes. But we look at it quite differently now...as simultaneously holding air and surface targets at risk. And if there is a pre-eminent role, it's the surface targets that are driving the requirement right now because the airplane will be so dominating air-to-air. The FA-22A will take on a capability not only to attack SAM radars but also to jam them."

• On September 19 the small diameter bomb fit check was completed. On the same date, F/A-22A, '4011 based at Edwards AFB experienced a loss of control during an ACM mission with a chase Lockheed Martin F-16. The F/A-22A entered a rolling maneuver at between 13,000 ft. and 15,000 ft. and loss some 10,000 feet before recovering from an inverted flat spin at 2,800 ft. No cause was determined at the time.

• On September 28 '4003 completed three test sorties in one day.

• On October 1 the F/A-22A received the prestigious Aviation Quality Award from *Aviation Week & Space Technology* magazine.

Top: **Line-up of F/A-22As on ramp at Nellis AFB, Florida during mid-2004. The closest aircraft bears 43rd FS markings on tail. Other discernible serial numbers include 01-4023, 02-4028, 00-4013, 01-4020, and 01-4022.** Lockheed Martin

Middle: **02-4032 at Marietta during static ground run.** Jay Miller

Bottom: **Unidentified F/A-22A provides an excellent front perspective and underscores the effectiveness of the low-observables intake design.** Lockheed Martin

• On October 12 '4010 made its first flight. This was considered to be the first production standard F/A-22A.

• On October 23 DD250 for '4010 was completed and, as of October 10, officially delivered (paperwork signed off) to the AF. This marked the first delivery of a production (PRTV) F/A-22A.

• On October 25 the stand-up of the first F/A-22A fighter squadron (325th Fighter Wing) took place at Tyndall AFB, Florida. On this same date, the AF and Boeing celebrated the opening of the new F/A-22A maintenance training facility at Tyndall AFB with a ribbon cutting and site dedication ceremony.

• On October 30 '4003 completed the first AIM-9 supersonic separation launch.

• During October it was announced by Lockheed Martin that the company had established a new avionics laboratory for the F/A-22A at its facilities in Fort Worth, Texas.

• On November 5 the first guided supersonic missile launch of an AIM-120 took place. The F/A-22A was flying at 1.5 Mach and 35,000 ft. The target was at 15,000 ft. and was approaching the aircraft nose-on. The missile was unarmed but was determined to have passed within lethal range.

• On November 7 it was revealed that the F/A-22A program was $690 million over budget. The figure caused the AF to announce that it would reduce its acquisition quantity from 339 aircraft (through 2013) to "fewer than 300". Much of the cost increase was attributed to the fact that labor costs had grown by more than 50% between 1995 and 2000.

• On November 18 Brig. Gen. Richard Lewis became the new F/A-22A POE and Brig. Gen. (select) Thomas Owen became the new F/A-22A Program Director. Lewis replaced Brig. Gen. William Jabour and Owen replaced Brig. Gen. Mark Shackleford.

• On November 19, Lockheed Martin replaced F/A-22A program manager Bob Rearden with Ralph Heath. The fall-out was the result of a projected $690 million cost over-run (later increased to $1 billion). As a result, the Air Force was seriously considering reducing the F/A-22 acquisition quantity from 339 aircraft to as few as 180. AF officials had argued that the service needed at least 381 F/A-22As to "populate" the Air Force's proposed ten deployable, rotating aerospace expeditionary forces and provide training, testing, and attrition/reserve aircraft.

• On November 22 an F/A-22A successfully launched an unarmed AIM-9M against a supersonic McDonnell Douglas QF-4 drone during a test over White Sands Missile Range, New Mexico. The F/A-22A was in "supercruise" flight without afterburners. The AIM-9M was fired at 1.4 Mach and 24,000 ft. The QF-4 was at 1.0 Mach and 14,000 ft.

• On November 26 DD250 of '4011 was completed.

• During a December 5 interview, Gen. Jumper noted that software stability remained an ongoing F/A-22A problem. Program experts claimed the integrated avionics software suite frequently "crashed".

• On December 19 the first F/A-22A MJU-10 countermeasure flare flight test was completed.

• On December 24, Lockheed Martin received three AF contracts totaling $922 million. The contracts included funding for production work on 42 aircraft.

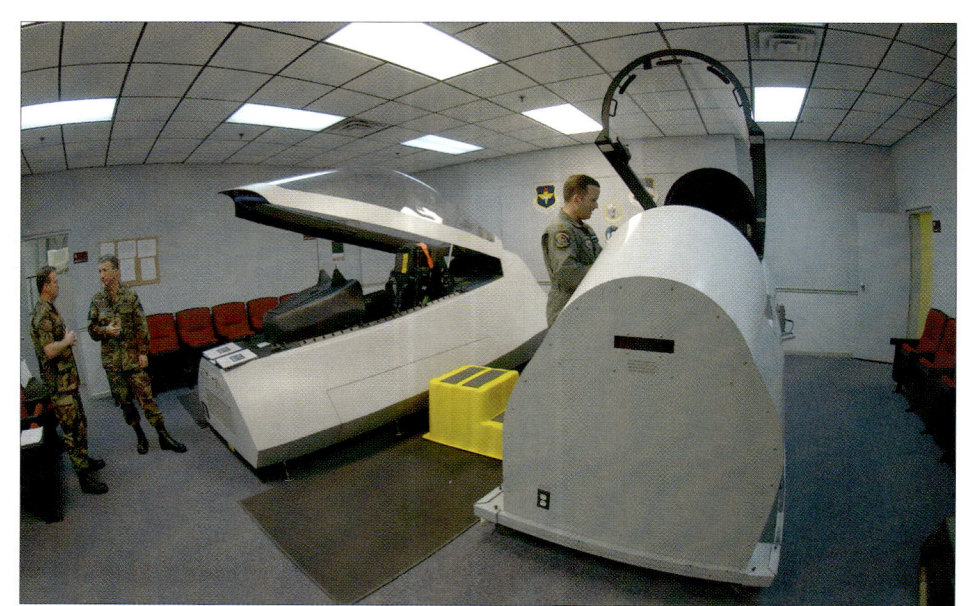

Top: **F/A-22A, 01-4021, on the main ramp at Tyndall AFB being prepared for an operational training sortie.** Eric Hehs

Left: **The F/A-22A simulator facility at Tyndall AFB includes a procedures trainer as well as a full-up flight simulator.** Eric Hehs

• On December 28 the first live-fire ground test from the F/A-22A was completed.

• On December 30 the first flight of '4009 took place from Marietta. Also on this date, the Air Force reduced its buy of F/A-22As from 325 to 276 aircraft. The reduction was to result in a FY 2003 reduction from 23 to 20 aircraft; a FY 2004 reduction from 27 to 22 aircraft, and a FY 2005 reduction from 32 to 24 aircraft. Concurrently, $876 million was shifted from buying aircraft to paying for increased development costs.

2003:

• On January 7, Lockheed Martin delivered the first F/A-22A, '4012, to the AF Air Warfare Center. The aircraft was to be flown to the AWFC's 422nd Test & Evaluation Squadron at Nellis AFB. An additional seven F/A-22As were expected to be assigned to the AWFC.

• Air Combat Command's Air Warfare Center at Nellis AFB, Nevada received its first F/A-22A. The aircraft was flown by Lt. Col. David "Logger" Rose, chief of the Nellis F/A-22A integration office. Seven F/A-22As scheduled for Nellis were to go to the 53rd Wing's 422nd Test and Evaluation Squadron and nine were to go to the 57th Wing for the AF Weapons School.

• On January 14 the final developmental flight test F/A-22A, '4009, was flown from Marietta to Palmdale for modification to Dedicated Initial Operational Test and Evaluation.

• On January 17 DD250 of '4012 was completed; and the first flight by an operational pilot, Lt. Col. David "Logger" Rose, took place.

• Historically, it should be noted that the AF's measure of software reliability was "mean-time between instability events" (MTBIE). By February of 2003, F/A-22As had an extremely poor record of dependability in terms of software system reliability. At this stage of the program, F/A-22As were having to initiate an avionics system restart every 1.9 hours...although the reliability goal was 20 hours or more (before a Type I failure occurred). Restarts took several minutes to cycle. In response to this, the AF and Lockheed Martin began issuing monthly upgrades. The net result was a 21.2 hour MTBIE for Type I failures. Type II failures, of somewhat reduced priority, were also attacked in a similar fashion with the net result being an improvement in their MTBIE from 1.39 hours to 5.29 hours. MTBIE has now been replaced with an MTBAA (mean-time between avionics anomaly) which combines Type I, Type II, and hardware (Type V) failure rates into one contiguous block.

• On February 13 two F/A-22As successfully demonstrated the capabilities of the Intraflight Datalink (IFDL)...a key component of the F/A-22A's avionics suite that is designed to enhance a pilot's situational awareness. During the almost four-hour test flight from the AFFTC at Edwards AFB, two F/A-22As, '4005 and '4006 demonstrated the basic functionality of the IFDL system which can broadcast and receive both voice transmissions and data. The IFDL is essentially an encrypted radio and wireless communications modem that allows F/A-22A pilots to covertly and securely talk to and share information with each other.

• On February 28 the F/A-22A flight test program recorded its 3,000th flight test hour.

• During early March the F/A-22A flight test force at Edwards AFB surpassed the program's 3,000th flight test hour. At the time, eight F/A-22As were assigned to Edwards.

• On March 4 the first DIOT&E F/A-22A was delivered to Edwards AFB.

• On March 27 the DAB approved the AF's awarding Lockheed Martin a $3 billion contract to build 20 additional production F/A-22As. Problems remained with the aircraft avionics and software as failure rates were once every 1.3 hours while the AF requirement called for once every 10 hours.

• On March 31, '4009 was returned to Edwards AFB following modifications and upgrades at Lockheed Martin's Palmdale, Cal-

ifornia facility. This was the last of four DIOT&E F/A-22As to be so upgraded. '4008 thru '4011 were all production-standard aircraft at this point.

• As of April 9 the F/A-22A test fleet had accumulated 3,220 hours during 1,501 sorties.

• On April 16 the AF awarded two F/A-22A contracts totaling more than $4 billion for Lot 3 procurement. Of that, $3.5 billion was for 20 F/A-22As and $630 million was for 40 F119 engines.By this date, the AF had taken delivery of nine F/A-22As.

• On April 29 '4014 completed its first flight and landed "Code One".

• On May 12 '4013 was ferried to the 422nd TES at Nellis AFB by Lt. Col. Dave "Logger" Rose.

• On May 13 the House Armed Services Committee voted to withhold $161 million from the F/A-22A program during 2004 unless Lockheed Martin corrected a persistent software problem. The money would be released only if the manufacturer guaranteed that it had fixed the problem, which sporadically resulted in MFD shut-downs.

• On May 22 DD250 of '4014 was completed.

• On May 29 '4014 was delivered to the 422nd TES at Nellis AFB by Lt. Col. Dave "Logger" Rose.

• On June 4 the F/A-22A fleet passed 3,500 flight test hours. Maj. Colin Miller flew the milestone test mission at Edwards AFB. During the flight he launched an AIM-120. The F/A-22A Combined Test Force (CTF) at Edwards AFB consisted of some 1,000 personnel from Lockheed Martin, Boeing, Pratt & Whitney, the AF, and various US Government offices at this time.

• On June 26 '4002 was flown on four missions in one day. The missions were to gather takeoff performance test points.

• On June 30 '4016 was delivered to the Air Force.

• On July 8 Secretary of the Air Force, James Roche, visited the Marietta facility.

• On August 21 '4017 was delivered to the Air Force.

• On August 29 seven F/A-22As were airborne at the same time. A four-ship ('4005, '4006, '4007, '4008 – the other three aircraft that were airborne at the same time were '4002, '4003, and '4009) flight test of the IntraFlight Data Link was conducted at Edwards AFB.

• On September 1, the F/A-22A CTF broke 4,000 flight hours.

Top: **Two F/A-22As , 01-4018 and 01-4019, during preflight in their new hangar at Tyndall AFB.** Eric Hehs

Below: **F/A-22A, 01-4021, during a sortie from Tyndall AFB over the Gulf of Mexico.** John Dibbs/*Plane Picture Company*

Facing page top: **Two EMD F/A-22As , 91-4002 and 91-4033, during a test flight to explore the compatibility of jettisonable wing tanks.** Lockheed Martin

Facing page bottom: **F/A-22A, 01-4021, during a sortie from Tyndall AFB over the Gulf of Mexico.** John Dibbs/Plane Picture Company

• On September 22 '4003 completed the first rolling high-g AIM-9 launch.

• On September 24 '4019 completed its first flight from Marietta.

• On September 26 DD250 of '4018 was completed and the aircraft delivered, three hours later, to the 325th Fighter Wing at Tyndall AFB, Florida. *Raptor 18*, 01-4018, piloted by 43rd FS commander Lt. Col. Jeffrey Harrigan, was delivered from Marietta to initiate operations with the squadron. The aircraft was the first of the LRIP batch. Plans called for the Wing to receive 50 F/A-22As with deliveries taking place every four to six weeks over the next two years. The 43rd will be the training unit for all F/A-22A pilots. Some fifty F/A-22As are expected eventually to be based at Tyndall.

• On October 10 an acceptance ceremony for '4018 was held at Tyndall AFB.

• During October, Pratt & Whitney completed the 100th F119-PW-100 engine at its Middletown, Connecticut facility. At the time, some 650 F119s were planned for production. Pratt & Whitney had support operations at Nellis AFB, Tyndall AFB, and one was planned for Langley AFB.

2004:

• Current production program called for 295 aircraft to be funded with additional F/A-22As – up to 339 aircraft total – to be produced if funding permits.

• On January 15, the F/A-22A fatigue test team set a new record for cyle rate in a single 24 hour period using '4000.

• On January 19 F/A-22A '4022 completed the F/A-22A's lightning test program. It later was restored to flightworthy condition, flight tested at Marietta, and delivered to Tyndall AFB.

• On January 21 '4020 was ferried to Tyndall AFB.

• On January 23, the first multiple missile launch from two F/A-22A's ('4005 and '4007) was accomplished; four missile launches took place on January 30.

• On January 30 two AFFTC F/A-22As launched three air-to-air missiles within seconds of each other. An AIM-9 was launched from one aircraft while it was traveling at 1.2 Mach at 5,000 ft. and in a 100° per second roll; using the F/A-22A's IntraFlight Datalink, two AIM-120s were launched moments later from

Above: **Another view of EMD F/A-22As, 91-4002 and 91-4003, flying with jettisonable wing tanks.** Lockheed Martin

Below: **F/A-22A, 01-4024, on final to Marietta with F-16B, 78-0088, flying chase.** John Wilhoff

two separate aircraft flying at 1.3 Mach and 30,000 ft. while looking down on their targets.

• On February 6 '4002 completed the first flight with two 600-gallon external fuel tanks mounted underwing. No problems were encountered.

• During the first week in February in-flight icing tests were successfully concluded. No problems were noted.

• On February 9 the F/A-22A Combined Test Force reached 5,000 hours of flight testing when Maj. James Dutton flew '4003 on an envelope expansion mission. Also on this date, '4015 had completed all required modifications and was ferried from Palmdale to Nellis AFB. Again on this date, '4014 was ferried to Palmdale to join '4017 for post-production mods. '4014 was the eighth of eleven aircraft slated for the mod program.

• During early 2004, the Pratt & Whitney F119 engine achieved 25,000 operating hours including 9,332 engine flight hours during 2,260 F/A-22A flights.

• By mid-February, '4023 had been DD250'd and was undergoing post-production modification on the new mod line in Marietta. '4021 had completed Mandatory Government Inspection (MGI) and was being prepared for DD250. '4024 was undergoing flight line operations, and '4025 was in fuel operations.

• On February 17 '4018 (assigned to the 43rd Sq.) returned to service following modifications to current production configuration. This was the first F/A-22A to be so modified at Tyndall AFB.

• On February 19 '4003 completed two successful AIM-9 separation launches. The first of these was a high roll rate launch with the aircraft at 1.4 Mach and 10,000 ft. The second was also a high roll rate launch but at 1.2 Mach and 5,000 ft. Only one missile shot test remained.

• On February 20 '4021 was ferried to Tyndall AFB where it was to be used for pilot and maintainer training. At the same time '4024 was being given its aero coatings while '4025 had begun post-rumble test inspection.

• On February 25 '4026 was rolled to the Marietta flight line.

• On March 3 '4018, '4019, and '4020 each flew twice in the same day during sorties from Tyndall AFB.

• On March 9 four F/A-22As flew a four ship IFDL test mission against eight F-15s and another F/A-22A.

• On March 18, '4003 successfully completed the first missile separation launches of AIM-9 and AIM-120 missiles during the same flight. The AIM-120 separation was at 1.5 Mach, 15,000 ft. and 0.5 gs; the AIM-9 separation was at 1.4 Mach, 10,000 ft., and 1 g while rolling. On the same date, two F/A-22As successfully completed the first hot pit refueling following a CTF mission. After landing, the two aircraft taxied through the hot pit – an isolated refueling area at Edwards AFB which allows aircraft to safely refuel with engines running and without complete cool-down.

• On March 19 the final missile test required prior to the start of IOT&E – the first launch of two AIM-120 AMRAAM missiles from a single F/A-22A – was accomplished. A total of 52 missile tests, a mix of guided and separation launches, were required prior to entry into IOT&E.

• During the first three weeks of March, the CTF flew eight four-ship IFDL missions.

• On March 22, the DAB reviewed the F/A-22A Program status, including avionics stability/functionality during OT&E Phase 1 and readiness for IOT&E. According to a Pentagon statement, DAB members were satisfied by the progress that had been made in improving avionics stability and preparing to start IOT&E. On the same date, F/A-22A '4016 was ferried from Marietta to Edwards AFB. The delivery mission followed several successful stability flights of the current production configuration software. Though assigned to Nellis AFB, '4016 was to be used at Edwards for further avionics stability testing before going through post-production modifications at Palmdale.

• On March 23 '4017 completed post-production modifications at Palmdale and was ferried to Nellis AFB. On the same date, '4013 was

Top: F/A-22A, 02-4032 at Marietta. Intake plugs and HUD protector have yet to be removed before static ground run. Jay Miller

Right: F/A-22A, 02-4031, immediately following touchdown at Tyndall AFB. The F/A-22A uses its toed-in rudders as airbrakes. The aircraft is not equipped with a drag chute. Norm Taylor

ferried from Nellis AFB to Palmdale for induction into the post-production mod line.

•On March 26 '4028, the first Production Lot 2 aircraft, rolled from the Marietta assembly line to the post-production modification line. At the same time, '4024 was being prepared for first flight while '4025 was undergoing engine runs. Also, '4026 and '4027 continued in flight line operations.

•During April the AF released a request for information calling for the beginning of studies leading up to a new interim bomber program. Lockheed's response has since become known as the F/B-22A.

•On April 1, Michael Wynne, acting Under Secretary of Defense, Acquisition, Technology & Logistics, signed the formal Acquisition Decision Memorandum which laid out the criteria for the F/A-22A to enter IOT&E.

•On April 15, certification testing of the F/A-22A's primary air-to-ground armament began.

Following successful ground jettison tests of 1,000 lb. GBU-32 satellite-guided JDAM, the first separation test took place during a flight of '4003 on April 23. The day before, inflight separation testing of the F/A-22A's 600 gallon external fuel tanks (for ferry missions) began. A total of sixteen tanks were dropped during eight inflight tests.

•On April 29, the AF officially released a "request for information" that entailed work Lockheed Martin had been pursuing under the auspices of the proposed FB-22 bomber banner. On the same day 24 F/A-22As were officially considered flightworthy and 36 more aircraft were under construction.

•On April 29 the AF announced the start of F/A-22A Initial Operational Test and Evaluation at Edwards AFB. IOT&E was to be utilized to evaluate the F/A-22A's lethality, survivability, deployability, and maintainability in a variety of operational missions.

•It was announced on April 30 that the F/A-22A had begun IOT&E on April 29. It was expected that IOT&E work would be completed during the following September. Concurrent to the announcement it was also stated that software anomalies had finally been overcome. Also on this date, '4009 completed the last RCS calibration flight. Prior to this, all operational test aircraft had completed the RCS calibration flights required before beginning IOT&E.

•On May 13 an F/A-22A made its first landing in Seattle, Washington. Flown from Edwards AFB by test pilot Randy Neville, the aircraft landed at Boeing Field and was displayed at the Museum of Flight for two days.

•During May the Air Force acknowledged that the F/A-22A was being groomed for cruise missile interception "well behind enemy lines". In order to accommodate this new role, advanced versions of the AIM-120 (referred to as the AIM-120C-6) was being developed. Additionally, a compressed-carriage AIM 120

Top: **F/A-22A, 02-4030 flying downwind at Tyndall AFB during 2004 *William Tell* meet.** Norm Taylor

Middle: **F/A-22A, 02-4028, taxiing back to parking ramp at Tyndall during 2004 *William Tell* meet.** Norm Taylor

Left: **F/A-22A, 02-4030, on static display at Tyndall AFB during 2004 *William Tell* meet.** Norm Taylor

was being considered that would allow for more than six of the missiles to be carried by the F/A-22A.

•On June 1, an F/A-22A participated in a fly-by during cadet graduation at the US Air Force Academy, Colorado Springs, Colorado. Lt. Col. Dawn Dunlop, a 1988 AF Academy graduate, was the pilot.

•On June 10 an F/A-22A from the Edwards test fleet demonstrated the aircraft's ability to roll and launch an AIM-9. The missile was launched at 1.7 Mach and 21,000 ft. while pulling 4 gs. Testing was conducted over the Naval Air Warfare Center's Weapons Division range near Point Mugu, California. Some seventeen AIM-9 launches were conducted in total over a wide range of conditions and throughout various parts of the F/A-22A's flight envelope.

•On July 1, approval for Lot 4 LRIP production was granted to Lockheed. This covered 22 aircraft raising the total number on oder as of this date to 74. An additional 50 aircraft were scheduled to be built through 2006.

•During July an F/A-22A was tested at the AFFTC's Benefield Anechoic Facility for the first time. The testing was undertaken to ensure the aircraft's defensive systems did not interfere with its communications, navigation, and IFF systems.

•On July 24 an F/A-22A from the Edwards test fleet lunched four guided AIM-120s against four separate targets. The aircraft was able to successfully identify, track, and link each target's data to the respective AIM-120 being launched. Each missile passed within lethal range of its target.

•IOT&E ended during September. Though details of the results remain classified, it was announced by the AF that the F/A-22A successfully met all challenges during the four-and-a-half months of testing. A total of 188 sorties using six F/A-22As were required to complete the IOT&E requirements. To date, 27 F/A-22As have been delivered to the AF with aircraft operational at Edwards AFB, California, Nellis AFB, Nevada, and Tyndall AFB, Florida. As of mid-2004, the AF requirement (not the number currently committed to buy) for F/A-22As sat at 381 aircraft.

•By the end of August, Tyndall AFB pilots had flown nearly 250 cumulative hours and more than 253 sorties in the F/A-22A.

•On September 2 an F/A-22A dropped a 1,000 lb. JDAM successfully hitting its designated ground target at Edwards AFB. This marked the first complete mission demonstra-

tion of the F/A-22A's air-to-ground attack capability.

•During September an unidentified F/A-22A was accidentally stressed to 10-11 gs due to an anomaly in the digital flight control software.

•On October 27 F/A-22A '4041 was officially rolled out at Marietta. Following completion of post-production preparation and initial test flights, this aircraft was to be the first delivered to the Air Combat Command's 1st Fighter Wing/27th Fighter Squadron (oldest in the US Air Force) at Langley AFB, VA. There, the aircraft will become the first for use as a combat dedicated aircraft. Actual delivery to Langley AFB was expected to take place during May 2005. IOC is expected to take place during early 2006. The 27th FS stood up as an F/A-22 squadron on October 6. An F/A-22A from the 4llth FLTS at Edwards AFB is to be transferred to Langley AFB during November for initiation of maintenance training. Two additional aircraft are expected to be assigned to Langley from the 43rd FS at Tyndall AFB during January and March of 2005. Other bases to be allocated F/A-22As had yet to be decided by late 2004 in consideration of the forthcoming (September 2005) base realignment and closure decision. Being considered, however, were Elmendorf AFB, Alaska; Eglin AFB, Florida; Tyndall AFB, Florida; and Mountain Home AFB, Idaho.

•During November, Lockheed Martin representatives briefed the AF F/A-22A Integrated Product Team on its proposed F/B-22A.

•On November 1 Thomas Christie, the DoD's Director of Operational Testing, announced that there had been "dramatic" improvements in F/A-22A combat testing, bringing the aircraft closer to approval for full production. Christie noted the changes included better software reliability and that canopy cracking problems had been resolved.

•On December 3 Lockheed Martin announced that Larry Lawson had been named to replace Ralph Heath as executive vice president, general manager of the F/A-22A program. Heath was promoted to executive vice president of the company.

•On December 20 F/A-22A, 00-0014 from the 422nd Test and Evaluation Squadron, 53rd Wing/Air Warfare Center crashed and burned (on base) while departing north from Nellis AFB at 15:45 on Runway 03.The pilot, who had about logged about 60 hours in the F/A-22A, ejected safely. The aircraft had logged some 150 hours of flight time at the time of the accident. No cause had been released as of this writing, but the crash was thought to have been caused by a digital flight control system anomaly.

•On December 30, news stories were published revealing that the drain on the Federal Budget caused by the ongoing war in Iraq was forcing Congress and the DoD to reassess funding allocations and acquisition numbers relating to many defense programs, including the F/A-22A. Among the numbers being discussed was a potential reduction in F/A-22A production from 276 (though the AF maintains a need for a minimum of 381) aircraft to as few as 180 (some sources indicate that even that figure could be reduced to 130). If approved (still unknown as of this writing during January of 2005), the production cuts would start taking effect after the 2007 budget year. F/A-22A production could end as early as 2010 (some sources indicated 2008).

Top: **F/A-22A, 02-4031 taxies during 2004 _William Tell_ weapons meet at Tyndall AFB during late 2004.** Norm Taylor

Right: **Final flight of EMD F/A-22A, 91-4005, as it arrives at Langley AFB, Virginia where it will be used as a permanently-grounded maintenance trainer. It is seen being escorted during January 2005 by Boeing F-15C, 83-0017, of Langley's 1st Fighter Wing.** Lockheed Martin

Top: **F/A-22A, 02-4030 at Tyndall AFB during 2004 *William Tell* meet.** Norm Taylor

Below: **First F/A-22A, 03-4041, is scheduled to become the first new Raptor to be delivered to the 1st Fighter Wing and the first fully operational Langley AFB F/A-22A.** John Rossino

• It was announced during the last quarter of the year that the Virginia Air National Guard's 192nd Fighter Wing would team with the 1st Fighter Wing at Langley AFB, VA to fly the F/A-22A. This will mark the first time the ANG has helped with the integration of new fighter system into the active AF inventory.

2005:

• The fiscal year 2005 defense budget includes a request for 24 Lot 5 aircraft (though two may be trimmed by Congress).

• Approximately 28 F/A-22As had been delivered as of January 1 with an additional 46 aircraft in production.

• On January 6 the AF cleared the F/A-22A to resume flight operations following a comprehensive review of procedural and engineering data in the wake of the December 20, 2004 accident at Nellis AFB. Accident investigation continued. It was also noted that the F/A-22A program had logged some 7,000 hours of flight time with an excellent safety record.

• On January 7, F/A-22A, 91-4005, made its final flight, landing at Langley AFB, VA where it will be used as a training tool to keep the 1st Fighter Wing maintainers proficient on the type. The wing's 27th FS pilots will begin flying operational missions later in the month following arrival of a second, flightworthy, F/A-22A.

• On January 7 it was announced that Gen. John Jumper, Chief of Staff of the AF, would be participating in F/A-22A qualification training at Tyndall AFB. He was to have his final qualification flight on January 12.

• On January 7 five F/A-22As were delivered together from Lockheed Martin's Marietta facility to the 43rd FS at Tyndall AFB. The arrival of these aircraft brings the squadron's inventory to 18 aircraft.

• The Fiscal Year 2005 defense budget includes a request for 24 F/A-22As to be built as part of production lot 5. Production lot 6 is expected to include 26 F/A-22As. During 2005 the AF is expected to make a decision to begin high-rate production in 2006, calling for some three aircraft per month to be built.

• Initial IOC at Langley AFB, Virginia under the auspices of the 1st Fighter Wing (assigned to the 9th AF, ACC [Air Combat Command] including the 27th and 94th Squadrons) is expected during December. This is defined as the unit having "enough trained pilots" and between 18 and 24 F/A-22As available and flightworthy for the first squadron.

2006:

• High rate production is expected to begin. Forty aircraft per year are expected to roll off Lockheed Martin production lines through 2013. A request for 28 aircraft in Lot 6 is planned for FY 2006.

2007:

• Full rate production of the F/A-22A at 32 aircraft per year is planned. Lockheed is proposing a production increase to 56 aircraft per year, which would call for completing production in 2009...two years earlier than planned and with resulting unit cost savings.

The original production plans for the F-22 and now F/A-22A initially called for 750 aircraft (including some two-seat trainers). This figure later was reduced to 648 aircraft and by 1993 had fallen to 442 (including 4 pre-production aircraft and 58 two-seat trainers). In turn, this number was reduced to 438 full-production single-seat F/A-22As (only; the 4 pre-production aircraft and all two-seat trainers were cancelled). By 1998, the production numbers

stood at 339 single-seat aircraft, and by early 2004, this figure had been reduced to 276.

Total planned production changes over the history of the F/A-22A program:

> October 1986 thru July 1991 – 750
> July 1991 thru January 1994 – 648
> January 1994 thru December 2000 – 442
> December 2000 thru November 2002 – 239
> Total aircraft on order/end of 2004 – 276

Actual EMD, PRTV, and full-production standard F/A-22A delivery dates and quantities were to go through a number of changes following completion and delivery (for flight test) of the first aircraft. The following is an accurate accounting of F/A-22A serial numbers and deliveries as of January 2005:

Serial numbers:

91-4001 thru 91-4009 (EMD aircraft, all went to Edwards AFB with ED tail code; '02 and '03 are categorized as flight sciences aircraft; '04, '05, '06, and '07 are utilized primarily for avionics testing [because it has full-up low-observable finishes, '07 is used for LO testing as well]; '08 and '09 are assigned to the AF's OT&E Center's Detachment 6)

99-4010 and 99-4011 (PRTV-I, both to Edwards with ED tail code; '10 and '11 are assigned to the AF's OT&E Center's Detachment 6; '10 now wears OT tail code)

00-4012 thru 00-4017 (PRTV-II, all to Nellis AFB with OT tail code)

01-4018 thru 01-4027 (Lot 1, '4018 first to Tyndall AFB with TY tail code)

02-4028 thru 02-4040 (Lot 2)

03-4041 thru 03-4061 (Lot 3, '4041 first to go to Langley AFB's 27th Fighter Squadron which will be the first of the three squadrons at Langley expected to transition to the F/A-22A; Langley eventually will have three squadrons with 24 aircraft in each...plus 6 back-up aircraft)

04-4062 thru 04-4083 (Lot 4)

Top and right: **Five F/A-22As (01-4027, 02-4032, 02-4033, 02-4035, and 02-4036) were delivered to Tyndall AFB on January 7, 2005. Above shows aircraft prior to departure from Marietta, and right shows the aircraft following their arrival at Tyndall AFB.** Lockheed Martin

Below: **Two views of F/A-22A, 02-4036, on final approach to Marietta. The aircraft has since been delivered to Tyndall AFB.** John Wilhoff

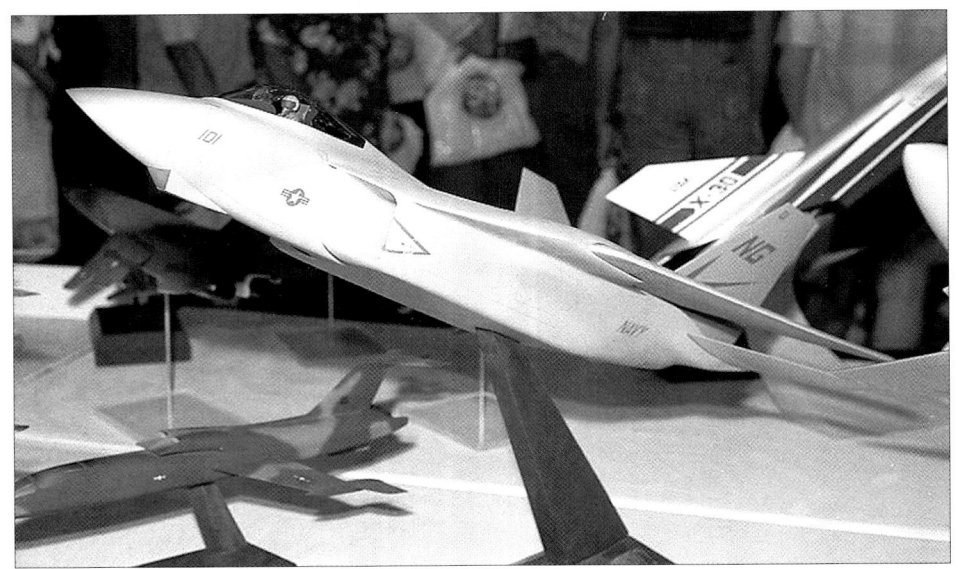

Note: Edwards AFB is home of the Air Force's Flight Test Center and location of the 411th FLTS; Nellis AFB is home of the Fighter Weapons School and the 422nd TES; and Tyndall AFB is home of the 325th Fighter Wing and 43rd FS (the 325th will serve as the initial training unit for the F/A-22A). The 1st Fighter Wing at Langley AFB is scheduled to have the IOC squadron during December of 2005.

Currently Planned Production and Delivery Quantities:
1997 – 1 prod./del. (91-4001)
1998 – 1 prod./del. (91-4002)
1999 – 2 prod. (91-4003/4004)
2000 – 2 prod. (91-4005/4006)
  2 del. (91-4003/4004)
2001 – 3 prod. (91-4007/4009)
  3 del. (91-4005/4007)
2002 – 4 prod. (99-4010/4011,
  00-4012/40013)
  5 del. (91-4008/4009,
  99-4010/4011, 00-4012)
2003 – 11 prod. (00-4014/4017,
  01-4018/4024)
  9 del. (00-4013/00-4017,
  01-4018/4020, 01-4022)
2004 – 19 prod. (01-4025/4027,
  02-4028/4040, 03-4041/4043)
  15 del. (01-4021, 01-4023/4027,
  02-4028/4036)

Three EMD aircraft, '4001, '4002, and '4003, were allocated to airframe structure evaluations at the beginning of the flight test program. Six EMD aircraft, including '4004, '4005, '4006, '4007, '4008, and '4009 became avionics systems testbeds. Each of the two groups of aircraft (airframe and avionics) had separate instrumentation configurations. The latter provided a system of test redundancy while also offering the flexibility of being able to switch missions, if required.

The nine EMD aircraft initially were committed to 4,337 hours of flying time and 2,409 sorties. Of these, 2,110 hours and 1,200 sorties were to be for airframe and systems testing. The remaining time and sortie allocations were to be used for mission avionics testing. During the third quarter of 2001, avionics flight testing time was reduced to 1,530 hours to make up for unforeseen test program delays.

Individual histories of the first nine aircraft are as follows:

'4001 was rolled out at Lockheed Martin's Marietta facility on April 9, 1997 as the *Spirit of America*. First flight took place on September 7,

Top, left and below: **Model and drawing of Lockheed Martin's F-22-based NATF study.** Jay Miller and Lockheed Martin (bottom)

Facing page: **Artist's images of F/B-22A (top photo, left aircraft). Noteworthy are the major physical differences between the standard F/A-22A fighter and the proposed bomber. The size of the latter's delta wing is particularly noteworthy.** Lockheed Martin x 2

1997. On February 5, 1998, after structural ground tests were completed, the aircraft was disassembled and airlifted to Edwards AFB. Following reassembly it was used for flying quality, flutter, and loads characteristics testing. On November 2, 2000 it was flown to Wright-Patterson AFB, Ohio and retired from flight test duty. It had logged 175 flights and 372.7 hours of flight time. After being stripped of useful components, it was used for live-fire testing, serving as a target for potential enemy weapons. Results of these tests are classified.

'4002 was rolled out at Lockheed Martin's Marietta facility on February 10, 1998 and eventually was nicknamed *Old Reliable*. First flight took place on June 29, 1998. It was flown to Edwards AFB on August 26. By the end of October 1998 it had logged 27 flights and 66.1 hours of flying time. It was used to expand the flutter and handling qualities envelope and was the first F/A-22A to achieve a 26° angle-of-attack in flight. During April of 1999 it was utilized for fit checks and captive-carry trials of the AGM-88 HARM. By September 8, 1999 the aircraft had logged 253 flights and 538.8 hours of flying time. The first F/A-22A AIM-9M launch was from this aircraft on July 25, 2000. The first F/A-22A AIM-120C launch also was from this aircraft on October 24, 2000. Other tasks assigned during flight test included performance evaluation, propulsion, high angle-of-attack, stores separation/jettison trials, and miscellaneous electronic warfare and infrared signature evaluations.

'4003's, center fuselage weapon bay was used for fit checks of the AIM-9 and AIM-120 at Lockheed Martin's Fort Worth facility during July of 1998 before the mid-fuselage section was delivered to Marietta. Upon completion, '4003 was rolled out at Lockheed Martin's Marietta facility on May 25, 1999. It was the first Block 2 aircraft and the first to have an internal structure that was fully representative of the production standard F/A-22A. The first engine runs were completed during October and taxi trials were undertaken during March of 2000. The first flight took place on March 6 and on its fourth flight on March 15 it was delivered to Edwards AFB. Ground testing and systems upgrades prevented an initial flight at Edwards AFB until September 19. Nearly a year later, on September 8, 2001, '4003 had logged 68 flights and 135.2 hours of flight time. This aircraft effectively took the place of '4001 and was used for loads testing, crosswind landing trials, arrester hook evaluations, and weapon bay environment studies. '4003 was used for the first AIM-120 launch at supersonic speeds on August 21, 2002 when a single missile was fired while the aircraft was flying level a 1.2 Mach and 12,000 ft. It was scheduled to serve as the M61A2 cannon and JDAM integration testbed as well.

'4004's mid-fuselage section was delivered from Lockheed Martin's Fort Worth facility to its Marietta facility on December 28, 1998. '4004 was the first EMD aircraft to be equipped with the Hughes CIP software, including that for the

AN/APG-77 radar, and instrument landing system. Block 1.1 avionics were installed while the aircraft was at Marietta and when it was first powered up electrically on August 31, 1999. The avionics were upgraded to Block 1.2 standard prior to taxi trials and initial flight testing at Dobbins Air Reserve Base, Georgia. First flight took place at Dobbins on November 15, 2000. It was ferried to Edwards AFB at the end of January 2001. The aircraft was assigned to avionics development. It was also tasked with low observables (RCS) and infrared signature evaluations and communica-tions/navigation/identification (CNI) testing. By September 8, 2001 it had logged 48 flights and 119.0 hours of flying time. Used for cold weather testing; on May 28, 2002, it was placed in the climatic hangar at Eglin AFB, Florida. Now permanently grounded following climate tests and used as a spare parts bin for remaining flightworthy EMD airframes.

'4005 was flown for the first time from Marietta on January 5. It was immediately tasked with AN/APG-77 radar, CNI, and armament development. Also became testbed for Block 3.0 software and served as the primary fire-control system evaluation platform. By September 8, 2001 it had logged 41 flights and 103.6 hours of flying time. On September 21, 2001, while flying over the Point Mugu test range, it made the first F/A-22A guided launch of an AIM-120C against a target drone. As of January 7, 2005, it is being used as a maintenance trainer at Langley AFB, Virginia.

'4006 was flown for the first time from Marietta on February 5, 2001. Used primarily for

integrated avionics and radar-cross-section testing. Later also used for systems effectiveness/military utility evaluation. By September 8, 2001 it had logged 16 flights and 33 hours of flying time.

'4007 was flown for the first time from Marietta on October 15, 2001. Officially became part of the Edwards F/A-22A DIOT&E test fleet on January 5, 2002. Used to support DIOT&E as a back-up aircraft. Originally intended to become the first two-seat F-22B, but with cancellation of the two-seat configuration, it was completed as a standard single-seat aircraft.

'4008 was flown for the first time from Marietta on February 8, 2002 and ferried to Edwards AFB on May 31. It became an avionics development mule and also was used for low-observables testing. With EMD aircraft '4007 and '4009 and PRTV aircraft '4010 and '4011, it was subsequently used for DIOT&E work and kept at Edwards AFB.

'4009 was to have been the second two-seat F-22B but, like '4007, was completed as a standard single-seat aircraft. Used primarily for avionics systems and software development and low-observables testing. Formally delivered to the AF for static maintenance trials (DLT&E) at Marietta on April 15, 2002. Last of the EMD class aircraft. Part of the DIOT&E fleet at Edwards AFB.

'4010 was flown for the first time on October 12, 2002 and was officially delivered to the AF on October 23. From Marietta, it was flown to Palmdale on October 30 where it was modified for flight test operations at Edwards AFB under the auspices of Det. 6. '4010 was the first PRTV

aircraft. It was allocated to DIOT&E and was used for additional service testing at Nellis AFB starting third-quarter of 2003.

'4011 was flown for the first time from Marietta on September 16, 2002 and was formally accepted by the AF on November 26. This was the second PRTV aircraft but the first to fly. It was also the last of the DIOT&E aircraft and sent to Nellis AFB starting third-quarter of 2003.

F-22B: This was the proposed two-seat training variant of the standard single-seat F/A-22A. Due to a dramatic increase in overall F/A-22A program costs, the F-22B officially was cancelled on July 10, 1996. As of this writing there are no plans to reinstate development and production.

F-22C: See NATF.

NATF:

As of this writing, Navy interest in the navalized F-22 (pre-F/A-22A era; some sources refer to the NATF F-22 as the "F-22C"), referred to as the Navy Advanced Tactical Fighter (NATF), no longer exists – though at one time as much as $8.5 billion was to have been spent on prototype design and development. The YF-22A Dem/Val program, however, provided approximately $1.2 billion in NATF technology transfers and generated some convincing arguments in favor of a navalized variant. Among the latter was a predicted 40% savings over a "stand-alone" Navy program. Additional life cycle savings were to have been generated through common F-22/NATF systems.

NATF production initially called for as many as 546 aircraft. This subsequently was reduced to 384 aircraft, and then to zero when the program was effectively cancelled. As of 1992, an option for program restart existed during the post-1997 period.

The NATF differed considerably from the Air Force F-22. Though utilizing many F-22 primary components, it would have been designed from the "deck up" for carrier suitability. Lockheed, in 1992, claimed to be in a position to produce up to four Navy F-22s per month if the service reversed itself and elected to move ahead with acquisition.

Though little concerning the exact physical characteristics of the NATF has yet surfaced in the public domain, artist's renderings indicate some commonality in the forward fuselage and empennage sections with virtually everything else being indigenous to the Navy requirement. The most striking difference would have been the addition of a totally new, variable-geometry wing and all-new horizontal and vertical tail surfaces.

Additionally, because of the multi-role (Combat Air Patrol [CAP]/strike escort) mission envisioned for the NATF, it would have carried a significantly different weapon system and associated weapon system sensor complement. Resulting from the latter would have been a considerably different lower nose configuration with an integrated low observables-optimized sensor fairing.

Range, loiter time, and such ATF fundamentals as low observables technology and supercruise capability all would have been different for the NATF in consideration of its mission. And because of aircraft carrier weight, launch, and landing constraints, the NATF's landing gear would have been considerably stronger, heavier, and more robust than that of the ATF.

F/B-22A: Due to a predicted short-fall in AF long-range weapons delivery capability starting in 2015, it has been proposed by Lockheed Martin that an interim bombing platform be created using the F/A-22A as a starting point (forward fuselage, avionics, software, flight controls, etc.). The proposed bomber, which was initially studied by Lockheed Martin during the fall of 2002, has been tentatively referred to as the F/B-22A and is viewed as being a multi-disciplined long-range strike-dedicated platform derived from the F/A-22A and optimized to accommodate bombing requirements from about 2015 to 2035.

The Air Force has actively sought proposals to meet the looming shortfall in bombing capability. As of early 2004, some 23 proposals (including at least six by Lockheed Martin) had been submitted by industry for AF consideration. Lockheed's F/B-22A contender is considered the front runner due to strong predicted performance figures and the fact that integrating a bomber version of the F/A-22A into the AF inventory would be a near-seamless undertaking. It will share 85% hardware and software

Top: **Computer-generated image of proposed F/B-22A parked next to standard F/A-22A.** Lockheed Martin

Left and facing page top and bottom: **Computer-generated images depicting an early F/B-22A study in flight. External stores mounted under delta wing are noteworthy in that they are optimized for reduced radar cross section. Inset depicts notional F/B-22A study without vertical tail surfaces.** Lockheed Martin

with the F/A-22A *Spiral 5* configuration (*Spiral 5* is a late iteration of a series of upgrades that is expected to be incorporated beginning with Lot V/Block 20/*Spiral 2* production aircraft to be delivered during 2007-2008; these will add a new AESA radar [developed in concert with the forthcoming F-35 radar]; Link 16 communication capability, various air-to-ground weapons and strike improvements will be added to Block 30/*Spiral 3 Global Strike Enhanced Raptors* to be delivered during 2008-2011; Block 40/50 *Spiral 40/50* aircraft are yet to be defined, but could feature improved electronic attack capabilities, an upgraded air-to-ground radar, and low-observable-optimized jettisonable wing tanks).

It is proposed by Lockheed that the F/B-22A eventually be equipped with state-of-the-art laser weapons, jamming equipment, an electrically charged skin coating that can change color in flight to improve camouflage capabilities, and passive sensors...all to accomplish a variety of combat roles. Additionally, it may be equipped with "morphing" skin panels to permit increased fuel capacity via flexible fuel tanks that expand and contract as fuel is added or consumed. Illustrations include underwing stealthy "wing weapons bays" (external weapons pods; 5,000 lb. capacity) and stealthy pylons, conformal antennas, and bulged weapons bay doors to accommodate weapons such as the GBU-31. The M61A2 gun would be eliminated.

As currently envisioned, the FB-22A is a semi-truncated delta wing (offering some three times the area of the standard F/A-22A wing; it would also be wet for increased fuel capacity) design with twin vertical tails (some early studies proposed eliminating the vertical tail surfaces; research was to have been conducted under the auspices of the now-defunct X-44 program) and a stretched fuselage (offering increased weapon bay size) with a tandem/two-seat cockpit.

Making the F/B-22A a two-seat configuration would permit a second pilot/weapons system operator to be carried. The second pilot would be necessary in light of the aircraft's planned 15-hour mission capability. Adding the second seat will not be difficult in light of the unrealized work that went into developing the never-built training version of the F/A-22A. The second seat will require a 60-inch plug, but no additional work on lowering the aircraft's RCS.

The F/B-22A would offer greater combat radius and greater payload capacity (up to 35 [v/s 8] small-diameter bombs) than the F/A-22A. Air-to-air capability and maneuverability (5 gs v/s 9 gs) would be somewhat less than the fighter. Only 30% of the F/B-22A's structure would be in common with the F/A-22A. Up to 90% of the avionics would be in common. It is also predicted that the engine chosen for the F/B-22A would be either the General Electric F110 or the Pratt & Whitney F135, though advanced F119 derivatives are strongly in the running (and currently being statically tested).

Thrust vectoring almost certainly would be eliminated in order to reduce production costs.

Sources indicate the aircraft, which will have a gross takeoff weight of up to 120,000 lb., will have an unrefueled range with weapons of from 1,500 to 2,000 nautical miles while carrying a 10,000 lb. to 30,000 lb. payload. Cruise speed would be approximately 1.5 Mach and maximum speed would be 1.92 Mach.

External, low-observable fuel tanks are being considered for the F/B-22A mission – and the aircraft would carry its own self-protection weapons, including AIM-9s and AIM-120s.

Final assembly and flight test probably would take place at Lockheed Martin's Marietta facility. Official Air Force review of the program was initiated during April of 2004. A very tentative AF schedule calls for first deliveries of up to 150 F/B-22As starting in 2011 and possible full-rate production during 2016. Unit costs are projected to be between $286 million and $400 million.

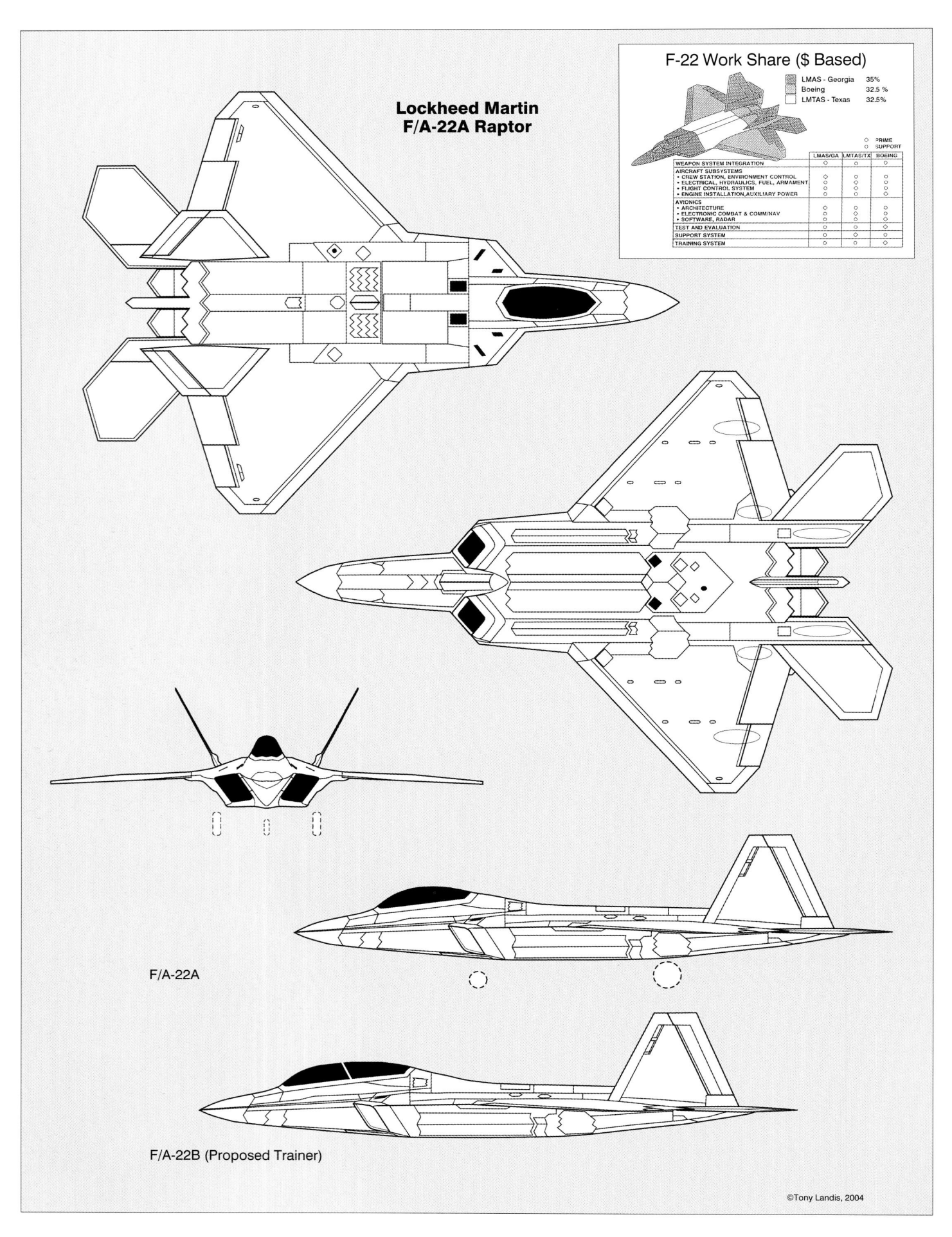

**Lockheed Martin
F/A-22A Raptor**

F-22 Work Share ($ Based)

LMAS - Georgia 35%
Boeing 32.5 %
LMTAS - Texas 32.5%

◇ PRIME
○ SUPPORT

	LMAS/GA	LMTAS/TX	BOEING
WEAPON SYSTEM INTEGRATION	◇		
AIRCRAFT SUBSYSTEMS			
• CREW STATION, ENVIRONMENT CONTROL	◇	○	○
• ELECTRICAL, HYDRAULICS, FUEL, ARMAMENT	○	◇	○
• FLIGHT CONTROL SYSTEM	○	◇	○
• ENGINE INSTALLATION, AUXILIARY POWER	○	○	◇
AVIONICS			
• ARCHITECTURE	◇	○	○
• ELECTRONIC COMBAT & COMM/NAV	○	◇	○
• SOFTWARE, RADAR	○	○	◇
TEST AND EVALUATION	○	◇	○
SUPPORT SYSTEM	○	◇	○
TRAINING SYSTEM	○	○	◇

F/A-22A

F/A-22B (Proposed Trainer)

©Tony Landis, 2004

Chapter Five

Construction and Systems

The F/A-22A is built by Lockheed Martin in partnership with Boeing. It is powered by Pratt & Whitney engines and made from parts and subsystems provided by approximately 1,000 subcontractors and suppliers in 43 of the 50 states.

Core components of the F/A-22A are manufactured at several different locations across the US (and, where appropriate, shipped to Marietta, Georgia) as follows:

Lockheed Martin in Marietta, Georgia – builds the forward fuselage. This includes the cockpit (avionics architecture, displays, controls, air data system, etc.), apertures, various edges, the tail assembly, the landing gear (installation only), and the environmental control system (installation only). Most importantly, final assembly and first flights of the aircraft take place here.

The Marietta facility also includes the special Radar Cross Section Verification Facility, which is a 50,000 sq. ft. fully enclosed structure optimized to test the stealth characteristics of each F/A-22A after it is completed. The main section of this building features a 45 ft. diameter turntable with precise positioning capability that permits full-scale testing. A separate 60 ft. by 210 ft. anechoic chamber is also an integral part of this building.

The Marietta facility also includes a Robotic Coatings Facility. This 43,000 sq. ft. building has separate areas for materials handling, sub-assembly painting, and a large bay where most of the exterior of each F/A-22A will be given their special RAM (radar absorbent material) and associated paint.

Lockheed Martin in Fort Worth, Texas – builds the center fuselage section.

Lockheed Martin in Palmdale, California – builds the nose radome and associated sub-assemblies.

Boeing in Seattle, Washington – builds the wings and the fuselage aft sections, accommodates the powerplant installation, builds the auxiliary power generation system, assembles the arresting gear unit, and is responsible for the avionics integration laboratory.

Four major classes of advanced composite materials were used on the YF-22A (which, how-

Top: **The first YF-22A, N22YF – the Pratt & Whitney F119-PW-100-powered prototype – entering final construction inside Lockheed Martin's famous Palmdale, California Skunk Works facility.** Lockheed Martin

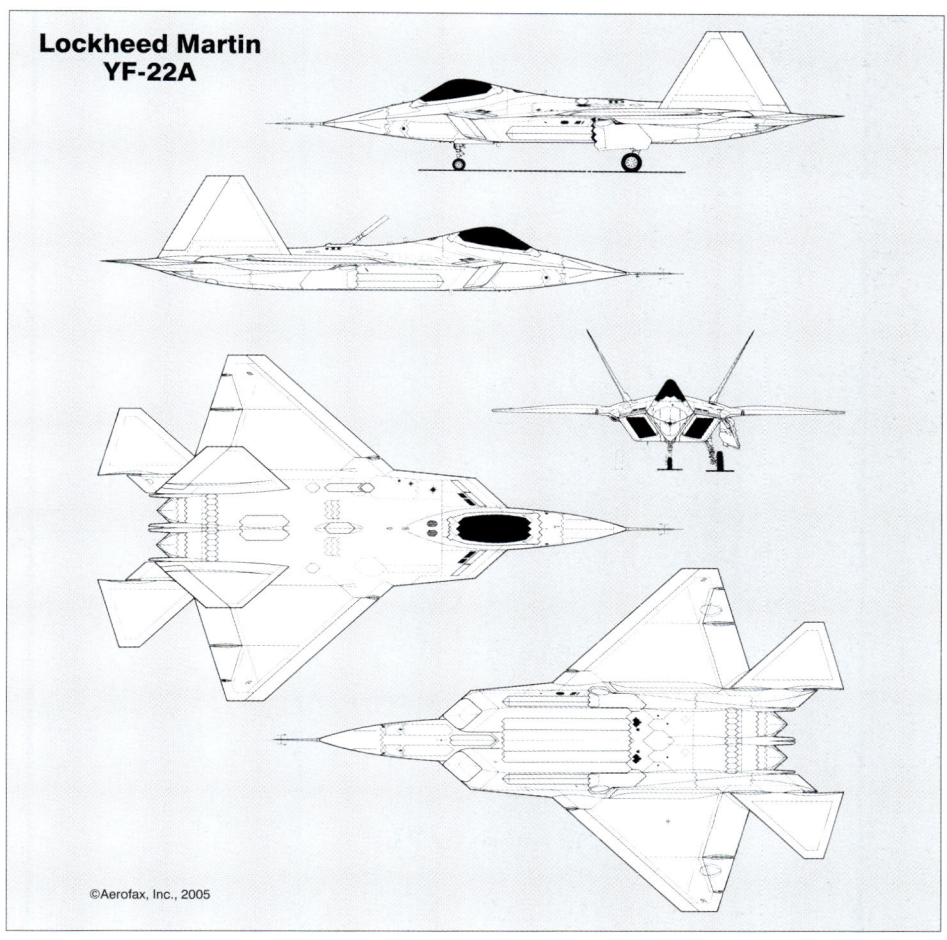

Lockheed Martin YF-22A

©Aerofax, Inc., 2005

ever, was primarily of metal construction) and now are used on the F/A-22A, demonstrating the contractor team's ability to design and manufacture parts from wet and dry thermoplastics as well as bismaleimide (BMI) and epoxy thermoset materials. Examples of the use of thermoplastics on the YF-22A were the single-piece wing skins. The various materials used in the construction of the YF-22A prototypes consisted of 13% graphite thermoplastics; 10% thermoset plastics; 33% aluminum; 2% advanced aluminum alloys; 24% titanium; 5% steel; and 31% other miscellaneous materials.

EMD F/A-22As are 1% thermoplastics; 37% titanium 6-4; 23% thermoset composites; 10% toughened epoxy composites; 15% aluminum; 6% steel; and 3% titanium 6-22-22.

The production F/A-22As differ in being 16% aluminum; 39 % titanium (36% Ti 6-4, 3% Ti 6-22-22); 6% steel; 1% thermoplastics; 24% thermoset composites; and 15% other miscellaneous materials.

Composite materials are combinations of two or more organic or inorganic materials. One material serves as a matrix; the other serves as a reinforcement in the form of continuous fibers dispersed in the matrix in an appropriate pattern. The function of the matrix is to bond the reinforcement together and to transfer loads between the fibers. The reinforcement supports the mechanical loads that the composite structure is subjected to in service.

Organic composite structural laminates are made up of stacks of oriented thin lamina that are consolidated under heat and pressure. Each lamina consists of a layer of high-strength, high-modulus, low-density reinforcing fibers embedded in a resin matrix. Fibers typically are materials such as carbon, boron, Kevlar 49, or fiberglass. The matrix can be either a thermosetting material such as epoxy, bismaleimide, or polyimide, or a thermoplastic material. If the matrix is thermosetting, a solid material is formed that cannot be reprocessed. Thermoplastic materials, however, can be reshaped by reheating and reforming.

Organic matrix composite parts currently being used on aircraft primarily are made up of thermoset materials that have been developed over the past twenty years. Thermoplastics for aerospace applications were introduced only a few years ago. An optimum mix of thermosets and thermoplastics were utilized on the YF-22A and are now utilized on the F/A-22A through complementary structural applications of each material class. In a program under contract to

Top: **F/A-22A forward fuselage section is manufactured in Marietta by Lockheed Martin.** Lockheed Martin

Middle: **F/A-22A center fuselage section is manufactured in Fort Worth by Lockheed Martin.** Lockheed Martin

Bottom: **F/A-22 aft fuselage section is manufactured in Seattle, Washington.** Boeing

the AFSC, the Lockheed ATF team built 12 main landing gear doors for the General Dynamics F-16 using thermoplastics and advanced processing. In a second phase of this program, the team also produced three generic fighter center fuselage sections while establishing and verifying various manufacturing methods that include filament winding, press forming, thermal forming, pultrusion, and adhesive bonding.

The external shape of both prototypes and the EMD series aircraft was optimized for low FICS. The blended wing/body configuration, which helped reduce FICS, also was structurally efficient and provided considerable internal volume for fuel carriage. Lockheed approached the complex problem of low observables from a systems engineering perspective. Requirements were established based on the mission. A configuration was then developed to satisfy the requirement. Configuration considerations included perimeter edge orientation and empennage interactions.

Additionally, low observable design efforts focused on subsystem performance. The engine intake/duct system, for instance, was required to balance low observables performance with propulsion system efficiency. Lockheed used a diamond-shaped intake/duct design which provided low observables performance without requiring special, low observables engine compressor face designs (which typically have had a severe impact on the engine's installed thrust).

Fuselage: The YF-22A fuselage, like much of the rest of the aircraft, was of mixed materials construction. Heavy emphasis was placed on low observables technology and accordingly, when assembly was completed, the metal components were covered with radar absorbent materials (RAM) and radar absorbent paint.

The fuselage was essentially modular in construction and was designed to provide maintenance access wherever possible without the use of ladders or access stools. Two large avionics bays were located in the fuselage nose section, these accommodating more than 100 common avionics modules in a liquid-cooled chassis. Each module was individually replaceable in the event of failure.

The YF-22A fuselage and F/A-22A fuselage differ physically in almost all respects, though materially they are quite similar. The F/A-22A fuselage is a blended wing/fuselage design with a semi-chined forebody that continues to the tip of the nose. The forebody, nose, and wing leading edges all contain conformal sensors of various types, including passive and active antenna assemblies.

Lockheed Martin has recently acknowledged that these buried sensors include the ability to gather electronic emissions from target sources at frequencies up to 18 GHz and to sort those emissions by time and angle of arrival. This permits determination of the source's location and also permits automatic analysis of the signature for rapid identification. When coupled with the F/A-22A's AN/APG-77 radar data, the pilot is provided an extraordinarily detailed overview of targets and threats.

All edge angles are aligned with the wing leading and trailing edges to most effectively accommodate reduced radar cross section (i.e., low-observables) requirements.

The fuselage has three integral weapon bays (two side and one main ventral).

The F/A-22A forward fuselage (manufactured by Lockheed Martin in Marietta) has a sub-structure of aluminum and composites. It consists of the structure aft of the radar bulkhead, the cockpit area, the nose wheel well, and the F-1 fuel tank. It comprises some 3,000 parts and includes wiring harnesses, tubing, cockpit instrument fixtures, avionics racks, and canopy mounts. It is just over 17 ft. long, just over 5 ft. wide, stands approximately 5 ft. 8 in. tall, and weighs approximately 1,700 lbs.

Built up in two sections, the forward fuselage is joined by two long and relatively wide side beams and two longerons that run the length of the assembly. The beams, made of composite material, also provide an attachment point for the F/A-22A's chine, a fuselage edge that provides smooth aerodynamic blending into the intakes and wings. The 17 ft. long aluminum longerons form the sills of the cockpit. The canopy rests on these.

The actual canopy transparency is a 3/4 in. thick fusion bonded (of two 3/8 in. thick sheets) and drape forged Sierracin Sylmar Corporation unit of tinted monolithic polycarbonate (approx. 140 in. length x 45 in. width x 27 in. height; unit weight is approx. 350 lb.). The canopy is supported by an aluminum frame that utilizes 8 lock units for latching. Heating/defrost/defogging are provided as an integral part of the frame assembly. The cockpit entry/exit ladder is pilot deployable.

The mid fuselage (manufactured by Lockheed Martin in Fort Worth) is the largest and most complex of the F/A-22A's major assemblies. It is approximately 17 ft. long, 15 ft. wide, and 6 ft. tall, and it weighs approximately 8,500 lbs. All F/A-22A systems pass through this section, including the hydraulic, electrical, environmental control, and auxiliary power systems, as well as the aircraft fuel. There are three fuel tanks, four internal weapons bays (the two side bays and the two sections of the main weapons bay that are separated), the 20 mm cannon, and the auxiliary power unit all located in the mid fuselage section.

The mid fuselage consists of three modules which are simultaneously assembled prior to mating. Some 35% of the mid fuselage structure is aluminum, 23.5% is of composite materials, and 35% is of titanium (one of the four one-piece titanium bulkheads is the largest sin-

Top: **F/A-22A mid-fuselage section in jigs.** Lockheed Martin

Middle: **YF-22A cockpit and associated instrument panel pod.** Lockheed Martin

Left and inset: **YF-22A instrument panel and side-stick controller. YF-22A ACES II ejection seat differed from that of F/A-22A. It moved from near vertical to reclined automatically. Pilots later rejected this option. Inset depicts original cockpit mockup with center stick.** Lockheed Martin and Jay Miller

gle piece of titanium ever used on an aircraft; the four main mid-fuselage section bulkheads are single-piece, closed-die, titanium forgings).

The rear fuselage (manufactured by Boeing in Kent) houses the two F119 engines and contains all or part of the aircraft's environmental control system and fuel, electrical, hydraulic, and engine subsystems. The aft fuselage is designed to withstand supersonic speeds for extended periods of time and extremely high-g maneuvers. The aft fuselage is approx. 67% titanium, 22% aluminum, and 11% composites. It is approx. 19 ft. long and 12 ft. wide and weighs approx. 5,000 lbs.

Approx. 25% of the aft fuselage is comprised of large electron beam welded titanium forward and aft booms. The largest of these, the forward boom, is more than 10 ft. in length and weighs approximately 650 lbs. The electron beam welded booms of the aft fuselage are extremely weight-efficient and reduce the use of traditional fasteners by approximately 75%.

The engine bay doors, located in the aft fuselage section are titanium honeycomb (produced by liquid-interface diffusion bonding).

The skins for all three fuselage sections are primarily graphite bismaleimide.

A pair of abbreviated tail booms are attached to the aft fuselage section. These are assembled using electron beam welding techniques.

Cockpit: The YF-22A cockpit was designed to permit greater situational awareness through an excellent field of view while minimizing pilot workload through the use of colored liquid crystal (LCD) multifunction displays (MFDs) with finger-on-glass (FOG) controls. LCDs permit lower weight, lower power requirements, reduced volume, and improved performance.

The LCDs used in the YF-22A involved active matrix technology for the presentation of real-time video or graphic images. The displays had a contrast ratio in excess of 12:1 in a 10k foot Lambert environment and a brightness of white in excess of 200 foot Lambert. A single display was packed into two line replaceable units (LRUs), the remote electronics unit (REU), and the display unit (DU).

There were two 6 in. x 6 in. primary multifunction displays (PMFD) and three 4 in. x 6 in. secondary multifunction displays (SMFD). The primary MFD and secondary MFDs were full-color liquid crystal units developed by Lockheed. These MFDs, in upgraded form, were carried over to the F/A-22A...though bezel buttons were provided for pilot format control in place of the FOG option.

In the EMD F/A-22A and production aircraft, displays consist of the following:

The Integrated Control Panel (ICP) is the primary means for manual pilot data entry for communications, navigation, and autopilot data. Located under the glare shield and the

Top: **F/A-22A, 00-4013, main instrument panel.**

Right: **F/A-22A left console with HOTAS-type throttle levers.** Jay Miller x 2

HUD in center top of the instrument panel, this keypad entry system also has some double click functions, much like a computer mouse for rapid pilot access/use.

There are six liquid crystal display (LCD) panels. These present information in full color and are fully readable in direct sunlight. LCDs offer lower weight and less size than the cathode ray tube (CRT) displays used in most current US military aircraft. The lower power requirement also provides a reliability improvement over CRTs.

The two Up-Front Displays (UFDs) measure 3 in. by 4 in. and are located to the left and right of the ICP. The UFDs are used to display Integrated Caution/Advisory/Warning (ICAS) data, communications/navigation/identification (CNI) data and serve as the Stand-by Flight Instrumentation Group and Fuel Quantity Indicator (SFG/FQI).

A total of 12 individual ICAW messages can appear at one time on the UFD and additional messages can appear on sub-pages of the display. Two aspects of the ICAW display differentiate it from a traditional warning light panel. First, all ICAW fault messages are filtered to eliminate extraneous messages and tell the pilot specifically and succinctly what the problem is.

The second is the electronic checklist. When an ICAW message occurs, the pilot depresses the checklist push button (a bezel) on the bottom of the UFD and the associated checklist appears on the left hand Secondary Multi-Function Display (SMFD). This function also provides access to non-emergency checklists for display to the pilot.

In addition to the visual warning on the display, the aircraft has an audio system that alerts the pilot. A caution is indicated only by the word "caution", while a warning is announced with the specific problem.

The Stand-by Flight Group is always in operation and, although it is presented on an LCD display, it shows the basic information (such as an artificial horizon) which the pilot needs to fly the aircraft. The SFG is tied to the last source of power in the aircraft, so if everything else fails, the pilot will still be able to fly.

The Primary Multi-Function Display (PMFD) is an 8 in. by 8 in. color display that is located in the middle of the instrument panel, under the ICP. It is the pilot's principal display for aircraft navigation (including showing waypoints and route of flight) and situation assessment.

Three Secondary Multi-Function Displays (SMFDs) are all 6.25 in. by 6.25 in. and two of them are located on either side of the PMFD on the instrument panel with the third underneath the PMFD between the pilot's knees. These are used for displaying tactical (both offensive and defensive) information as well as non-tactical information (such as checklists, subsystem status, engine thrust output, and stores management).

On the YF-22A, the UFCD was for presentation of communications, navigation, and identification (CNI) data as well as caution, warning, and advisory messages.

The F/A-22A's CNI system includes GPS, Tacan, and twin Litton LN-100F ring laser gyroscope inertial reference units. The latter are placed nose-to-nose behind the radar on the aircraft's centerline and are operated off separate data buses to provide independent measurement data. The LN-100Fs are fused with the GPS.

The GEC-built HUD (wide field of view – 30° horizontally and 25° vertically) presents primary flight reference, weapon-aiming, and weapon release information. The HUD, which is 4.5 in. tall and uses standardized symbology developed by the AF Instrument Flight Center, is fully night-vision-goggle compatible. Back-up flight performance information is provided on a full-time basis by the standby flight group (SFG).

The pilot's ability to assess and manage the tactical situation and to prosecute the attack is enhanced by automation of sensors, threat assessment, and attack management tasks. This relieves the pilot of many routine tasks and provides the decision aids and situational awareness needed to maintain the advantage over an adversary.

The caution warning and advisory system is designed to eliminate indications that lead to a proliferation of unwanted and unneeded warning lights. Messages are displayed on the up-front control/display unit and are backed up by a voice annunciation system. The pilot is not only informed of what is wrong, but also is presented with the corrective actions required.

There is a side-stick controller (contrary to earlier plans calling for a conventional center stick) and conventional rudder pedals. The HOTAS (hands-on throttle and stick) philosophy allows the pilot to prosecute an attack from beyond-visual-range (BVR) to a one-on-one "dogfight" without having to remove his hands from the stick or throttles to manage offensive and defensive sensors and weapons. The integrated throttle control also provides the pilot with a single grip for control of both engines. Tailoring the throttle grip provides a comfortable hand rest and easy HOTAS switch manipulation. Auxiliary controls for independent management of each engine also are provided.

Right: **Full view of F/A-22A instrument with panel MFDs lit for photography.** Lockheed Martin

Below: **Instrument panel pod (including inset) and raster-type holographic HUD.** Jay Miller x 2

HOTAS contains 20 controls permitting 63 functions.

Cockpit interior lighting is fully NVG compatible, as is the exterior lighting. The cockpit panels feature extended life, self-balancing, electroluminescent (EL) edge-lit panels with an integral life-limiting circuit that runs the lights at the correct power setting throughout their life.

The cockpit is sized to accommodate 99% of the Air Force pilot population and is arranged to provide the pilot with a safe, comfortable working environment. Required controls and displays are within comfortable reach and view.

The ejection seat is an improved version of the ACES II (Advanced Concept Ejection Seat). The seat has a center mounted (between the pilot's legs) ejection handle. Improvements over extant ACES seats include:

• The addition of an active arm restraint system to eliminate arm flail injuries during high-speed ejections.

• An improved fast-acting seat stabilization drogue parachute system to provide increased seat stability and safety for the pilot during high-speed ejections. The drogue is located behind the pilot's head, rather than in the back of the seat. It is mortar-deployed.

• A new electronic seat and aircraft sequencing system that improves the timing of the various events that have to happen in order for the pilot to eject (initiation, canopy jettison, and seat catapult ignition).

• A larger oxygen bottle gives the ejecting pilot more breathing air to support ejection at higher altitudes (if required).

The ACES II ejection system utilizes the standard analog three-mode seat sequencer that automatically senses the seat speed and altitude, and then selects the proper mode for optimum seat performance and safe recovery of the pilot. Mode 1 is low-speed, low-altitude; Mode 2 is high-speed, low-altitude; and Mode 3 is high-altitude.

When sitting in the seat, the pilot's view over the nose is -15°.

The development of a new tactical life support system (TLSS) flight suit and associated equipment has offset the need for the articulated seat. The TLSS provides increased protection against high-g by providing both an upper and lower-body g-suit and a positive pressure breathing system. Chemical and cold water immersion protection is provided by the same garment. Comfort is aided by a personal thermal control system to control air temperatures from the environmental control system.

The pilot is provided a Meta Research life support system pressure suit and currently, a HGU-86/P helmet. The latter will eventually (not

currently on aircraft being delivered due to "technical problems") transition to an advanced technology helmet integrating the Boeing-developed Joint Helmet Mounted Cuing System (JHMCS). The latter allows a pilot to aim air-to-air missiles at close-range targets simply by head movement. The unit is designed to counter the off-boresight capabil-

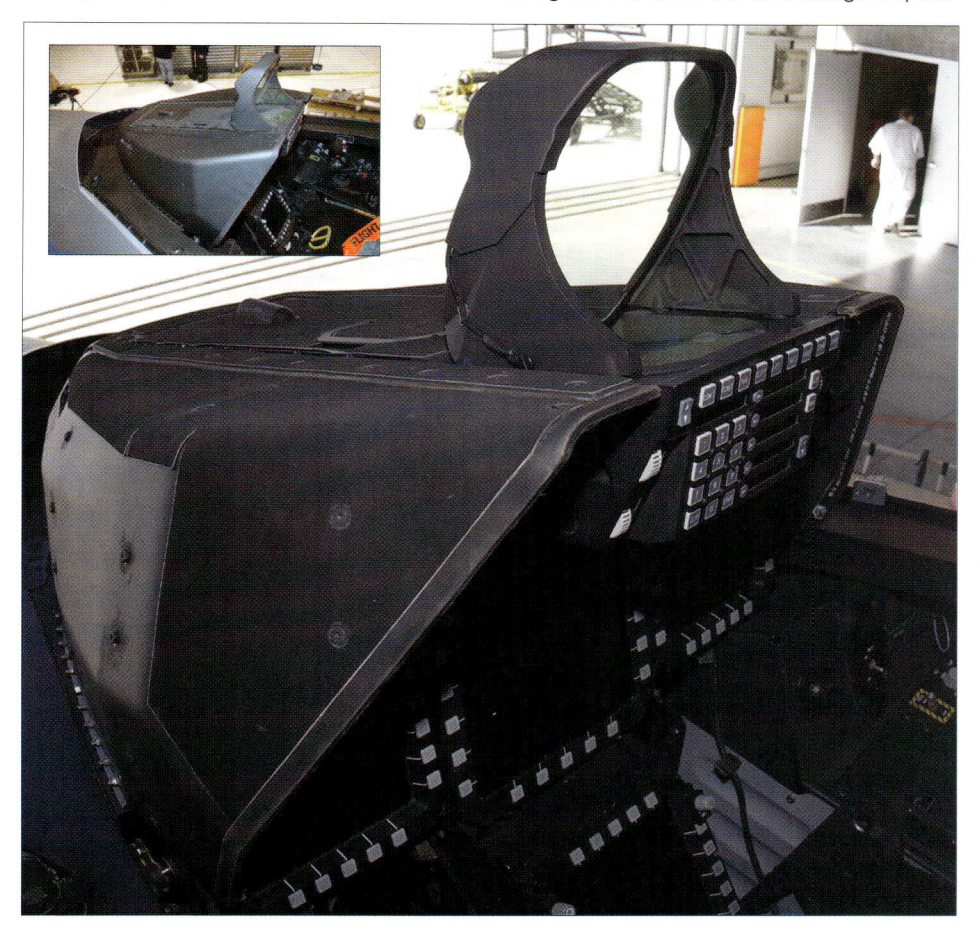

ity currently found in many of the most advanced Russian fighters. The pilot is also provided with ILC Dover life support chemical/biological/cold water immersion gear.

EMD aircraft utilize a considerably different MFD control arrangement. Difficulties with the FOG system, due primarily to a lack of tactile feedback, led to a decision to return to a conventional push button switch system around the screen bezels.

Sorted and fused information is displayed on six Sanders/Kaiser (OIS) color active-matrix, liquid-crystal, multifunction displays; primary multi-function display (PMFD) measures 8 in x by 8 in (20 cm by 20 cm), two up-front displays (UFDs) of 3 in by 4 in (7.6 cm by 10 cm), and three secondary multi-function displays (SMFD) of 6.25 in. by 6.25 in. (16 cm by 16 cm). There is also an integrated caution, advisory, and warning (CAW) system with up to twelve filtered messages appearing at any time on the UFD below the instrument panel glare shield. Additional messages on sub pages are available on the display.

Two Little LN-100G laser-gyros are provided for the inertial reference system. GPS data is also available.

The HUD is a GEC-Marconi wide-angle unit (30° horizontally, 25° vertically). In the event of canopy impact (bird strike, etc.), the HUD will collapse in order to avoid fracturing the transparency. The aircraft is also equipped with a Sanders graphics processor video interface unit (GPVI); an airborne video tape recorder (AVPR); an operational debrief system (ODS); and a common automated test system (CATS). There is also a fiber network interfaces unit (FNIU); an avionics bus interface (ABI), and a Harris Government Aerospace fiber optic bus component.

The aircraft is equipped with a microwave landing system. The glide-slope antenna is mounted inside the nose landing gear door.

The F/A-22A's cockpit environmental control system/thermal management system (ECS/TMS) is manufactured by Honeywell. It is an open-loop air-cycle system that serves to cool flight-critical avionics while supplying the pilot's life support system. A primary heat-exchanger

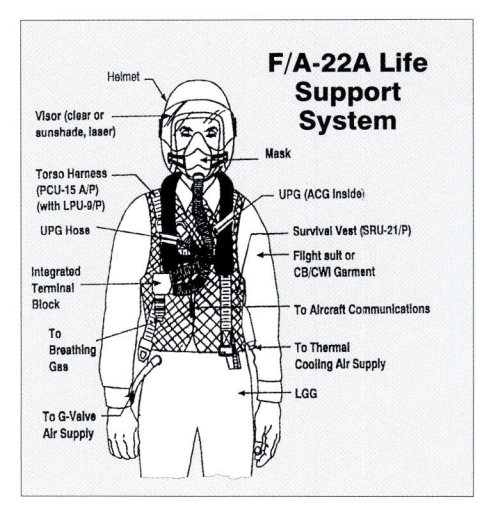

cools an engine /auxiliary power unit bleed air supply to an air-cycle refrigeration pack. A closed-loop vapor-cycle system provides liquid-cooling (using polyalphaolephin [PAO] coolant) for mission-critical avionics. Temperature is a constant 68° F. The aircraft fuel supply serves as the system's heat sink. The thermal management system cools the fuel.

There is a Normalair-Garrett-manufactured on-board oxygen generation system (OBOGS) which supplies oxygen to meet pilot requirements.

Fire protection is provided via infrared and UV sensors and a Halon 1301 gas (eventually to be replaced by an agent less harmful to the environment) extinguisher system. Fire protection is provided for the aircraft's engine bays, the APU, the landing gear wells, the side-of-body cavities, the LLAHS, the OBIGGS, the left and right ACFCs, and the ECS bay.

A CFC ram-air intake (positioned in the boundary layer diverter) injectors suck air into ram ducts when the aircraft is sitting statically.

Aircraft start-up and taxi have been reduced to three steps: the pilot places the battery switch to "on"; the pilots places the auxiliary power unit (APU) switch momentarily to "start"; and the pilot places both throttles in "idle". The aircraft is ready to taxi in less than 30 seconds following initiation of the starting procedure.

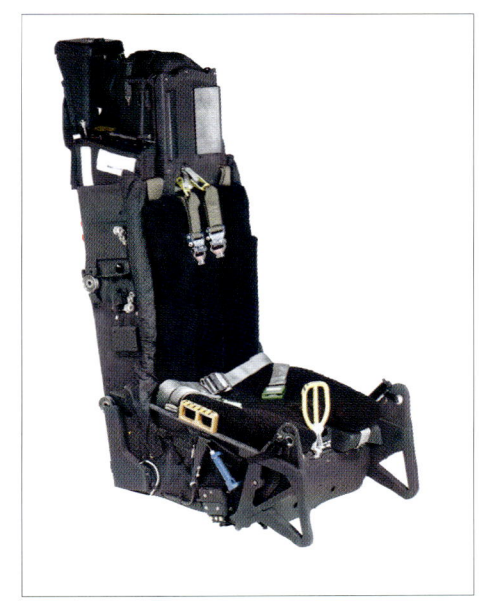

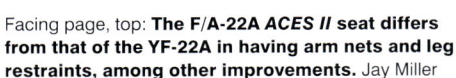

Facing page, top: **The F/A-22A ACES II seat differs from that of the YF-22A in having arm nets and leg restraints, among other improvements.** Jay Miller

Facing page, bottom left: **View of aft cockpit area behind ejection seat includes canopy raise/lower worm drive and canopy hinge.** Jay Miller

Above left: **ACES II ejection seat for F/A-22A differs in many respects from earlier ACES II designs. Among the changes, it is electronically sequenced; the firing handle actuates dual squibs that light thermal batteries. At that point, all the squibs are electrically signalled to function.** AF/Lockheed via Kevin Coyne

Right, bottom two: **Various views of the F/A-22A canopy. Canopy consists of multiple laminates including one optimized to reduce cockpit radar returns.** Jay Miller x 2 and Lockheed Martin

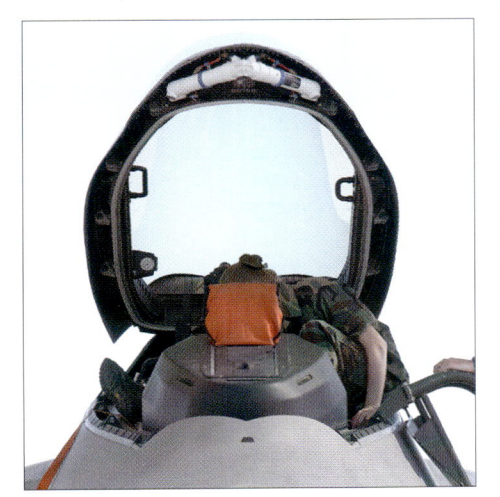

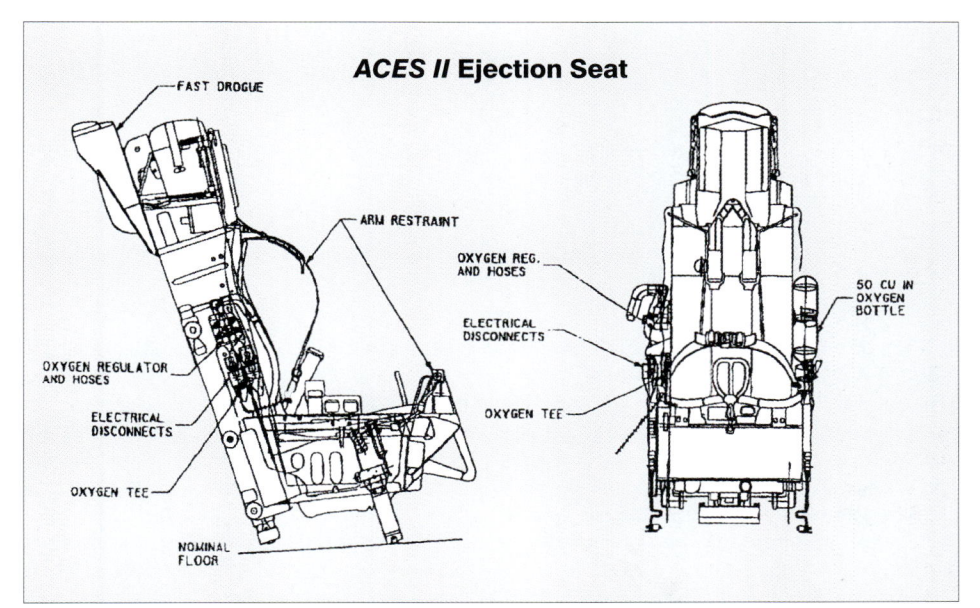

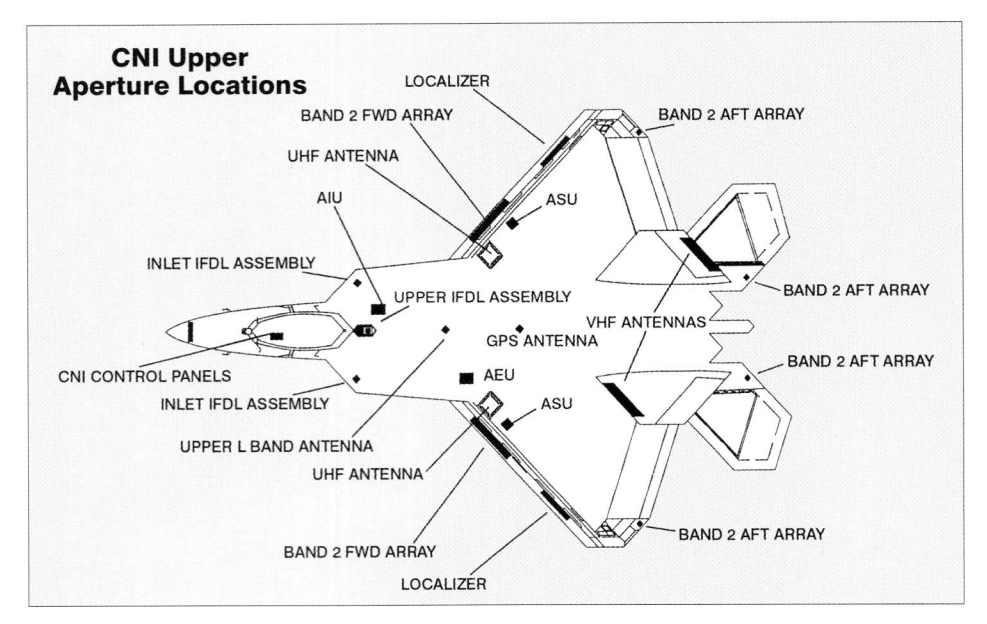

CNI Upper Aperture Locations

LOCALIZER
BAND 2 FWD ARRAY
BAND 2 AFT ARRAY
UHF ANTENNA
AIU
ASU
INLET IFDL ASSEMBLY
UPPER IFDL ASSEMBLY
BAND 2 AFT ARRAY
VHF ANTENNAS
GPS ANTENNA
BAND 2 AFT ARRAY
CNI CONTROL PANELS
AEU
INLET IFDL ASSEMBLY
ASU
UPPER L BAND ANTENNA
UHF ANTENNA
BAND 2 AFT ARRAY
BAND 2 FWD ARRAY
LOCALIZER

To reduce pilot workload, the F/A-22A incorporates a unique caution and warning system called ICAW (Integrated Caution, Advisory, and Warning system). ICAW messages normally appear on the 3 in. by 4 in. UFD just below the glare shield. A total of 12 individual ICAW messages can appear at any one time on the UFD with additional message space available on sub-pages of the display.

Flight Control System: The YF-22A's flight control system, developed by General Dynamics was a full fly-by-wire system. Development began during 1987 and involved about 60 employees at its peak. General Dynamics participated in decisions concerning the sizes and shapes of control surfaces, the types of control surface actuators, and the degree of maneuverability needed to accommodate the ATF's mission objectives. Additionally, the company's flight control engineering team participated in the wind tunnel test program and designed the aircraft's control laws.

A quadruply-redundant digital flight control computer (FLCC) configuration was chosen for the YF-22A primarily to take advantage of simpler redundancy management techniques. The FLCC output to the surface actuators was triple-redundant. Command signals to the flight control computers were initiated by applying position or force commands to the throttles, sidestick controller, or rudder pedals. These signals were processed by the flight control computers along with data from the air data sensors, rate gyros, and accelerometers.

Fly-by-wire was required in part because the F/A-22A utilizes longitudinal relaxed static stability. It also has automatic structural load limiting that permits the use of maximum allowable load factors throughout the flight envelope.

The F/A-22A utilizes a Lear Astronics vehicle management system (VMS) that integrates flight and propulsion controls in a nearly seamless exercise. The integrated vehicle subsystem control (IVSC) operates utilities via the digital databus. A total of 18 Raytheon 1750A common processor modules are used for VMS, IVSC, and stores management.

The VMS is also integrated with a Rosemount low-observable air data system that includes two angle-of-attack probes and four sideslip plate-type sensors on the nose.

The F/A-22A is the first aircraft of its class to utilize a triplex digital flight control computer arrangement with no electrical or mechanical back-up. The system is capable of automated control reconfiguration any time there is an actuator or hydraulic system failure. The VMS controls 14 surfaces and doors, including the horizontal tail, the ailerons, the flaperons, the rudders, the leading edge flaps, and the inlet bleed and bypass doors.

The F/A-22A has no angle-of-attack limitation. Over-stressing the airframe, however, is rendered moot by computer-dictated limitations to roll rate and load factor. Built-in to the equations are fuel status, stores/pods, and overall aircraft flight condition.

Avionics: The F/A-22A is optimized to provide a highly integrated avionics suite suitable for single-pilot operation and quick reaction. Per the Lockheed Martin engineering team's mandate, the F/A-22A is designed to exploit information while concurrently denying information to the enemy. Accordingly, avionics systems in the aircraft are designed to gather information from many sources and then process that information into a simple, intuitive picture of the tactical situation for the pilot.

The radar, radar warning and receiving (RWR), and communications/identification systems are all managed concurrently through a system optimized for operation by a single crew member. Electronic emissions are controlled in stages starting with totally passive...and escalating to fully active as dictated by the pilot and the tactical situation. The two CIPs (central integrated processors) control all avionics system functions including self-protection, radio, and panel presentations. They are capable of automatically reconfiguring themselves to compensate for faults. The two CIPs (space is available for a third) are linked by a 400 Mbits/s fiber optic network.

A closed-loop vapor-cycle system provides liquid-cooling (polyalphaolephin coolant [PAO]). This cools mission-critical avionics. The aircraft's fuel supply is used as a heat-sink.

Some F/A-22A antennas, such as communication, navigation, and IFF are integrated into the airframe as conformal hardware and are integral with the aircraft's wing and vertical tail leading edges. Select antennas are multifunction and use shared assets to perform radar track warning, missile launch detection, and threat identification.

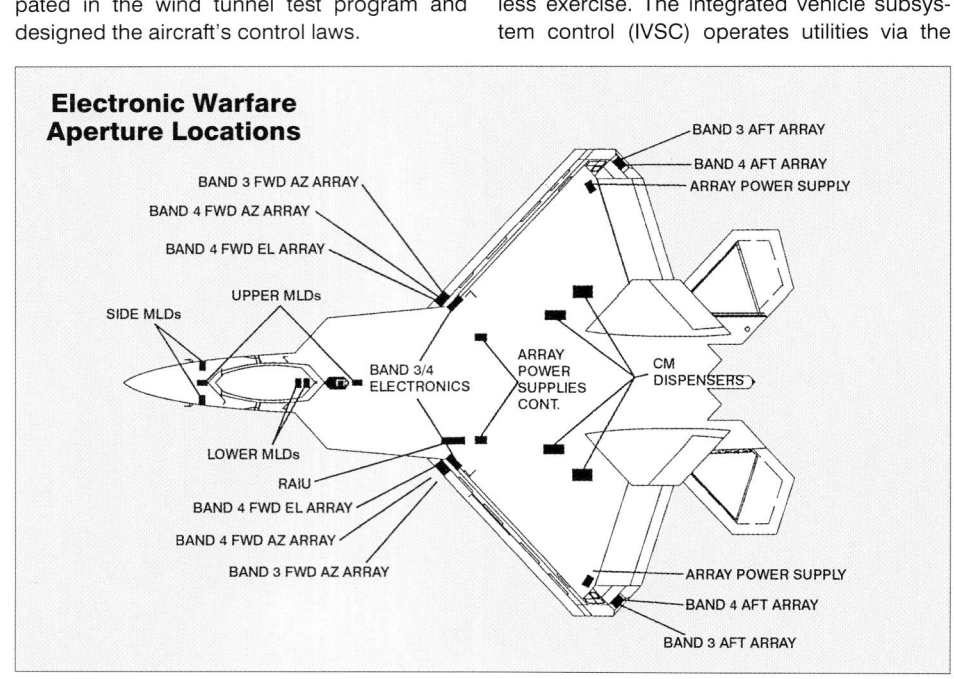

Electronic Warfare Aperture Locations

BAND 3 FWD AZ ARRAY
BAND 4 FWD AZ ARRAY
BAND 4 FWD EL ARRAY
UPPER MLDs
SIDE MLDs
BAND 3/4 ELECTRONICS
ARRAY POWER SUPPLIES CONT.
CM DISPENSERS
BAND 3 AFT ARRAY
BAND 4 AFT ARRAY
ARRAY POWER SUPPLY
LOWER MLDs
RAIU
BAND 4 FWD EL ARRAY
BAND 4 FWD AZ ARRAY
BAND 3 FWD AZ ARRAY
ARRAY POWER SUPPLY
BAND 4 AFT ARRAY
BAND 3 AFT ARRAY

The technology Lockheed developed for the fire control radar and other avionic apertures met the F/A-22A's low observable requirements without impacting aperture performance. The integration of these apertures into a low observable vehicle was critical to mission survivability.

Under what is referred to as a "Federated" system, the avionics, including the radar, the IRST, the threat receivers, the CNI (communications/navigation/identification), weapons system, miscellaneous aircraft systems, and countermeasures system all feed into a 1-megabyte-per-second serial bus. The CNI also includes a JTIDS (receive-only) terminal.

The F/A-22A electronic combat suite combines multiple functions to counter advanced radars and long-range, multispectral weapons. The suite includes a radar-warning receiver, missile approach warning, infrared and FIF countermeasures, and electronic support measures functions. A precision direction-finding capability aids situational awareness. All of these functions are contained on approximately 70 Standard Electronics Model E (SEME) format modules which fit together with a central integrated processor Hughes Aircraft Radar Systems Group (CIP) computer.

On the prototype (YF-22A) aircraft, the left primary MFD (No.1) could be removed when required and replaced either by a flutter excitation system panel or stabilization recovery chute control panel. The right primary MFD never was installed. Instead, a special programmable cathode ray tube (CRT) display was installed and served to provide flight test nose boom air data information. Four different types of display format could be selected by the pilot, depending on the type of testing being performed.

The secondary MFDs (Nos. 4, 5, and 6) were used to present the following types of display formats: subsystem status display; fuel status display; stores management display; and subsystem control display. For communication/navigation/identification the following were displayed: communication option page; TACAN option page; IFF option page; and INS option page. For head up and vertical situation displays the following were displayed: HUD declutter page and VSD declutter page. For integrated flight/ propulsion control the following were displayed: engine controls page and flight test aid page. For mission data base the following were displayed: communication list page; TACAN list page; and waypoint list page. The flight test aid page enabled the pilot to: select different pre-programmed control law options; perform automatic pitch, yaw, or roll doublets; adjust the load factor times weight

(NzW) limiter to various percentages of the maximum allowable; and vary exhaust nozzle area ratio and nozzle trim angle.

The electronics and software that make up the prototype avionics suite for the YF-22A began flight tests on April 18, 1990 from Boeing's Seattle, Washington facility. A four-month check-out was undertaken utilizing Boeing's 757 FTB (Flying Test Bed; originally it was referred to as the Avionics Flying Laboratory [AFL]) test aircraft. Prototype YF-22 sensors flown aboard the FTB included the Northrop/Grumman (formerly Westinghouse) Raytheon AN/APG-77 active VLO electronically-scanned active array radar (first flight with the AN/APG-77 installed took place on November 21, 1997). Integral with the radar was the F/A-22A's integrated composite radome and integrated CIP (common integrated processor) assembly. Two side array units, scheduled for eventual integration (for beam concentration during proposed computer network attack missions under what is currently referred to as Project *Sutor*) also were tested. The TRW communi-

cations/navigation/identification system, the Lockheed Sanders/General Electric electronic combat system, and the General Electric infrared search-and-track unit also were flight tested on the Boeing 757 FTB.

The FTB, during the course of tests, was flown against targets of opportunity including commercial, general aviation, and military aircraft. Individual tests were used to evaluate the installed performance of each sensor, the integrated avionics suite, and the mission avionics sensor management and sensor track integration functions.

Software, developed by Lockheed Martin's Sanders division, has been delivered the F/A-22A program in Blocks. Block 0 was utilized in initial flight tests. Block 1.1 (primarily for radar and avionics suite code source lines) was installed on '4004 during 1999. Block 2 was installed on and only tested on the Boeing 757 FTB during October of 1999 (served as sensor integration software: radio frequency coordination, select electronic warfare functions). Block 3S served and introduced CNI and ECCM

Top: **The F/A-22A's radome is an integral part of the AN/APG-77 radar package.** Jay Miller

Right: **Angular nose radome cross-section is the end product of low-observables requirements.** Jay Miller

capabilities. Block 3.0, offering full sensor integration and weapon delivery capability, was initially flown aboard the Boeing 757 FTB during the fourth quarter of 2000 and, tested aboard an F/A-22 for the first time on January 5, 2001. Block 3.1 integrated GBU-32 JDAM, JTIDS integration and GPS capability and was the software initially installed in IOC-level aircraft. Block 4.0 offered helmet mounted sighting capability, AIM-9X and JTIDS data transmission. Blocks 5.0 and 6.0 are not yet finalized. Initial installation is scheduled for 2006 and will offer enhanced air-to-ground capability (inclusive of the Small Diameter Bomb [SDB]).

All operational F/A-22As will have the Northrop Grumman Radio Systems developed IntraFlight Datalink (IFDL) system as part of the Communications, Navigation and Identification (CNI) suite. IFDL allows F/A-22A formations to discretely share information provided by each other's on-board and off-board sensors, including target tracking information provided by the aircraft's AN/APG-77 radar. Such information will help prevent weapons from being unnecessarily launched or dropped on targets already being engaged by another F/A-22A. The IFDL also helps the flight leader keep track of wingmen and the formation's weapons load-out and fuel status so that missions can be successfully executed. Using IFDL, all aircraft and pilots involved in a mission can maximize their combat effectiveness.

The Boeing FTB was used initially to prove the IFDL's capabilities both in the air and on the ground with but a single F/A-22A pilot at Edwards AFB. During three days of testing, the FTB showed that the IFDL can share data with a wingman, even when the F/A-22A pilot executes a series of fast and slow rolls and high-g maneuvers. Previous IFDL flight tests involving the FTB and the ground-based Avionics Integration Laboratory (AIL) at Boeing's facility in Seattle. Avionics testing onboard the Boeing 757 testbed helped reduce both risk and future F/A-22A flight test hours by enabling extensive in-flight testing, evaluation, and trouble shooting prior to installation on production aircraft.

Radar: The Northrop Grumman/ Raytheon third-generation AN/APG-77 multi-mode radar currently found on all F/A-22As through production Lot 4 aircraft, is a very low observables, active, electronically scanned array (AESA) antenna design that is integral with the aircraft radome (manufactured by Lockheed Martin in Palmdale, California) and CIP. It is capable of interleaving air-to-air search and multi-target tracking. It also has a weather mapping mode, a side array scan capability, and provision for air-to-ground capability if needed.

AESA radars are comprised of a number (often many hundreds) of stationary transmitter/receiver units that can be programmed individually to accommodate different tasks. These latter can include simultaneously searching, tracking, and imaging target aircraft and, in some cases, jamming enemy aircraft radars and associated communications systems. The latter capability, under the auspices of the currently-under-development Thor jamming system, is to be an integral part of the F/A-22A's ECM capability by 2008.

Sources indicate the radar is capable of tracking targets as small as 10.76 sq. ft. at a range of over 125 miles. It is a multi-mode unit and has a wide field of view. ADA software (with 800K lines of code) has been demonstrated.

On June 11, 2004, Northrop Grumman Corporation successfully conducted the first flight test of its new, fourth-generation AN/APG-77 variant. It is understood that the new version of the An/APG-77 is intended to reduce the production and maintenance costs of the earlier radar by adapting the design that was implemented successfully in the AN/APG-81 radar for the Lockheed Martin F-35 Joint Strike Fighter and the AN/APG-80 for the Block 60 Lockheed Martin F-16.

The new AN/APG-77 version requires significantly fewer parts than the third-generation model and the production line relies on a greater degree of automation. The new unit will have high-resolution mapping-of-ground-targets capability which will permit true all-weather, precision strike capability. This will

All three: **The F/A-22A's Northrop Grumman/ Raytheon AN/APG-77 multimode, electronically scanned radar is arguably the most advanced radar of its kind in the world. These three images depict prototype units and are not representative of the actual AN/APG-77 as installed in the F/A-22A. As part of the effort to meet low-observables requirements, the AN/APG-77 is rigidly mounted in an upward-facing position.** Lockheed Martin and Northrop Grumman/Raytheon

transform the F/A-22A into a true multi-mission asset. The company currently expects to deliver 203 of the new AN/APG-77s for the F/A-22A program.

Starting with Lot 5 production (est. late 2008), the F/A-22A's AN/APG-77 radar will be replaced with a further-improved AN/APG-77 AESA-type radar with an advanced air-to-ground capability and probably, significant jamming capability. Instead of the often broadband, omni-directional jamming of current and immediate past systems, the new AESA radar will note and discriminate threats and specifically target their frequencies. Particular emphasis will be placed on data transmission and air defenses. In so doing, it will reduce the amount of electronic clutter and thus permit the monitoring of enemy communications and other electronic sources for important data.

Wings: The truncated delta wing of the YF-22A and F/A-22A differed somewhat in materials and construction. Thermoplastics were utilized in the YF-22A prototypes, but production aircraft use a less expensive thermoset alternative. On the production aircraft, the wing skins are made of monolithic graphite bismaleimide. The main spars (front) are machined titanium forgings while the intermediate spars are a mix of resin transfer molded (RTM) sine-wave composites and titanium (which help reduce the vulnerability of the wing fuel tanks to damage). The rear spars are also manufactured of composites and titanium. Materials by weight are 35% composites, 42% titanium, 23% aluminum, with some miscellaneous materials in the form of steel for fasten-

ers, clips, etc. Each wing is 16 ft. by 18 ft. (leading edge) and weighs approximately 2,000 lbs.

The wing root and control surface actuator fairings are titanium HIP castings. The wing control surfaces are manufactured of a combination of co-cured composite skin/substructures and non-metallic honeycomb core construction.

Each wing is equipped with a single trailing edge aileron outboard and a large, single piece flaperon inboard (driven by Parker Bertea actuators). The leading edge flap (driven by Curtiss-Wright Flight Systems actuators) is also a single piece unit and extends to the wing tip.

The wing leading edge sweep angle is 42° for the F/A-22A (48° for the YF-22A). The trailing edge sweep angle (forward) is 17° (same for the YF-22A). The latter increases to 42° outboard of the ailerons.

The Lockheed Martin-designed wing airfoil section is approximately 3.8% and is optimized for transonic operation. Some blending at the root section accommodates both RCS and aerodynamic requirements without compromising either. The wing taper ratio is 0.169. Wing leading edge anhedral is 3.25° and root twist is 0.5°. Tip twist is a negative 3.1°. Thickness/chord ratio is 5.92% at the root and 4.29% at the tip.

Roll control is provided by a combination of differential movement of the ailerons (+/-25°), flaperons (+25° or -35°), and horizontal stabilators (leading edge +30° to -25°). Symmetrical movement of the full-span leading edge flaps (normally +3° to -35°; maximum is +5° to -37°), ailerons, and flaperons is scheduled as a function of angle-of-attack, Mach number, and landing gear position. All control surfaces are hydraulically actuated. All surfaces droop during low-speed flight to accommodate lift requirements.

Tail Surfaces: The horizontal and vertical tails utilize "tow placed" composite pivot shafts supporting an aluminum honeycomb core. The skins, like those of the wings, are of solid graphite bismaleimide. The spars are constructed of graphite epoxy RTM. They have

Top left: **F/A-22A forward fuselage section and intake.** Jay Miller

Top right: **Wing undersurface. Diamond patterns are covers for external stores pylon mounting points.** Jay Milller

Far left: **Left wingtip formation light.** Jay Miller

Left: **Left Intake top edge and upper intake panel surface detail.** Jay Miller

Bottom two/insets: **Vertical tail and rudder detail. Outward cant of vertical tails is the result of radar cross section requirements.** Jay Miller x 4

been designed to provide unrestricted maneuvering and battle damage redundancy. The rudder actuator housing is a hot isostatic pressed (HIP) casting.

Pitch control is provided by symmetrical movement of the horizontal stabilators (+30° to -35° leading edge) and engine nozzles. Production F/A-22As utilize vertical tails made of metal-matrix composites (MMC). The rudders provide directional control and coordinate the aircraft in roll. The horizontal tail leading edge surfaces have a sweep angle of 42° (consistent with the wing). They have no dihedral and no twist.

The vertical tail surfaces each cant outward 28° in an attempt to reduce the aircraft's RCS. Leading and trailing edge sweep angles are 22.9°. The airfoil section is bi-convex. Rudders move +/-30° in rudder mode and 30° outboard in airbrake mode.

The F/A-22A's flight control system is a triplex, digital, fly-by-wire system with GEC side-stick controller. It uses line-replaceable electronic modules to reduce maintenance requirements. The F/A-22A does not have an airbrake but instead uses differential rudder and wing trailing edge surfaces for speed control.

Landing Gear: The fully retractable Menasco-manufactured tricycle landing gear is conventional in layout and design. It is stressed for no-flare landings of up to 10 ft. per second.

The nose gear, which is turned hydraulically for steering and is mechanically driven to align itself correctly during retraction, retracts forward.

The two AirMet 100 main gear assemblies retract outward, toward the wingtips. Retraction is via independent hydraulic ram-type actua-

tors. Each Honeywell-manufactured main gear wheel is equipped with an Allied Signal Carbonex 4000 carbon mainwheel anti-skid disc brake assembly.

Each main gear well is covered by a single piece composite door. The nose gear well is covered by a two-piece door. RCS considerations dictated the design of the forward edge of the main gear door panels.

The nose wheel tire is either a Goodyear or Michelin 23.5 x 7.5-10, 22-ply tubeless; the main wheel tires are Goodyear or Michelin 37 x 11.50-18, 30-ply tubeless.

A Kaiser-manufactured arresting hook is faired into the underside of the fuselage between the engine nacelles.

Top both including inset: **F/A-22A nose landing gear retracts forwad into well. Steering is via hydraulic actuator.** Jay Miller x 3

Below and right: **Main landing gear retract outward toward wingtips. Multiple doors cover main gear wheel wells.** Jay Miller x 2

On the YF-22A, an F-15-style, hydraulically actuated speed brake was located between the vertical stabilizers, aft of the inflight refueling receptacle. It is hinged at its forward end. This feature was eliminated from the production F/A-22A aircraft.

Hydraulic System: The F/A-22A is equipped with two 4,000 psi hydraulic systems driven by four independent pumps capable of delivering up to 72 gallons per minute. These power the single Parker Bertea actuators used to drive each of the aircraft's control surfaces. There is no actuator redundancy (a weight-saving measure). The leading edge flaps are driven by Curtiss-Wright actuators.

Electrical: The F/A-22A uses a Smiths Industries 270 volt, direct current (DC) electrical system. It uses two 65 kilowatt generators.

The F/A-22A is also equipped with an Allied Signal Aerospace auxiliary power generation system (APGS), consisting of an auxiliary power unit and a self-contained stored energy

Nose Landing Gear

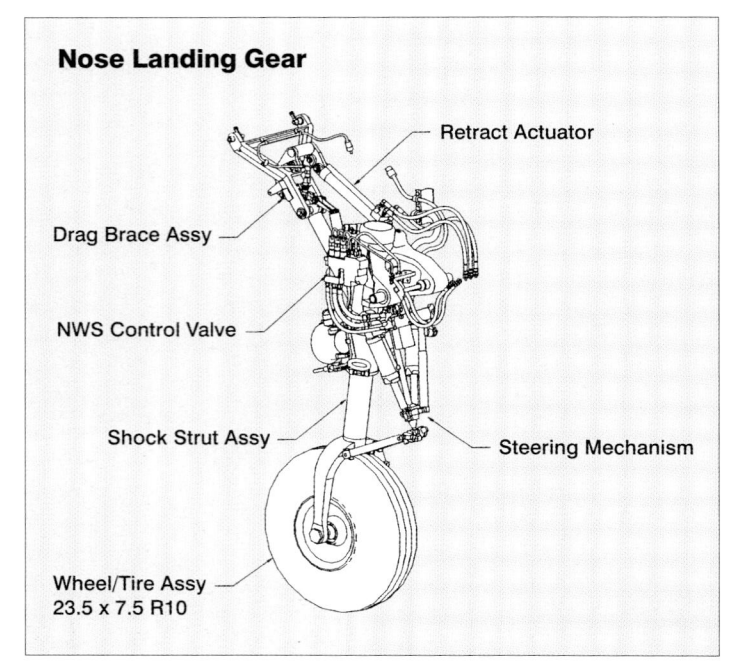

- Retract Actuator
- Drag Brace Assy
- NWS Control Valve
- Shock Strut Assy
- Steering Mechanism
- Wheel/Tire Assy 23.5 x 7.5 R10

Main Landing Gear

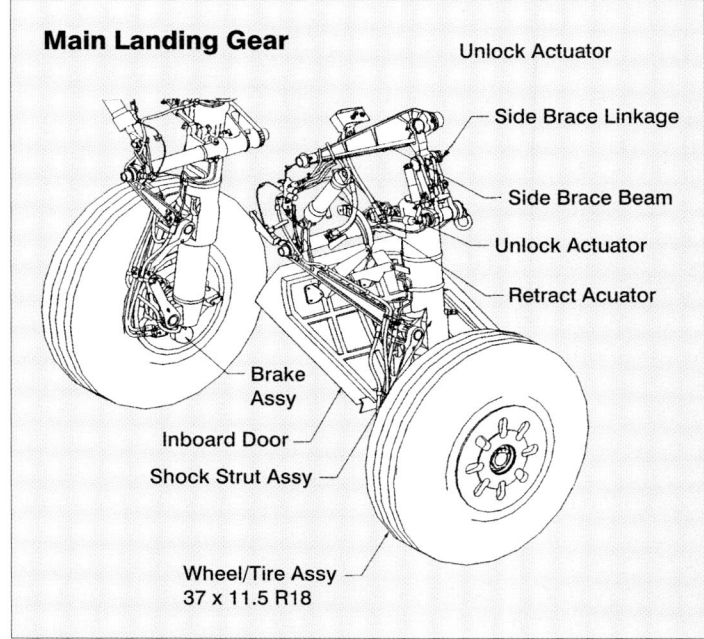

- Unlock Actuator
- Side Brace Linkage
- Side Brace Beam
- Unlock Actuator
- Retract Acuator
- Brake Assy
- Inboard Door
- Shock Strut Assy
- Wheel/Tire Assy 37 x 11.5 R18

system (SES). The latter consists of a Honeywell G250 auxiliary power unit (APU) that, when required, provides 335 kW (450 hp) of power to drive a Hamilton Sundstrand 27 kW generator and a 26.50 gallon per minute hydraulic pump.

External lighting consists of integral position and anti-collision lights (including strobes) on the wings. The low-voltage electroluminescent formation lights are located at critical positions for night flight operations on the aircraft (on both sides of the forward fuselage) under the chine, on the tip of the upper left and right wings, and on the outside of both vertical stabilizers.

Weapons/Sensors: Weapons are carried internally. There are two side bays positioned integral with the intake cheek assemblies each covered by a hydraulically actuated (Curtiss-Wright developed) two-panel hinged thermoset composite door (doors are equipped with a system to store missile fins from externally mounted missiles during ferry flights). The side bays are optimized to carry a single (heatseeking) infrared-guided AIM-9M/X each on a trapeze-type hydraulically-actuated LAU-141/A launcher.

The AIM-9M and the forthcoming AIM-9X are short-range, heat-seeking air-to-air missiles. The missiles are carried on a Lockheed Martin Tactical Aircraft Systems-manufactured LAU-141A trapeze-type launcher. This unit is basically a wingtip launch rail from an F-16 with a swing out mechanism that extends rapidly. Each launcher is fitted with a missile engine plume deflector which prevents damage to the bay as the missile departs the aircraft.

AIM-9 particulars are as follows:

- Manufactured by Raytheon Company and Loral Autoneutronics
- Powered by a single Thiokol Hercules Mk.36 Mod 11 (AIM-9M) solid propellant rocket engine
- Guidance is via a solid-state infrared (IR) homing unit

- Warhead is a high-explosive, blast fragmentation unit weighing 20.8 lbs.
- AIM-9M dimensions include a length of 9 ft. 5 in. (AIM-9X is slightly longer); a body diameter of 5 in.; and a fin span of 2 ft. 1 in.
- AIM-9M weight is 191 lbs.
- Cruising speed to target is approximately 2.0 Mach
- Range following launch is approximately 10 miles
- Loading is by hand from ground level on the same side as the bay

Ventrally, there is a single main bay covered by a two-part hydraulically actuated four-panel hinged door (also of thermoset composites) and partitioned into two sub-bays. Each sub-bay is large enough to accommodate three (in each sub-bay the center missile is staggered ahead of the inboard and outboard missiles to avoid fin interference problems) radar-guided AIM-120C AMRAAMs on Edo LAU-142/A pneudraulic AMRAAM-dedicated vertical ejection launchers (AVEL; each launcher weighs 113 lbs. and is made primarily of aluminum; it has a 9 in. stroke and ejects the missile from the bay at more than 25 fps with a force of 40 gs).

The AIM-120C has multiple target engagement capability, increased maximum launch range, a reduced-smoke rocket engine, and improvements in maintenance and handling. The AIM-120 has no official name, but is often called *Slammer* by pilots.

AIM-120C particulars are as follows:

- Manufactured by Hughes Missile Systems and the Raytheon Company
- Powered by a single Aerojet two-stage solid propellant rocket engine
- Guidance is via inertial midcourse, with active radar terminal homing
- Warhead is a high-explosive, directed fragmentation unit weighing 48 lbs.
- AIM-120C dimensions include a length of 12 ft. 0 in.; a body diameter of 7 in.; and a fin

span of 1 ft. 6 in. (later AIM-120 variants have smaller span dimensions)

- AIM-120C weight is 345 lbs.
- Cruising speed to target is approximately 4.0 Mach
- Range following launch is approximately 30 miles
- Loading is from the opposite side of the F/A-22A using an MJ-1 load vehicle (called a *jammer*)

At a later date, as improved versions of extant missiles, or advanced missiles such as the *Have Dash 2* air-to-air missile or *Have Slick* air-to-surface missile, enter the inventory, they will be easily accommodated by the F/A-22A's weapon bays.

The F/A-22A also is equipped with an improved, internally-mounted 20 mm General Electric M61A2 multi-(long-)barrel rotary cannon positioned on the right side of the aircraft above and aft of the intake. The gun port is equipped with a hinged, hydraulically-actuated gun door (opens to 90°) in concert with the aircraft's low-observables requirements. A gun gas purge door opens in concert with the gun port door.

The gun is provided with a closed-loop ammunition feed and storage subsystem housed integrally under the right wing root/fuselage for easy ammo upload and download (of empty casings). The ammunition magazine capacity is 480 rounds with a linear linkless ammunition handling system (LLAHS).

The LLAHS consists of a 480 round ammunition storage container with drive train and integral access (reload) unit, an ammunition conveyor assembly, a hydraulic drive unit, a rounds limiter, and a last round switch. There are no links between rounds. The latter eliminates completely any potential jamming of the gun breech assembly.

The M61A2 is a lightweight version of the older M61A1. Most of the weight saving was

Right: **Left main gear. Countermeasures dispenser bay is located just ahead of the green panel in front of main gear well.** Lockheed Martin

Middle and insets: **The F/A-22A is equipped with a stainless steel and titanium tailhook for runway trapping in emergencies. The hook resides in a special fairing between the aft ends of the engine nacelles.** Jay Miller x 2 and Lockheed Martin

Bottom left: **Main weapon bay is divided by aircraft structural keel. Trapeze launchers are visible to rear of bay.** Jay Miller

Bottom right: **Main weapon bay is the only bay that can accommodate the AIM-120 AMRAAM.** Lockheed Martin

achieved by machining down the barrel wall thickness. A 42 hp fixed displacement motor powers the gun and is, in turn, powered by hydraulic pressure supplied by the F/A-22A's hydraulic system. Each of the gun's six barrels fires only once during each revolution of the barrel cluster. Firing rate is 6,000 rounds per minute. The M61A2 is government furnished equipment (GFE).

In place of the six AIM-120 AMRAAM missiles in the main under-fuselage weapon bay, a load of two 1,000 lb. (ea.) GBU-32 JDAM (Joint Direct Attack Munition) PGMs can be carried. The JDAM is actually a tail guidance kit that converts existing unguided free-fall bombs into near precision-guided "smart" munitions. It also includes strap-on strakes that attach to the bomb's body to improve aerodynamic stability.

The JDAM kit is manufactured by Boeing. Integral with the kit is an inertial navigation system (INS) and a global positioning system (GPS). For F/A-22A purposes, the JDAM kit is optimized to fit on a standard Mk. 83 1,000-lb.-class bomb. With the JDAM kit added, total weight of the weapon is 1,015 lbs.

In service, JDAM can be launched from altitudes of 40,000 ft. or higher. Targets as distant as 15 miles can be destroyed. Circular error probable (CEP – a measurement of accuracy) is stated to be under 15 m. A recent upgrade has now reduced the CEP to under 10 m.

Like the AIM-120, the JDAM is loaded from the opposite side of the F/A-22A in order to provide necessary MJ-1 load vehicle clearance under the aircraft.

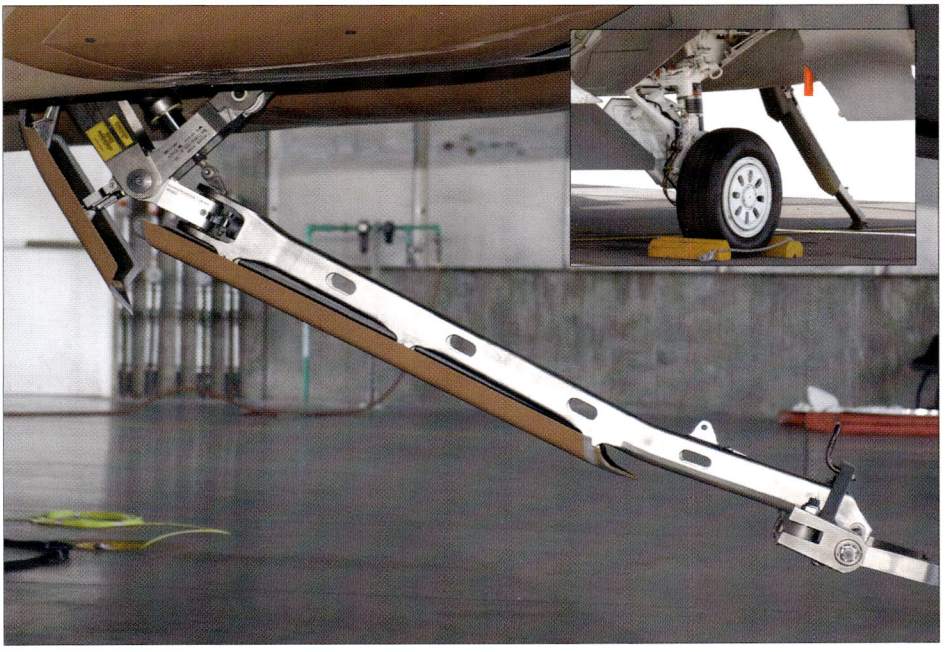

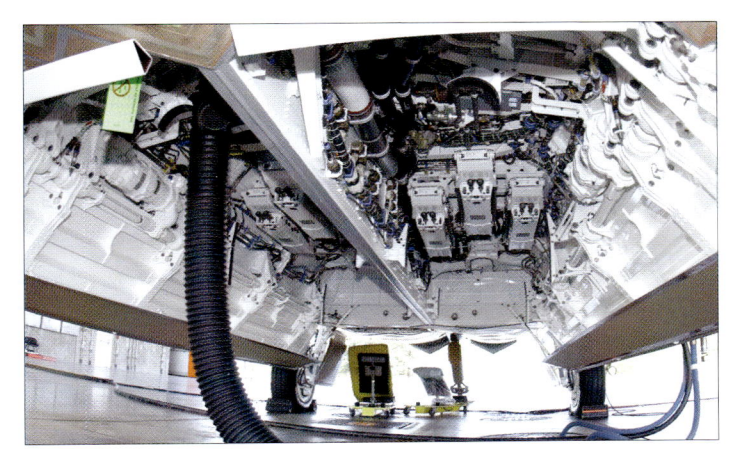

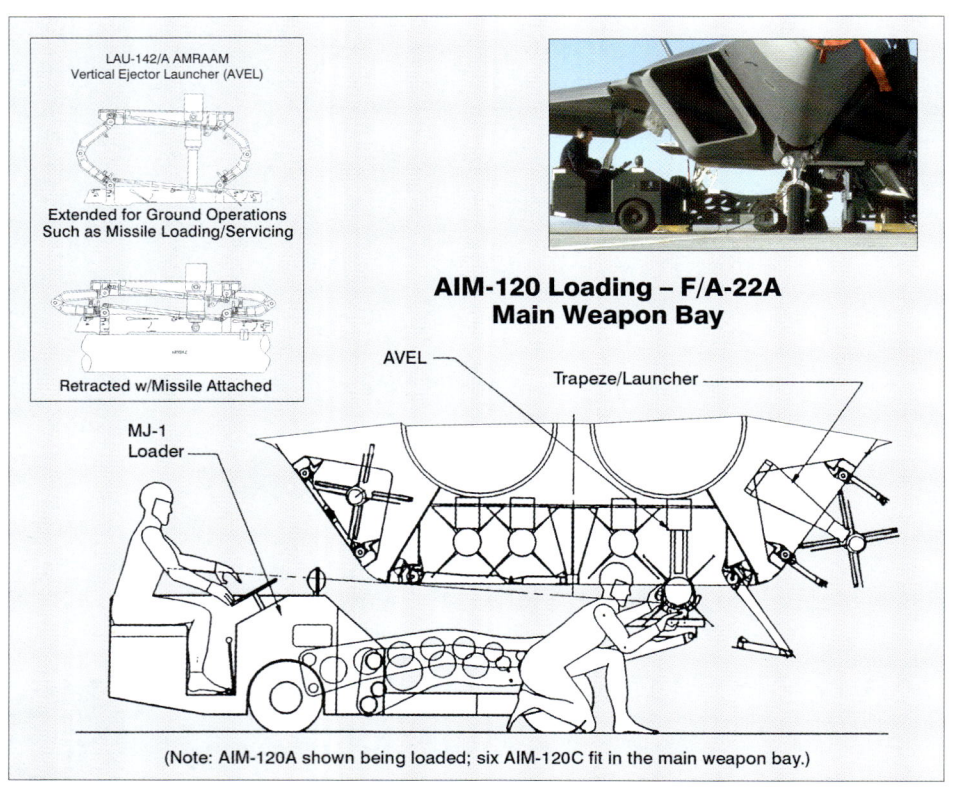

AIM-120 Loading – F/A-22A
Main Weapon Bay

LAU-142/A AMRAAM
Vertical Ejector Launcher (AVEL)

Extended for Ground Operations
Such as Missile Loading/Servicing

Retracted w/Missile Attached

MJ-1 Loader

AVEL

Trapeze/Launcher

(Note: AIM-120A shown being loaded; six AIM-120C fit in the main weapon bay.)

Miscellaneous weapons available for F/A-22A delivery include the BLU-109 *Penetrator*, the wind-corrected munitions dispenser (WCMD), the AGM-88 HARM, the GBU-22 *Paveway 3* guidance unit on a 500 lb. bomb, the Small Diameter Bomb (SDB; eight can be carried), and the low-cost autonomous attack system (LOCAAS) submunitions dispenser package.

During late August of 2003 the AF selected Boeing as the developer of the Small Diameter Bomb. Boeing is expected to produce about 24,000 SDBs and 2,000 "smart racks" to carry them. These numbers are expected to be increased; the SDB is a 250-pound-class weapon. Four can be hung from a smart rack; the F/A-22 will carry them internally. The SDB is a highly flexible munition because it can handle a range of dissimilar targets.

The SDB has wings that, after release from the aircraft, extend to provide a standoff range of up to 46 miles, depending on altitude. It is guided by an advanced, antijam GPS-aided inertial navigation system. It can further refine its GPS satellite location information by getting data from ground-based differential GPS units around the world – giving the bomb an accuracy of within 13.2 feet.

The F/A-22A also has four underwing stores stations positioned 125 in. and 174 in. respectively, from the aircraft centerline. These can accommodate loads of up to 5,000 lbs. each and can be used to mount weapons externally, including AIM-9s and AIM-120s on LAU-128/A rail launchers.

For self-defense, the F/A-22A is equipped with a BAE Systems AN/ALR-94 electronic warfare subsystem. Integral with this is radar warning and countermeasures devices and a missile launch detection capability. An AN/ALE-52 flare dispenser is integral with the airframe. A next-generation missile warning system (MWS) is planned for future integration. This advanced IR system increases detection range over existing ultraviolet MWS. Northrop Grumman and Lockheed Martin are competing for this contract. Lockheed Martin's AAR-56 Missile Launch Detector is currently used on the F/A-22A.

Air Data Systems: Both YF-22As were equipped with flight test nose booms which provided air data as well as AoA and side slip information to a special flight test cockpit display and the instrumentation package. The nose boom was totally independent from the production low-observable pneumatic air data system (PADS). This system consisted of two fuselage-mounted air data probes, one on each side of the fuselage located aft of the radome, and four flush-mounted static ports

Middle: **LAU-142/A trapeze launcher was developed by Edo Corporation for F/A-22A.** Edo

Left: **Up to six AIM-120Cs can be carried in the F/A-22A's split main weapon bay.** Lockheed Martin

(two on each side of the fuselage) which also were located aft of the radome above and below the chine. Total pressure, static pressure, and AoA information were derived from the air data probes. The set of static pressure ports above the chine were used to measure angle of sideslip at low AoA and the lower set was used at high AoA. Air data computers converted the pressure inputs to electrical signals and corrected for local flow effects.

The PADS provided air data to the flight control system (and other aircraft systems) within the conventional AoA. As AoA increased above approximately 33°, the flight control inputs transitioned from the pneumatic value to an inertially derived AoA. Pneumatic angle of sideslip was used up to much higher AoA until it too transitioned to an inertially derived angle of sideslip above 60° AoA. At negative AoA the transition occurs at -5° and -20° respectively.

Vehicle Management System (VMS): The Lear Astronics VMS consists of the following computer subsystems and their common bus interfaces: flight control computers and bus controllers; left and right engine control computers; head up display (HUD); integrated vehicle subsystem controllers; fuel management system; pneumatic air data system transducers (PADS); inertial navigation system (INS); mission display processors (MDP); and the integrated flight propulsion control (IFPC) 1553B buses.

The VMS subsystems and their associated bus structure are flight-safety critical in nature with the exception of the MDP and its interface to the other aircraft avionics. For example, the pilot has no control over the engine except via the IFPC buses, and the FLCCs would not operate safely without the PADS. The IVSCs are required to turn on the emergency power unit in the event of a dual engine flameout or the simultaneous loss of the generators. The HUD provides the pilot with attitude and air data information in the event of loss of avionics and displays. The INS provides the aircraft velocity vector used by the flight control system in the computation of inertial AoA and sideslip angles when the aircraft is outside the range of the PADS as well as attitude information. In short, the VMS provides the pilot with everything needed to fly and land the aircraft safely under all recoverable failure situations.

Integrated Vehicle Subsystem Control (IVSC): The Lear Astronics IVSC is part of the vehicle management system. The IVSC interfaces pilot commands to subsystems, commu-

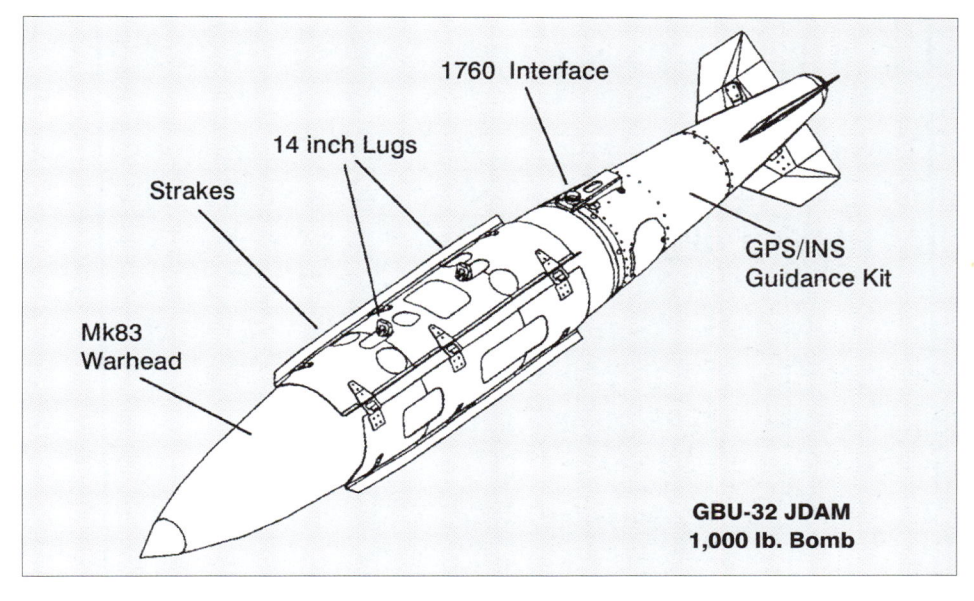

Strakes

14 inch Lugs

1760 Interface

GPS/INS Guidance Kit

Mk83 Warhead

GBU-32 JDAM
1,000 lb. Bomb

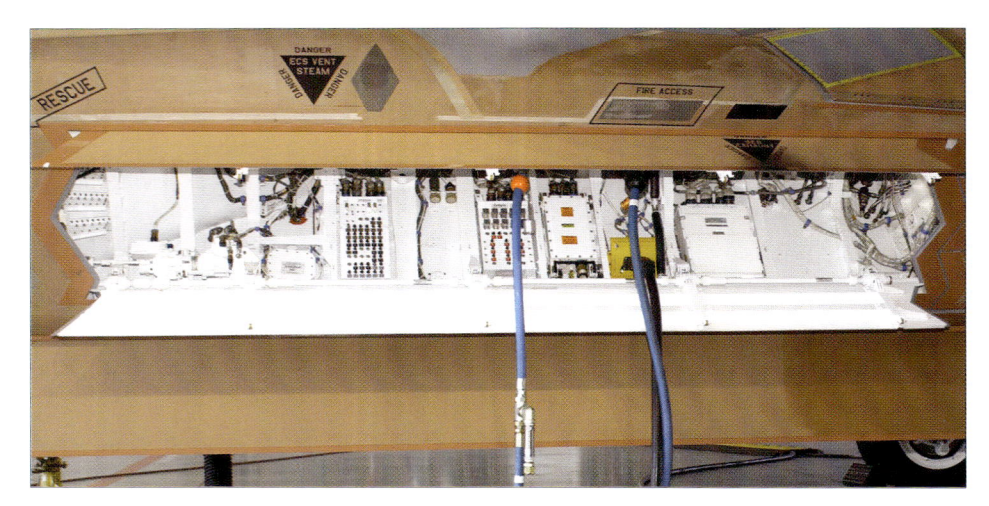

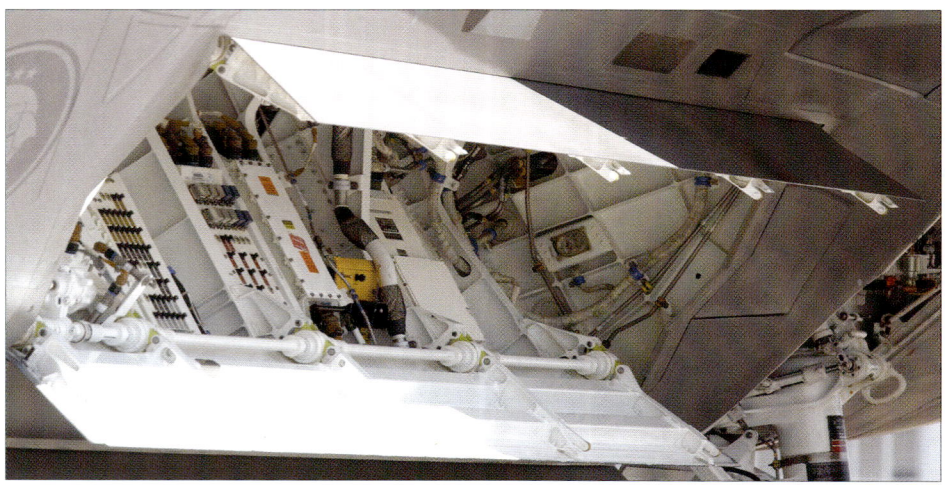

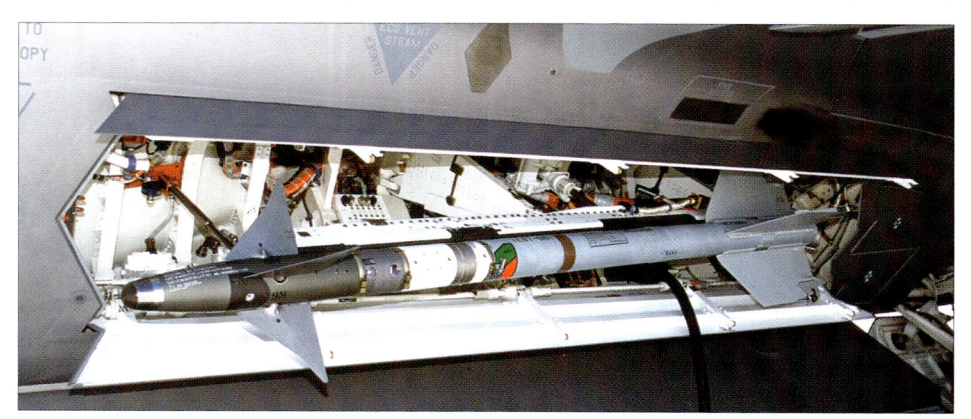

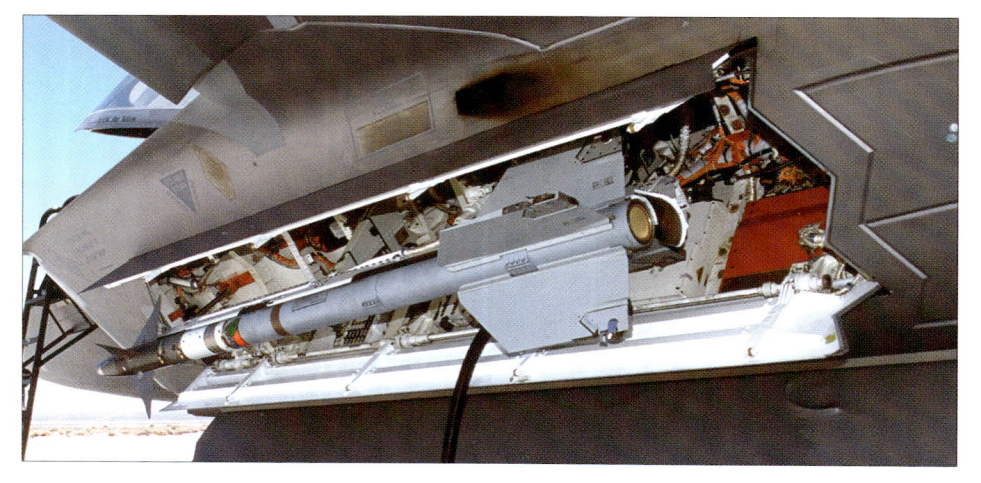

Multiple views of the F/A-22A's side weapon bay arrangement. The aircraft has a bay on each side of the fuselage. These are currently optimized to hold one AIM-9M/X each. The two lower photos show partially extended AIM-9M in launch position. *Jay Miller x 2 and Lockheed Martin x 2*

nicates subsystem status to the pilot, and performs monitoring and control of certain subsystem functions. The IVSC also provides status, alerts, warnings, and diagnostics to assist the pilot in fault detection and corrective actions. These functions are accomplished for the following subsystems via the IFPC digital data bus, dedicated cockpit switches and lights, mission display processors, and multifunction displays (MFDs): landing gear system (IVSC controls retraction); 4,000 psi hydraulic system; environmental control system (IVSC controls); electrical system; auxiliary power system (IVSC partially controls); pilot's life support systems (IVSC controls); fire protection system (IVSC controls); master caution annunciation (IVSC partially controls); and cockpit controls and indicators as required for the above subsystems or functions (IVSC partially controls). The IVSC replaces all relay logic with software. It also reduces the number of dedicated displays, panels, and switches historically associated with each subsystem.

YF-22A Flight Test Instrumen-tation: Baseline flight test instrumentation requirements were apportioned in accordance with each prototype's planned flight test assignments. The system was designed with the flexibility necessary to permit some expansion, and as areas of concern were identified during flight test, limited additional instrumentation was added to support problem identification and resolution.

The measurements were transmitted to ground receivers via encrypted and unencrypted telemetry links. Specialized data was also acquired and recorded by dedicated systems. The instrumentation system acquired the following types of data: signals from dedicated flight test instrumentation transducers (approx. 50 accelerometers; approx. 260 strain gauges; approx. 150 pressure transducers; approx. 150 thermocouples; and approx. 15 position indicators); aircraft electrical signals (approx. 20); selected words from MIL-STD-1 553 buses (approx. 100); HUD video; bulk data from MIL-STD-1 553 buses; and armament system high speed photography (4 cameras).

The pulse code modulation (PCM) data acquisition system was a semi-distributed system with one master controller and a maximum of 24 remote signal conditioning/digitizing/multiplexing units. The remote units are able to accept analog and digital information. Under control of the master unit, two modules are capable, as passive listeners, of acquiring preselected MIL-STD-1553B data bus messages for inclusion with other PCM data. The PCM system has an integral time code generator. The central controller is programmable to provide flexibility for data frame formatting. PCM

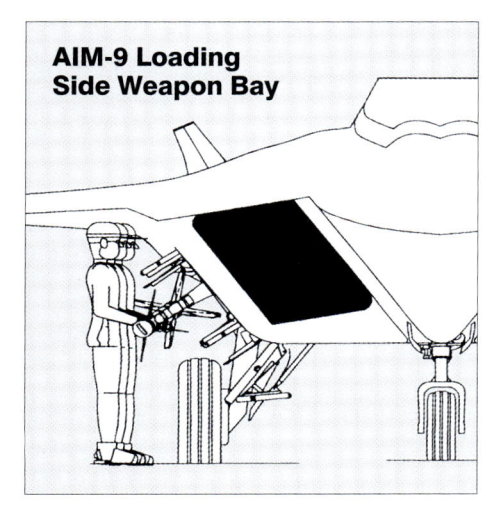

AIM-9 Loading Side Weapon Bay

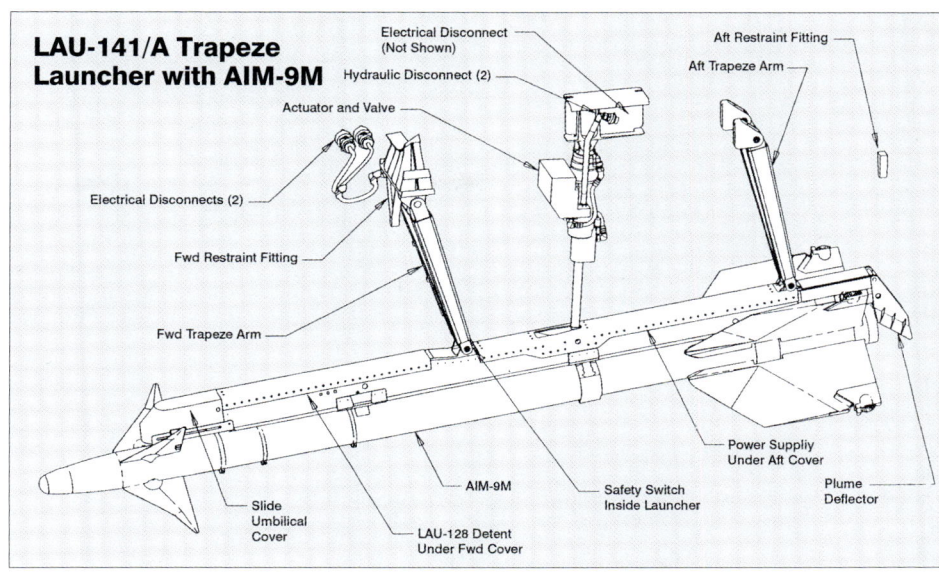

LAU-141/A Trapeze Launcher with AIM-9M

Electrical Disconnect (Not Shown)
Hydraulic Disconnect (2)
Actuator and Valve
Aft Restraint Fitting
Aft Trapeze Arm
Electrical Disconnects (2)
Fwd Restraint Fitting
Fwd Trapeze Arm
Power Supply Under Aft Cover
Plume Deflector
AIM-9M
Safety Switch Inside Launcher
Slide Umbilical Cover
LAU-128 Detent Under Fwd Cover

data acquisition is limited to information for which a frequency response of 100 Hertz (Hz) is required. A passive system for recording bulk MIL-STD-1553B bus data also was installed. This system is capable of acquiring data from multiple buses. A small constant bandwidth frequency modulation (CBWFM) system also is used for high frequency engine data and weapons bay acoustic measurements. PCM data was encrypted for transmission to one or more ground monitoring facilities via telemetry link. The CBWFM data was transmitted in the clear.

Pratt & Whitney instrumentation information was in a RS-232 formatted Universal Asynchronous Receiver/Transmitter (UART) data stream. A special interface unit was designed and installed to convert the UART data stream to a PCM stream.

PCM, CBWFM, bulk 1553 bus and Pratt & Whitney engine data were recorded on a 28-track instrumentation tape recorder. A VHS format video recorder was installed to record HUD symbology and video information. Sixteen millimetre cameras operating at 200 frames per second were installed to photograph weapon releases. Time correlation for the cameras was provided by recording the unmodulated IRIG "B" signal on the edge of the film. The cameras could be controlled manually by the pilot or automatically by the weapon separation signal.

A special flight test nose boom and high accuracy digital transducer was installed on, and in, the nose radome for the acquisition of free stream total and static pressures and AoA and sideslip. Nose boom indicated airspeed, pressure altitude, rate of climb, AoA, and sideslip were displayed in the cockpit on a special programmable CRT display.

F/A-22A Simulation: Boeing has developed a total training system package for the Air Force to permit support of all F/A-22 pilot and main-

tenance training requirements throughout the life cycle of the aircraft. The F/A-22A training system will feature extensive multi-media computer-based training which will be compliant with the Aviation Industry Computer-Based Training Committee (AICC) guidelines and standards. F/A-22A computer-based training will utilize state-of-the-art training technologies developed for the Boeing 777 commercial airliner. The efficiency of the F/A-22A training system development process is enhanced by a direct linage between the aircraft and training design databases. Hughes Training Systems will provide the three pilot training system devices (full-mission trainer ([FMT]), weapons and tactics training (WTT), and aircraft egress procedures trainer (EPT), and the so-called "complex" maintenance training devices (seat and canopy trainer, armament trainer, base-level forward fuselage trainer, engine LRU trainer, the landing gear trainer, the cockpit and forward fuselage trainer, and the aft fuselage trainer.

A total of 32 full-mission trainers, which allow the pilot to practice the entire mission from engine start-up to engine shut down, are scheduled for the F/A-22A program. The FSM will feature a high-resolution, full 360° visual

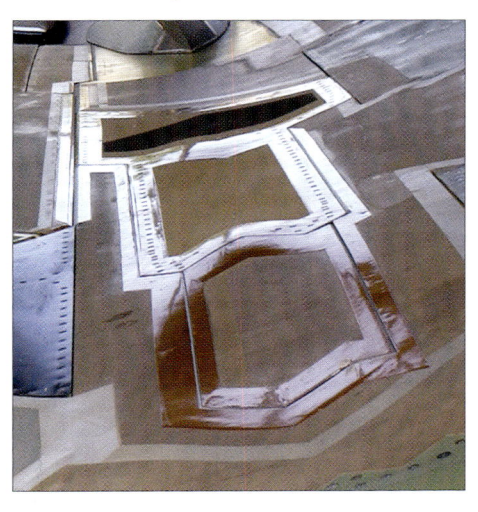

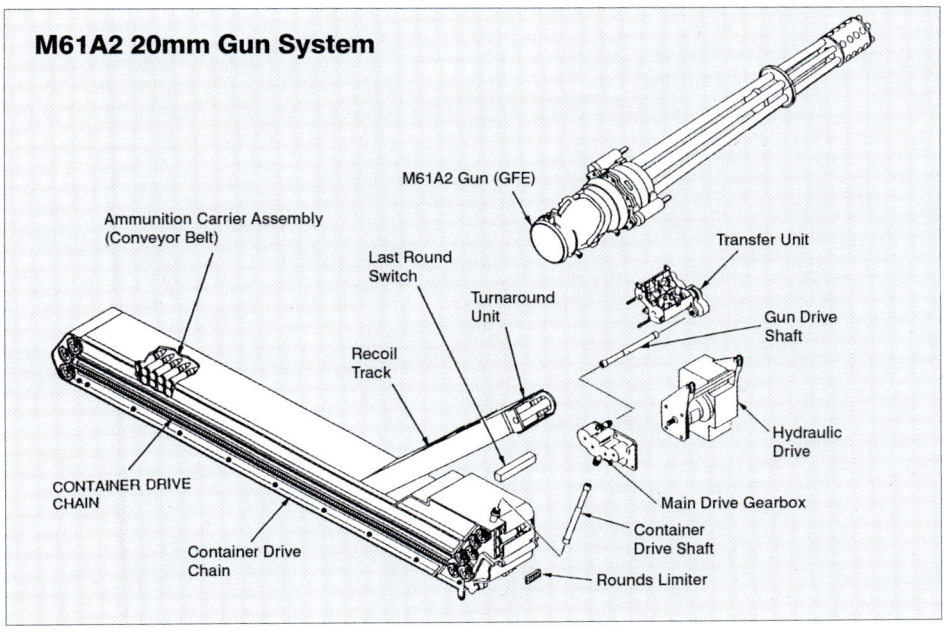

M61A2 20mm Gun System

Ammunition Carrier Assembly (Conveyor Belt)
Last Round Switch
M61A2 Gun (GFE)
Transfer Unit
Turnaround Unit
Recoil Track
Gun Drive Shaft
Hydraulic Drive
CONTAINER DRIVE CHAIN
Main Drive Gearbox
Container Drive Shaft
Container Drive Chain
Rounds Limiter

Internal Weapon Complement

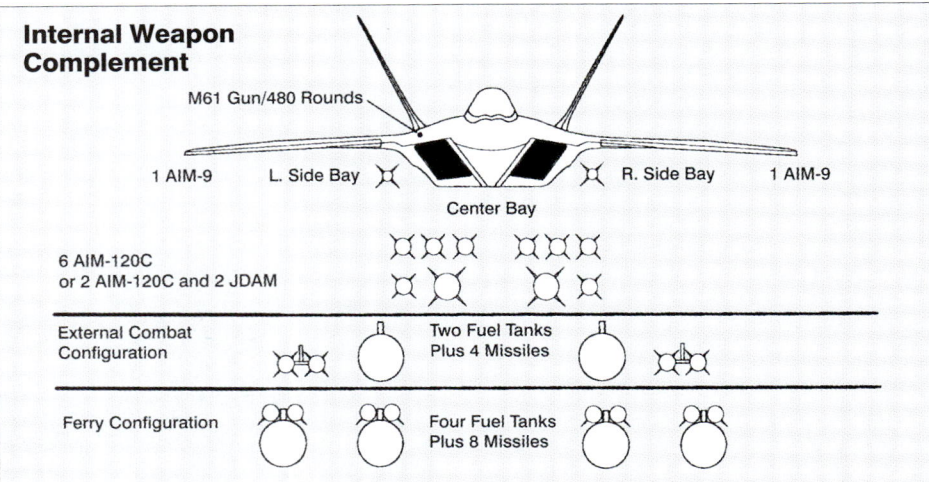

M61 Gun/480 Rounds

1 AIM-9   L. Side Bay   R. Side Bay   1 AIM-9

Center Bay

6 AIM-120C
or 2 AIM-120C and 2 JDAM

External Combat Configuration   Two Fuel Tanks Plus 4 Missiles

Ferry Configuration   Four Fuel Tanks Plus 8 Missiles

system (it will not be motion based). The FMT will support flight training, air refueling, takeoff and landing, emergency procedures, and visual-range combat. A total of 78 pilot training devices are scheduled for the F/A-22A program. A total of 447 maintenance training devices also have been planned for the F/A-22A program. All are expected to be delivered between April and August of 2005.

An F/A-22A maintenance training facility was opened by Boeing and the AF during October of 2004 at Tyndall AFB, Florida. A simulator center for pilot training is expected to open at Tyndall as well. The latter will offer four full mission trainers (FMTs) three weapons and tactics trainers (WTTs), six electronic classrooms, and twenty electronic workbook stations. The FMTs and WTTs are being manufactured under sub-contract to Boeing by L-3 Communications' Link Simulation & Training division.

An Air Combat Simulator (ACS) was built and placed in operation at Lockheed Martin's Marietta, Georgia facility during 2000. The ACS was originally developed as a software laboratory and used for F/A-22A cockpit development, but later was expanded to have the capability to evaluate the F/A-22A's mission effectiveness during IOT&E. The ACS proved so effective that it allowed the reduction of operational IOT&E flights from 700 to just 240.

Miscellaneous Systems, Sub-Systems, and Facts:

• Once completed, new F/A-22As exit the Lockheed Martin factory at its south end. From the plant an aircraft is moved to the fuel tank flushing facility. There, its fuel system is flushed ten to twenty times with JP-8. Each flushing runs through a group of filters ranging from coarse to fine. Following that, the aircraft is filled and then towed to one of several engine run stations where it is tied down using the aircraft tailhook and cables. The engines are then started and run for approximately one hour while being cycled several times between idle and maximum afterburner. The APU is tested at this point as well.

Once cleared for flight, the F/A-22A is assigned to a company test pilot. First flights usually concentrate on airframe systems and typically last just about an hour. During the first flight, the envelope is explored out to 1.5 Mach and 50,000 ft. Pressurization checks, mil power runs, a climb to 30,000 ft., aerial refueling system checks, auxiliary power starts, engine airstarts, engine transients, landing gear cycling and instrument landing system checks are all part of the first flight routine.

The second flight checks avionics including the autopilot, the weapons system, the communications systems, navigation, IFF, and electronic warfare. High AoA is also explored during this flight as is aircraft symmetry, the g-limiter, and trim checks.

Once the aircraft is declared fully flightworthy, it is moved into the paint shop where it is given its low-observables coating. In the interim, it is assigned to a government pilot who then verifies – through a series of flights – that the aircraft meets AF acceptance standards. Once these tests are passed, the aircraft is formally accepted and, shortly afterwards, flown to its receiving base.

• The F/A-22A's air cycle system takes hot (1,200°/2,000° F.) bleed air from the engines and cools it down in the primary heat exchanger (PHX) to approximately 400° F. From the heat exchanger, the air is fed into the air cycle refrigeration package (ACRP). The air must be dry, so the system also includes water extractor. When the air exits the ACRP, its temperature is approximately 50° F.

• Production F/A-22As are coated with a Boeing-developed low-reflectivity (i.e, radar absorbent) paint. This was first applied to the second EMD aircraft, 91-4002, during March of 2000. All succeeding F/A-22As have been delivered painted.

• Venting cut-outs are covered by titanium screens containing thousands of precision-cut (using an abrasive water-jet) holes in a special alignment pattern to reduce to negligible levels radar reflections.

• There is a Lockheed-developed airborne video recorder in the F/A-22A's cockpit.

Top: **EMD F/A-22A, 91-4002, test firing M61A2 20mm gun over Nellis AFB test range.** Lockheed Martin

Left: **F/A-22A, dispensing flares over Nellis AFB test range. Flare dispenser units are located just aft of main gear wells.** Lockheed Martin

Right top: **Small air blast deflectors automatically extend from the front edge of the bay cavity when main weapon bay doors open for missile launch or bomb drops.** Jay Miller

Right top: **Small air blast deflectors automatically extend from the front edge of the bay cavity when main weapon bay doors open for missile launch or bomb drops.** Jay Miller

Right: **Four small diameter bombs suspended next to an AIM-120C in the left main weapon bay of an F/A-22A.** Boeing via AF

Below: **F/A-22A in paint bay at Marietta. Coating applications are very critical to the maintenance of low-observables capability.** Lockheed Martin

• The F/A-22A airframe has provisions for the mounting of a ventral (forward fuselage) infrared search-and-track unit and a side-mounted phased-array radar unit.

• Thermoplastics have been used in all appropriate parts of the aircraft where high tolerance to damage is required. This includes the landing gear and weapon bay doors.

• The F/A-22A has an intra-flight data link system allowing the sharing of tactical information between two or more aircraft during a mission.

• All avionics and miscellaneous subsystems on both the YF-22A and F/A-22A are purposefully located on the aircraft to permit ground level access for maintenance. A brassboard *Pave Pillar* avionics architecture was utilized and demonstrated.

• General Dynamics has been tasked with providing dedicated versions of an advanced electronic warfare suite and a new communications/ navigation/identification system. Both will be derived from integrated electronic warfare systems (INEWS) and integrated communications and navigation avionics technology.

• The bottom of the F/A-22A sits only 36 in. off the ground, allowing maintenance personnel to have shoulder-height access (or lower) to nearly every component or system without the use of ladder or workstands.

• There is an extensive Built-In Test (BIT) capability. The diagnostics system can test down to the Line Replaceable Module (LRM – the individual electronics cards) to determine faults.

• An On-Board Oxygen Generating System (OBOGS) provides breathable air to the pilot.

• An On-Board Inert Gas Generating system (OBIGGS) is used to fill the fuel tanks with nitrogen as a safety measure when fuel is depleted during flight.

• The F/A-22A is capable of being refueled, rearmed, and returned to combat under the Integrated Combat Turn (ICT) system. This allows for simultaneous gun ammunition and missile reloading.

• The F/A-22A Integrated Maintenance Information System (IMIS – which is supported by the Maintenance Support Cluster [MSC] and the Maintenance Work Station [MWS]) integrates the Tech Order Data (TOD), maintenance forms into an onboard system for maintenance and support in the field.

• The F/A-22A is equipped with two Hughes common integrated processing (CIP) units.

The CIPs utilized in the F/A-22A support all signal processing, data processing, digital input/output (I/O), and data storage functions using a single integrated hardware and software design. They are distinguished from federated or partially integrated architectures because they provide the requisite high-performance computing capability with lower installed weight, volume, power, and cost.

The integrated architecture incorporates the *Pave Pillar* concepts and implements Joint Integrated Avionics Working Group (JIAWG) standards. The latter includes the parallel-interface (PI) bus, the test-maintenance (TM) bus, and the data processing element (DPE) which employs a high-performance 32-bit central processing unit (CPU) and the Intel 80960 reduced instruction set computer (RISC) processor. The 80960 instruction set architecture (ISA) is one of two 32-bit ISAs chosen by the JIAWG as the basis for standardization of 32-bit embedded avionics computers.

The CIPs also utilize mission-specific information delivered to the system through a Fairchild-manufactured data transfer equipment/mass memory (DTE/MM) system that contains mass storage for default data and air vehicle operational flight programming. It also serves as a stores management system.

Processing capacity of each CIP is generally rated at more than 700 million instructions per second (Mips). Growth capacity of this system is up to 2,000 Mips. Signal processing capacity is greater than 20 billion operations per second (Bops). Expansion capacity is up to 50 Bops

Each CIP contains more than 300 megabytes of memory and can be expanded to 650 megabytes if and when required. Some 132 board slots in the CIPs (1 and 2) are available and some 41 of these were unused at the time of initial F/A-22A delivery.

• A maintenance computer enables maintenance crews to conduct operational checks on the ground, eliminating the need to get into the cockpit during engine runs. It contains a library of some 1,300 technical orders.

• In operational service, the F/A-22A is expected to have a fifteen minute turnaround time for high sortie rates.

• All F/A-22A maintenance will be "on the plane" or at depot level, with the sole exceptions being the tires and battery. Ground support equipment is not needed as there has been a near-elimination of wing-level maintenance shops and personnel. Portable maintenance aids (in the form of a lap top) are an integral part of the F/A-22A maintenance package.

• A squadron of 24 F/A-22As is expected to require less than the capacity of eight C-141 transport and 258 support personnel for a 30 day airlift deployment.

• The F/A-22A is expected to have an 8,000 hour structural, systems, and avionics life.

• The F/A-22A is compatible with existing aircraft shelters

• The first AF Reserve pilot to fly the F/A-22A was Lt. Col. Alan Norman who was then assigned to the 412th Operations Group at Edwards AFB.

• As of this writing, Bret Luedke is Lockheed Martin's chief of flight test for the F/A-22A program.

Specifications and Performance

	YF-22A	F/A-22A
Length	64 ft. 2 in./19.60 m.	62 ft. 1 in./18.92 m.
Wingspan	43 ft. 0 in./13.1 m.	44 ft. 6 in./13.56 m.
Wing chord		
(theoretical @ root)		32 ft. 3.5 in./9.84 m.
(reference @ tip)		5 ft. 5.5 in./1.66 m.
(actual @ tip)		3 ft. 90 in./1.14 m.
Wing anhedral		3°15'
Wing aspect ratio	2.2	2.36
Wing area (gross)	840 sq. ft./78 sq. m.	840 sq. ft./78 sq. m.
Leading edge flap area (total)		51.20 sq. ft./4.76 sq. m.
Flaperon area (total)		55.0 sq. ft./5.10 sq. m.
Aileron area (total)		21.40 sq. ft./1.98 sq. m.
Vertical tail area (total)	218 sq. ft./20.26 sq. m.	178 sq. ft./16.54 sq. m.
Rudders/speedbrakes area (total)		54.80 sq. ft./5.09 sq. m.
Horizontal stabilator area (total)	134 sq. ft./12.45 sq. m.	136 sq. ft./12.63 sq. m.
Horizontal tail span		29 ft. 0 in./8.84 m.
Height	17 ft. 8.9 in./5.39 m.	16 ft. 8 in./5.08 m.
Vertical tail span (tip to tip)		19 ft. 7 in./5.97 m.
Wheelbase		19 ft. 9.75 in./6.04 m.
Weapon bay ground clearance		3 ft. 1 in./0.94 m.
Weight empty	31,000 lb./14,043 kg.	31,670 lb./14,365 kg.
Weight maximum takeoff	58,000 lb./26,308 kg.	66,500 lb./30,125 kg.
Weight (internal fuel)	22,000 lb./9,979 kg.	22,000 lb./9,979 kg.
Wing loading		71.43 lb. per sq. ft./348.7 kg. per sq. m.
Max power loading		0.86 lb. per lb. thrust/87 kg. per kN
Max. level flight speed (supercruise)	1.58 Mach @ 30K ft. (1,075 mph)	1.82 Mach (1,220 mph)
Max. level flight speed (in afterburner @ 45,000 ft.)	2.0 Mach @ 30K ft. (1,075 mph)	2.25 Mach (1,500 mph)
Max. level flight speed (in afterburner @ s.l.)		1.40 Mach (921 mph)
Roll rate		100° per sec.
Service ceiling	50,000 ft. plus	65,000 ft.
Takeoff/landing field length req.	3,500 ft./1,067 m.	
Unrefueled combat radius (est.)	750 to 800 n. mi (1,389 km. to 1,481 km.)	450 mi.
Normal range		2,000 mi.
g Limit	+7.9	+9.0/-3.0
Sustained g at 1.8 Mach	6	6
Fuel Fraction (est.; fuel wt. divided by max. takeoff wt.)	?	0.29

F/A-22A AIRFRAME SUBCONTRACTORS
- Aerojet – Aft forward fuselage booms (for Boeing)
- Alliant Techsystems (ATK Composites) – IM-7, IM-8 fibers, composite parks on horizontal stabilator (for Vought)
- Amcast Precision – investment castings
- Astech/MCI – structural materials
- BASF Structural materials – 5250-4 bismaleimide resin
- Colt Industries/Menasco Aerosystems – prototype main and nose landing gear (for Lockheed Martin)
- Dow-UT – composite wing spars, fairings, other structural components
- ICI Fiberite – 977-3 toughened epoxy
- GenCorp Aerojet Propulsion Division – booms for fuselage-to-wing and vertical stabilator interfaces (for Boeing)
- GKN Aerospace Services – aft boom fairings, sine wave wing spars (for Boeing), horizontal stabilator skins, engine transition ducts, air intake lips, fan and augmentor ducts, composite parts (for Lockheed Martin)
- Hexcel – IM-7/Cycom composite materials
- Howmet (Alcoa) – titanium casting, including body and aileron parts and arresting gear
- Marion Composites – composite parts, including vertical stabilator skin, fairings, and door assemblies (for Lockheed Martin)
- Michelin – tires
- PCC Schlosser – titanium castings
- PCC Structurals – investment castings (for Boeing)
- Quadrax – composite materials including Radel 8320 polyarylsulfone
- RMI Titanium – 6-22-22 titanium mill products (sole supplier)
- Sierracin – preproduction canopies
- Vought Aircraft – composite lower wing skins
- Weber Aircraft (Kidde) – ejection seat
- XAR Industries – inflight refueling receptacle

F/A-22A ENGINE SUBCONTRACTORS
- Goodrich (Rohr) – titanium engine bay doors
- Hamilton Sundstrand (UTC) – FADEC for F119
- Honeywell – main fuel throttle on engine, engine anti-ice valves, engine augmentor fuel controls
- Parker Bertea (Hannifin) – actuators, pumps, fuel injection nozzles

F/A-22A ELECTRONICS SUBCONTRACTORS
- IDD Aerospace – display bezels
- Kaiser Electronics – active matrix LCD panels
- Astronics/LSI – illuminated cockpit control panels
- BAE Systems – head-up display; multifunction full-color cockpit displays; integrated electronic warfare system; intraflight datalink for ICNIA; GPVI module; mission planning equipment; phased array nearly-conformal antenna
- Aydin Telemetry – common airborne integrated flight test system
- TRW – integrated CNI/IFF avionics
- Intel – 32-bit microprocessor
- Motorola – computer security module

- Raytheon (TI/Hughes) – VHSIC central processing computer module; CIP; vehicle management system core
- Harris – avionics bus interface module; high-speed data bus; transmit/receiver module
- Honeywell – fuel management controls; ring laser inertial navigation system
- Lear Astronics – vehicle management system modules
- Digital Equipment – workstations; software development computers
- Northrop Grumman (Litton/Raytheon TI Systems) – GPS/INS; fire control radar
- Lockheed Martin – electro-optical sensor system; advanced infrared search and track

F/A-22A WEAPON SYSTEMS SUBCONTRACTORS
- EDO Corp. – air-to-air missile launchers, BRU-46 bomb racks (for Lockheed)
- Kaman Aerospace – composite hat stiffeners on weapon bay doors; gun breech screens
- Raytheon (E-Systems) – actuator valve assembly for AIM-9 trapeze launcher
- Smiths Aerospace – actuator for trapeze launcher

F/A-22A MISCELLANEOUS SUBCONTRACTORS
- Dowty Aerospace Yakima – hydraulic actuators
- Electrodynamics – crash survivable memory unit
- Gentex – HGU-55P pilot helmet
- Hamilton Sundstrand (UTC) – environmental control system; auxiliary power generator system; electrical generators; fuel pumps
- Honeywell – (AiResearch/Bendix/Garrett) – wheels and brakes; digital brake anti-skid system; auxiliary power generating system
- Howmet – titanium forgings
- Kaiser Electroprecision – arresting gear components
- Kaman Aerospace – coaxial cables
- Kidde-Graviner Ltd. – fire retardation equipment
- Korry Electronics – switches; control panels; cockpit control panel
- Loral – integrated aircrew training system
- Lucas Aerospace – converter regulator; power takeoff shafts
- MPC Products – throttle quadrant assembly
- National Waterlift/Parker Hannifin – flight control actuators
- Normalair-Garrett – onboard oxygen generation system
- Parker Bertea – actuators
- Precision Castparts (Wyman Gordon) – titanium forgings
- Rosemount – air data probes
- Sargent Aerospace – throttle quadrant
- Sargent Fletcher – external fuel tanks
- Schlosser Casting – titanium forgings
- Simmonds Precision Products – fuel management system
- Smiths Industries – electrical power distribution centers
- Sterer Engineering and Manufacturing – nose wheel steering actuation system
- Thompson Saginaw – pylon conversion actuator ball screws
- Trilectron Industries – ground power conversion and cooling
- Trinova Corp. Vickers Operations – primary and auxiliary driven pumps
- Westinghouse Electric – variable speed, constant frequency generator

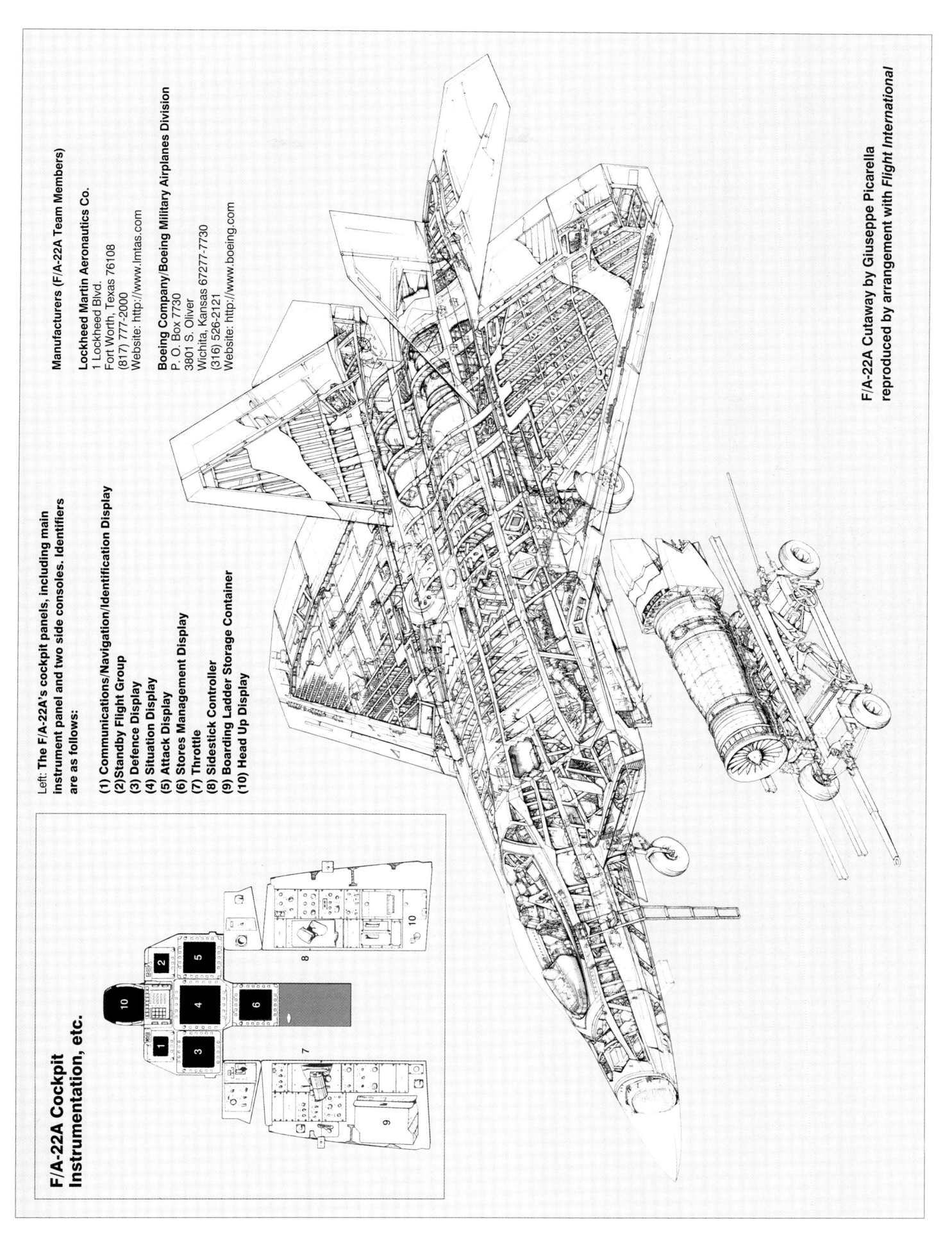

F/A-22A Cockpit Instrumentation, etc.

Left: **The F/A-22A's cockpit panels, including main instrument panel and two side consoles. Identifiers are as follows:**

(1) Communications/Navigation/Identification Display
(2) Standby Flight Group
(3) Defence Display
(4) Situation Display
(5) Attack Display
(6) Stores Management Display
(7) Throttle
(8) Sidestick Controller
(9) Boarding Ladder Storage Container
(10) Head Up Display

Manufacturers (F/A-22A Team Members)

Lockheed Martin Aeronautics Co.
1 Lockheed Blvd.
Fort Worth, Texas 76108
(817) 777-2000
Website: http://www.lmtas.com

Boeing Company/Boeing Military Airplanes Division
P. O. Box 7730
3801 S. Oliver
Wichita, Kansas 67277-7730
(316) 526-2121
Website: http://www.boeing.com

F/A-22A Cutaway by Giuseppe Picarella
reproduced by arrangement with *Flight International*

Chapter Six

Powerplant

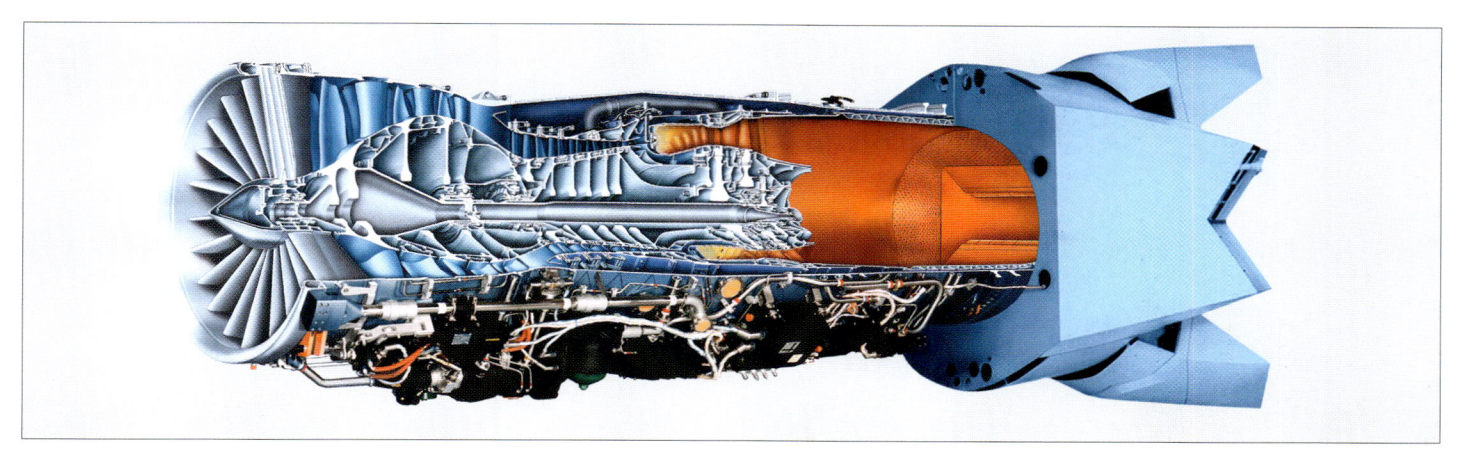

Two different engine designs developed under the auspices of the Joint Advanced Fighter Engine (JAFE) program, one by Pratt & Whitney in East Hartford, Connecticut (but tested in West Palm Beach, Florida; other Pratt & Whitney F119 manufacturing sites include Middletown and New Haven, Connecticut; North Berwick, Maine, and Columbus, Georgia), and one by General Electric in Evendale, Ohio, were tested on the YF-22A prototypes. Both were capable of self-starting, and both were equipped with autonomous ground checkout systems. Design objectives were centered on very high thrust-to-weight ratios (F/A-22A is estimated to have a thrust-to-weight ratio of approximately 1.4 to 1 at combat weight) and high reliability.

For Pratt & Whitney, initial development in a dem/val program sponsored by the ASD began during 1983 under the auspices of the company's PW5000 engine...which later was designated F119 by the AF. During 1984, component rigs were designed and models were tested; during 1985 the demonstrator engine design was completed, the component rigs were fabricated, and testing was initiated; during 1987-1989 additional component core and engine testing was undertaken; and during

1989, the first flight test work was initiated using prototype engines.

Ground testing of the F119 resulted in the simulation of more than six years of operational usage on a single engine. The 18th of 25 flight test engines was designated the durability test engine. It was run through 4,325 thermal cycles (representing six to eight years of operational service). The engine survived this test series without major failures or anomalies and in late 2002 was utilized for a continuance test series of equivalent duration. The F119's design life is 8,650 cycles or the equivalent of 15 years of service.

The transformation from development to production required a transformation of the Pratt & Whitney assembly line. As of this writing, a slow transition from production of 3 engines per

month during 2003/2004 to 8 engines per month during 2008 is expected. Production is expected to peak at 74 engines during 2009 and is scheduled to wind down during 2012 unless more F/A-22As are ordered. At its peak, F119 production is expected to account for almost one-third of the total Pratt & Whitney commercial and military engine workload at the Middletown plant. The F119 is priced at approximately $10 million per engine.

It should be noted that Pratt & Whitney has not sat on its laurels with the F119. The company is, in fact, working on advanced versions of the engine and is hoping that the resulting improvements in performance will merit F/A-22A upgrades to include the newer F119 derivatives. Among these is an axisymmetric thrust-vectoring nozzle which has fewer parts

Facing page: **Multiple views of the Pratt & Whitney YF119-PW-100 pre-production series engine as used on YF-22A, N22YX.** Pratt & Whitney (top) and Jay Miller x 3

Top: **Cutaway of the standard production series F119-PW-100 engine as used on the F/A-22A. The blue and red indicate the cooler and hotter sections of the engine.** Pratt & Whitney

Right: **YF119-PW-100 on display at the USAF Museum, Wright-Patterson AFB, Ohio.** Jay Miller

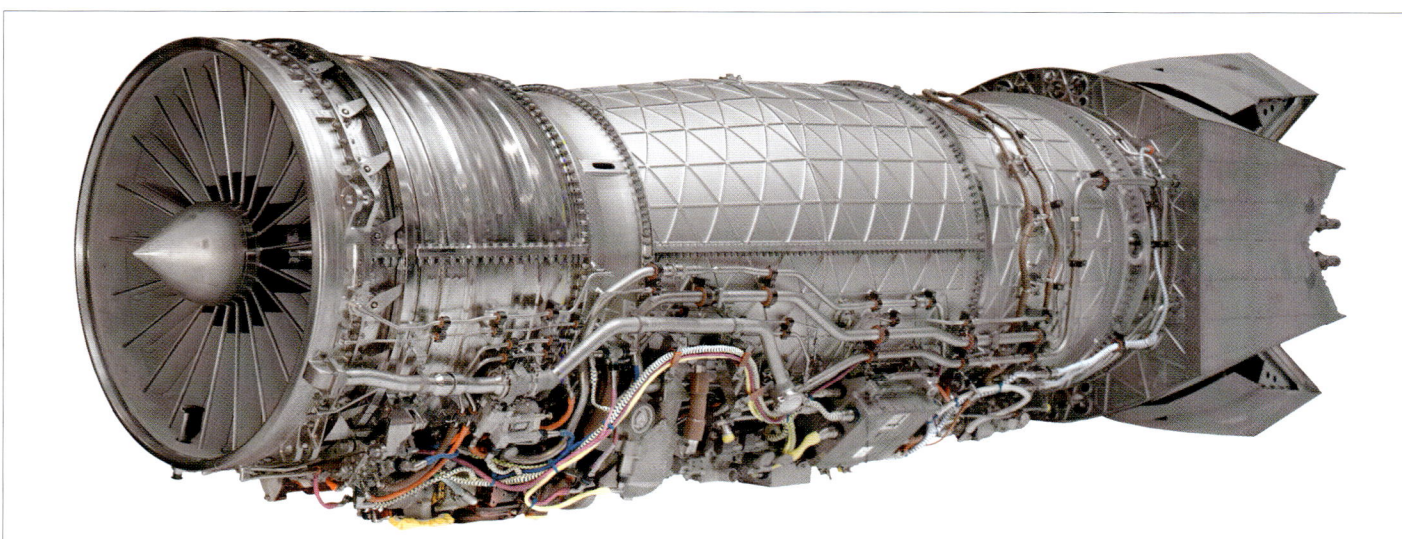

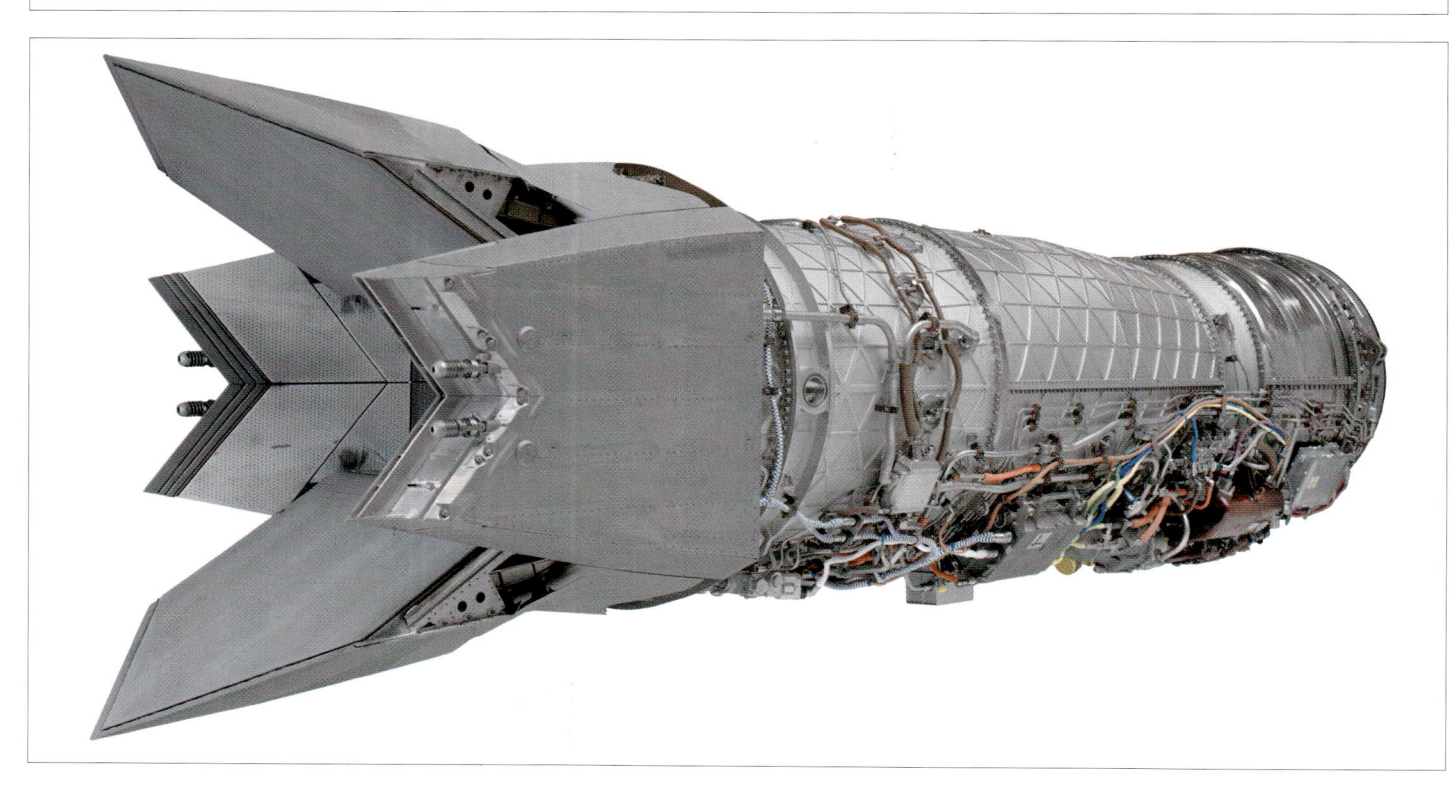

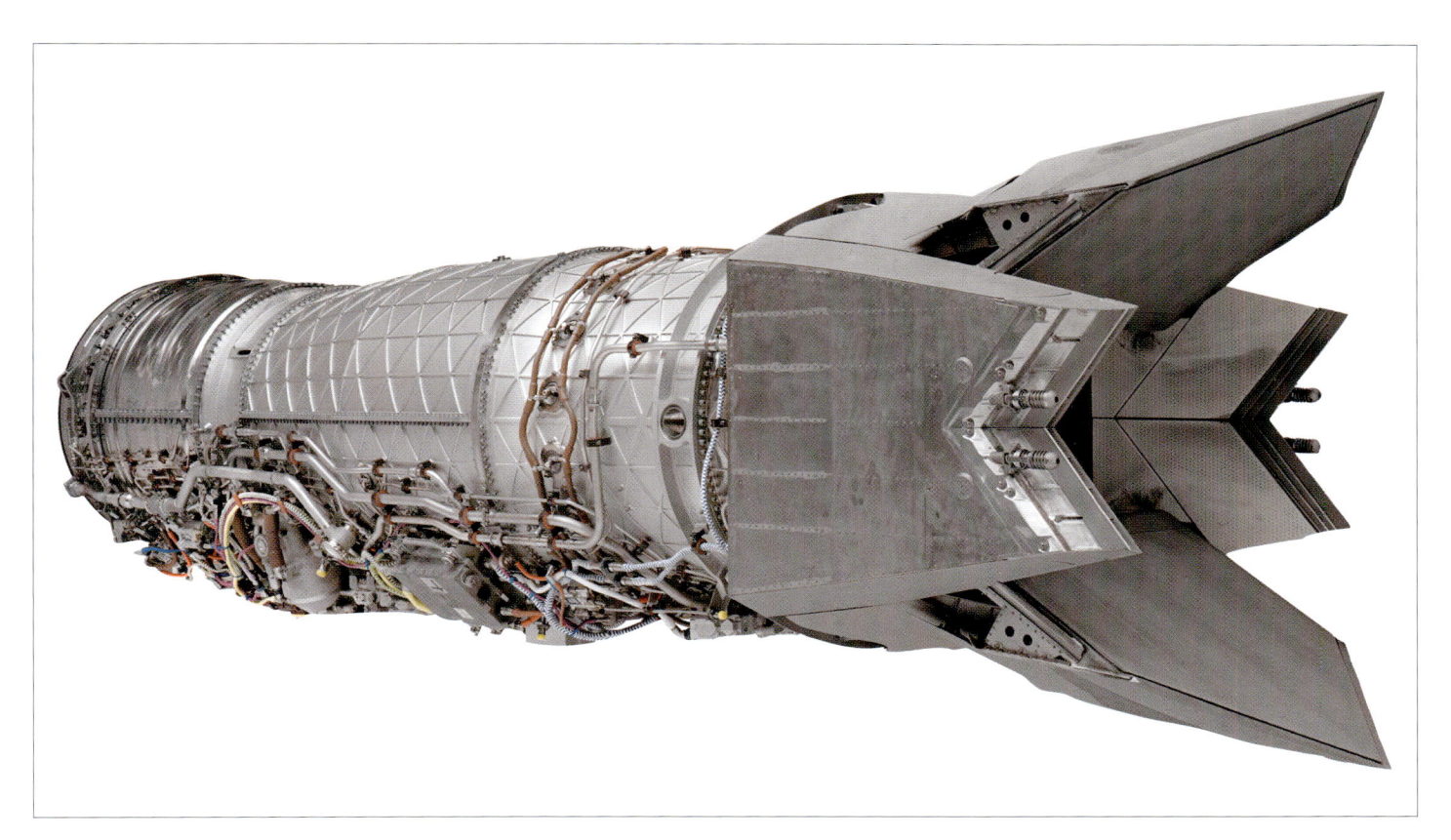

Facing page and this page top and below: **F119-PW-100 has been designed with considerable emphasis on maintainability and replaceable parts accessibility. Exhaust nozzle with associated vectorable components is delivered as an integral part of the engine.** Pratt & Whitney x 5

Right: **F119-PW-100 exhaust nozzle is claimed to add only minimal weight to the base weight of the engine.** Pratt & Whitney

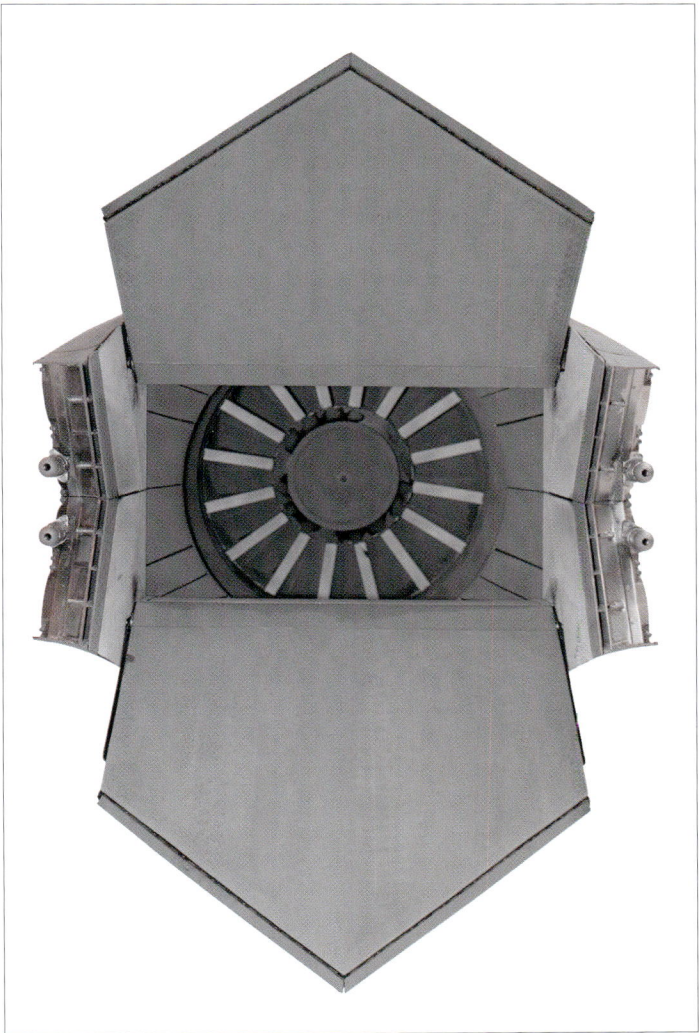

and is less expensive than the current nozzle. It is expected to be available during 2009.

In the YF-22A and F/A-22A, the powerplants are fed by separate fixed ramp, diamond-shaped intakes. These provide low distortion air to the engines while also providing a high recovery rate. Low observables requirements played a preeminent role in the intake design and the resulting configurations provided 100% line-of-sight blockage to the engine face and thus all but eliminated return energy leaks. On the F/A-22A, the intakes are positioned somewhat farther aft when compared to the YF-22As, thus giving the aircraft a different forward fuselage profile.

The intake tunnels are provided boundary layer bleed systems which dump air through covered slots located just behind the upper intake lip. The auxiliary intakes also are mounted dorsally.

When the Pratt & Whitney YF119-PW-100 was selected as the ATF propulsion system winner over the General Electric YF120-GE-100, the long term production potential for the engine equated to some 1,500 units with production to be initiated during 1997. Experience with the engine by late 1992 totaled over 3,000 hours of ground and air time. Some 1,500 of those hours included tests with two-dimensional exhaust nozzles.

The YF-22A's pre-production Pratt & Whitney YF119-PW-100 and the F/A-22A's production F119-PW-100 are counter-rotating, dual rotor, augmented turbofan engines. The low-pressure rotor consists of a three-stage fan driven by a single-stage low-pressure turbine. The high-pressure rotor consists of a six-stage high-pressure compressor driven by a single-stage high-pressure turbine. High-pressure compressor exit guide vanes are cast as an integral part of the strutless diffuser. The exhaust system consists of a fully modulating cooled augmenter and a rectangular, two-dimensional, convergent-divergent nozzle with a thrust vectoring (TV) capability (plus or minus 20° in the vertical plane).

The flight control system commands the nozzle vector angle through the engine control system. Nozzle exit area and thrust vector angle are set by upper and lower divergent flaps which are each independently powered by a pair of hydraulic actuators.

The engine is controlled by a redundant, engine mounted full-authority digital engine control (FADEC) which interfaces with hydraulic actuators on the nozzle, fuel throttling valves, and compression system variable geometry. Hydraulic and electrical power for the control system are supplied by an independent engine-mounted hydraulic system and engine-mounted generator.

All engine accessories are positioned at the bottom of the engine for easy maintenance access. An engine change can be accommodated in under 90 minutes using a single Boeing-developed, six-axis A/M32M-34 trailer for support and movement. The trailer is approximately 14 ft. in length and 6 ft. wide. When fully lowered by means of its mechanically actuated scissor lift assembly, the trailer's height is only 38 in. Maximum height is 5 ft.; The trailer's empty weight is 3,400 lbs. and maximum payload capacity is 7,500 lbs.

An AlliedSignal G250 APU is located in the F/A-22A's port wing root and supplies engine starting power and initial electrical power. There is a stored energy system (SECS) bottle for engine-out restart.

The F119-PW-100 is rated in the 35,000 lb. th. in afterburner class. Military power is approximately 23,500 lb. th. Production engines differ from those utilized in the ATF prototypes only in having a slight increase in fan section diameter and a somewhat different exhaust nozzle configuration.

The F119 has 40% fewer major parts than current fighter engines, and each part is more durable and does its job more efficiently. Computational fluid dynamics (CFD) – the study of airflow using advanced computers – led to the design of engine turbomachinery of unprecedented efficiency, giving the F119 more thrust with fewer turbine stages.

The F119 cuts requirements for support equipment and labor by half, which, among other things, reduces the amount of spares required for transportation during combat zone deployments. It is estimated the F119 will require 75% fewer shop visits for routine maintenance than predecessor engines.

F119 features include:
- Integrally bladed rotors: in most stages, disks and blades are made from a single piece of metal for better performance and less air leakage.
- Long chord, shroudless, hollow (for weight savings) fan blades: wider, stronger fan blades eliminate the need for the shroud, a ring of

Below left: **F/A-22A fuel system static test rig included plumbing for four jettisonable wing tanks.** Lockheed Martin

Below right: **Inflight refueling receptable, normally covered by two hydraulically actuated doors, is mounted dorsally on the F/A-22A's centerline.** Lockheed Martin

metal around most turbofan engine fan sections; both the wider blades and shroudless design contribute to engine efficiency.

• Low-aspect, high-stage-load compressor blades; wider blades offer greater strength and efficiency.

• Alloy C high-strength burn-resistant titanium compressor stators: Pratt & Whitney's innovative titanium alloy increases stator durability, allowing the engine to run hotter and faster for greater thrust and efficiency.

• Alloy C in augmentor and nozzle: the same heat-resistant titanium alloy protects aft components, permitting greater thrust and durability.

• Floatwall combustor; thermally isolated panels of oxidation-resistant high cobalt material make the combustion chamber more durable, which helps reduce scheduled maintenance.

• Fourth-generation full-authority digital electronic engine control (FADEC): dual-redundant digital engine controls – two units per engine, two computers per unit – ensure unmatched reliability in engine control systems. The same experience that introduced full-authority digital control to fighter engines works with the aircraft

Right: **Boeing developed the A/M32M-34 trailer to ease the installation and removal of the F119-PW-100 engine.It permits extremely precise vertical and lateral movement of the engine.** Jay Miller

Right: **Lower vectorable exhaust nozzle flap.** Jay Miller

Below: **When sitting statically, vectorable exhaust nozzle flaps are in fully extended non-symmetric position.** Jay Miller

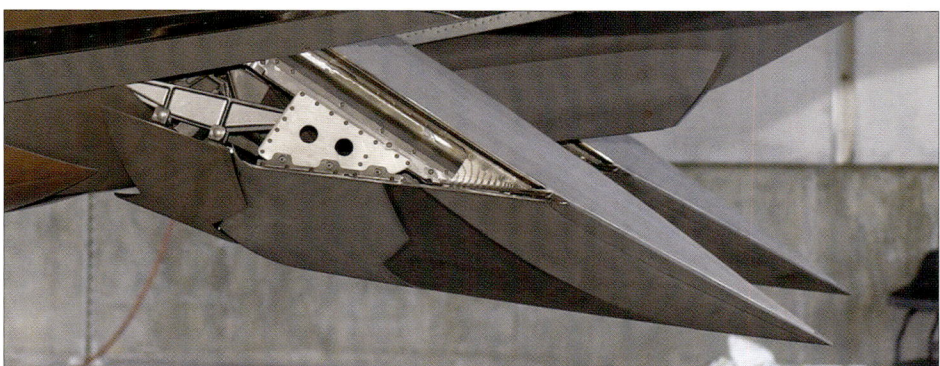

Above: **F119-PW-100 vectoring capability is demononstrated by this multiple-exposure photograph.** Pratt & Whitney

Left and bottom: **Two images depicting F119-PW-100 static test rig. Water injection cools exhaust and helps attenuate noise.** Pratt & Whitney x 2

Facing page, right: **F119-PW-100 vectored exhaust in full afterburner.** Pratt & Whitney

Facing page, bottom: **Right and left fixed-ramp intakes are optimized to meet low observables requirements.** Jay Miller x 2

system to make engine and aircraft functions as a single flight unit.

• No visible smoke: reduces the possibility of an enemy visually detecting the F/A-22A.

• Improved supportability: all components, harnesses, and plumbing are located on the bottom of the engine for easy access, all line replaceable units (LRUs) are located one deep (units are not located on top of one another), and each LRU can be removed with just one of the six standard tools required for engine maintenance.

The F119 nozzle is the world's first full production vectoring nozzle, fully integrated into the F/A-22A/engine combination as original equipment. The two-dimensional nozzle vectors thrust 20° up and down for improved aircraft agility. This vectoring increases not only rate of pitch, but also the F/A-22A's roll rate by 50% and has features that contribute to the aircraft's low-observables requirements.

Heat resistant components give the nozzles the durability needed to vector thrust, even in afterburner conditions. With precision digital controls, the nozzles work like another aircraft flight control surface. Thrust vectoring is an integral part of the F/A-22A's flight control system, which allows for seamless integration of all components working in response to pilot commands. The nozzle is manufactured at Pratt & Whitney's West Palm Beach, Florida facility.

The F/A-22A also has an airframe mounted accessory drive (AMAD). Built by Boeing the AMAD transfers shaft power from the Air Turbine Starter System (ATSS) to the F119s for engine starts, and from the engines to a generator and hydraulic pumps for the electrical and hydraulic systems. The AMAD transmits power required by the F/A-22A throughout its flight envelope and incorporates a high-reliability lubrication system that services the AMAD-

mounted generator and ATSS as well as gearbox components.

The General Electric YF120-GE-100 was also a counter-rotating, dual rotor, variable-cycle, augmented turbofan engine. It was controlled by a triplex, engine-mounted, full-authority digital engine control unit (ECU). The low-pressure rotor consisted of a two-stage fan driven by a single-stage high-pressure turbine. The variable cycle technology enabled the engine to operate as a conventional turbojet at supersonic speeds, while exhibiting the characteristics of a more fuel efficient turbofan at subsonic cruise speeds. The nozzle was a two-dimensional convergent/divergent design with a thrust vectoring capability.

One of the primary low observables areas of concern was the F/A-22A's exhaust system. In order to maintain the low observables objectives of the rest of the design, the exhaust system and associated empennage area were required to meet edge orientation and surface discontinuity specifications. Additionally, they

were required to incorporate high-temperature technologies. These were required to provide broadband low observable performance without inhibiting the exhaust system's propulsion performance.

The F/A-22A's JP-8 (naphthalene-based) fuel load is carried in eight tanks located in the forward fuselage, mid-fuselage, wings, and each of the tailbooms. Provision for additional fuel in the form of saddle and fin tanks has been made in all production aircraft. Additionally, the aircraft is capable of carrying up to four external F-15-type fuel tanks (two per wing on Edo BRU-47A racks attached to hardpoints) – each carrying 600 US gallons – for long range ferry missions. All fuel tanks on the F/A-22A are inerted using OBIGGS-generated nitrogen.

A Xar Industries inflight refueling receptacle, covered by two butterfly doors with integral low-voltage lights for night refueling, is exposed upon pilot command and is located dorsally, at about the mid-fuselage point on centerline.

Chapter Seven

YF-22A and F/A-22A Gallery

The General Electric YF120-GE-100 -powered YF-22A, N22YF during its first flight on September 29, 1990. Lockheed's Bob Ferguson was pilot.

Pratt & Whitney YF119-PW-100 engine and exhaust nozzle as installed on YF-22A, N22YX.

Pratt & Whitney YF119-PW-100 -powered YF-22A, N22YX. Pratt & Whitney logo is visible on intake cheek.

Pratt & Whitney YF119 -PW-100-powered YF-22A, N22YX (foreground) and General Electric YF120-GE-100 -powered YF-22A, N22YF.

EMD YF-22A, 91-4002, with left main weapon bay door open. Three AIM-120s are visible.

Boeing's prototype 757, N757A, served as a flying laboratory for the YF-22A and F/A-22A avionics and weapon systems.

Second EMD F/A-22A, 91-4002, was – among several tasks – the spin test airframe. It was temporarily equipped with a spin recovery chute system.

Main instrument panel of F/A-22A, 00-4013. Noteworthy is the lack of analog instrumention of any kind. Landing gear handle is visible on left.

Second EMD F/A-22A, 91-4002, undergoing static engine run at night.

The second EMD F/A-22A poses for a special photo session under the auspices of chief Lockheed photographer, Eric Schulzinger.

F/A-22A, 01-4027, sans paint. It has since been delivered to Tyndall AFB, Florida. Various radar absorbent panels are readily discernible.

F/A-22A, 02-4035, turning final to Marietta, Georgia. Aircraft since has been delivered to Tyndall AFB, Florida.

An unidentified EMD F/A-22A over the Edwards test range. Deflected full-span leading edge flaps are noteworthy.

Another view of the second EMD F/A-22A, 91-4002, with spin recovery chute system attached via tripod mount. Chute was ballistically deployed.

Unusual head-on view of F/A-22A, 01-4018, hangared at Tyndall AFB, Florida.

With the moon sitting in the background, Edwards-based post-EMD F/A-22A, 91-4010, takes on fuel from Boeing KC-135R, 60-366.

F/A-22As move down the production line at Lockheed Martin's Marietta, Georgia facility. Production tolerances are measured to .0001 inch.

EMD F/A-22A, 91-4007, during departure from Edwards AFB. Position of exhaust deflectors is noteworthy.

Unidentified EMD F/A-22A, probably 91-4002, with main weapon bay doors open. Test instrumentation package is positioned in the right bay half.

F/A-22A, 02-4032, during ground inspection and prior to static engine run in bay at Lockheed Martin's Marietta, Georgia facility.

F/A-22A, 01-4025, on final to Marietta, Georgia and prior to delivery to Nellis AFB. Tailhook fairing is readily visible between engine nacelles.

F/A-22A, 02-4032 overhead at Marietta, Georgia. Aircraft has since been delivered to Tyndall AFB, Florida.

F/A-22A, 02-4032, inside engine ground run hangar at Marietta, Georgia on November 8, 2004.

Exhaust nozzle vector flaps work in unison during inflight maneuvering. They are seen in their maximum "open" position in this view of 02-4032.

Ten Pratt & Whitney F119-PW-100 afterburning, vectorable-thrust, turbofans in depot at Marietta, Georgia awaiting installation in new F/A-22As.

Vectorable exhaust nozzle assembly is an integral part of the Pratt & Whitney F119-PW-100.

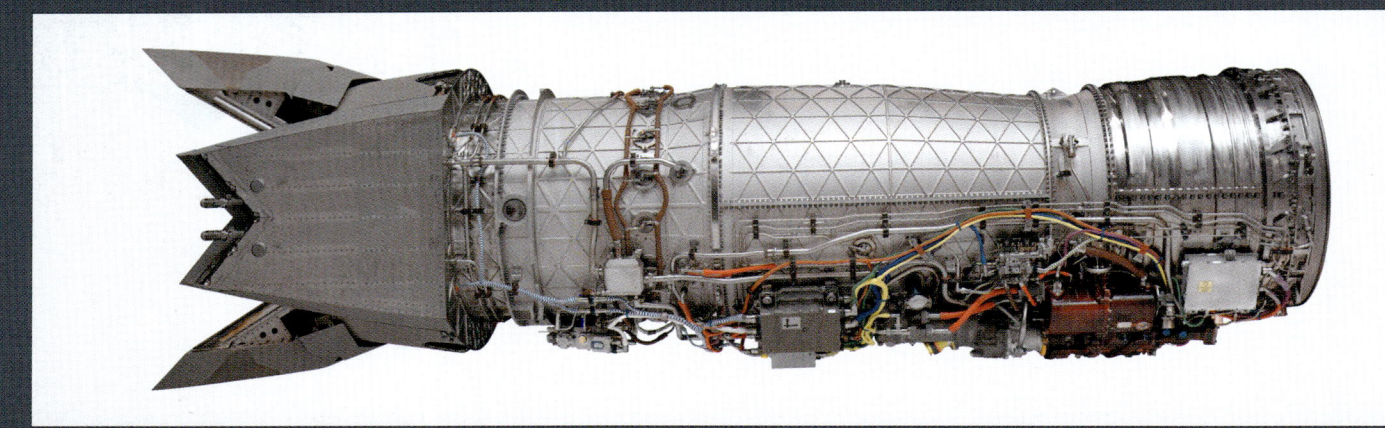

Right-side view of a production-standard Pratt & Whitney F119-PW-100 afterburning turbofan engine with vectorable exhaust nozzle.

Left-side view of a production-standard Pratt & Whitney F119-PW-100 afterburning turbofan engine with vectorable exhaust nozzle.

Pratt & Whitney F119-PW-100 on Boeing A/M32M-34 trailer.

Exhaust assembly view of Pratt & Whitney F119-PW-100.

Twin exhaust nozzle assemblies and associated vectorable ramps of Pratt & Whitney F119-PW-100 as installed in F/A-22A, 02-4032.

We hope you enjoyed this book . . .

Midland Publishing offers an extensive range of outstanding aviation titles, of which a small selection are shown here.

We always welcome ideas from authors or readers for books they would like to see published.

In addition, our associate, Midland Counties Publications, offers an exceptionally wide range of aviation, military, naval and transport books and videos for sale by mail-order worldwide.

For a copy of the appropriate catalogue, or to order further copies of this book, and any other Midland Publishing titles, please write, telephone, fax or e-mail to:

Midland Counties Publications
4 Watling Drive, Hinckley,
Leics, LE10 3EY, England
Tel: (+44) 01455 254 450
Fax: (+44) 01455 233 737
E-mail: midlandbooks@compuserve.com
www.midlandcountiessuperstore.com

US distribution by Specialty Press – see page 2.

Aerofax
LOCKHEED'S SR-71 'BLACKBIRD' FAMILY

James Goodall and Jay Miller

Though only 50 of these craft were built, everything about them was unique. The stories of the development program, the General Dynamics 'Kingfish' competition, the M-21 and D-21 effort, the F-12 saga, and the operational history of the A-12 and SR-71 under the auspices of the CIA and the USAF are all covered in detail. The high-speed, high-altitude recce overflights performed by SR-71As from bases in the US, Japan and the UK during the Cold War are also covered.

Softback, 280 x 215 mm, 128 pages, 205 b/w, 43 colour photos, plus illusts
1 85780 138 5 **£15.99**

Aerofax
BELL BOEING V-22 OSPREY
Multi-Service Tiltrotor

Bill Norton

This technologically challenging tiltrotor project established in 1982. A transport aircraft style fuselage, able to carry 24 troops, is topped by a wing with two swivelling pods housing Rolls-Royce engines, each driving three-bladed prop-rotors. The USAF should receive the CV-22B for special missions, the US Marines the MV-22B assault transports and the Navy the HV-22B CSAR/fleet logistics version, but the program suffered setbacks, with initial operating capability now set for 2005.

Softback, 280 x 215 mm, 128 pages
174 colour, 60 b/w photos, 33 dwgs
1 85780 165 2 **£16.99**

Aerofax
SAAB GRIPEN
Sweden's 21st Century Multi-role Aircraft

Gerard Keijsper

Today's Swedish Air Force has as its spearhead the Saab Gripen. A fourth-generation fighter that embraces state-of-the-art technology, the Gripen has an impressive multi-role capability, making it a more than worthy successor to the Viggen and Draken.

First flown in 1988, operational capability with the Swedish Air Force was achieved in October 1997. Production continues and sales are being made to South Africa, Hungary, Poland and the Czech Republic.

Softback, 280 x 215 mm, 144 pages
230 colour photographs, plus dwgs
1 85780 137 7 **£19.99**

MCDONNELL DOUGLAS F-4 PHANTOM II
Production and Operational Data

William R Peake

The McDonnell Douglas F-4 Phantom II is an aircraft with a long history and global presence. Although the F-4 is no longer in production, the 5,000+ airplanes have yet to be accurately chronicled on an individual basis.

The book lists each airplane in production order, and list block number, serial number, attrition date and circumstances, aerial 'kills', retirement date and circumstances, tail codes, and other essential details.

Softback, 280 x 215 mm, 360 pages, 191 colour photographs
1 85780 190 3 **£27.99**

AIR ARSENAL NORTH AMERICA Aircraft for the Allies 1938-1945 – Purchases & Lend-Lease

Phil Butler with Dan Hagedorn

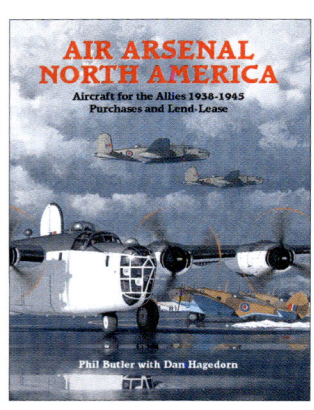

A detailed analysis of aircraft purchases made in North America by the British Commonwealth and European democracies during 1938-1945 and the subsequent operation of the Lend-Lease Acts and Canadian Mutual Aid.

All of the many aircraft types are described and illustrated; supplemented by sections covering their operation by each of the countries involved, including aircraft serials, delivery routes, and various appendices.

Hardback , 282 x 213 mm, 320 pages
600 b/w photos, some colour
1 85780 163 6 **£40.00**

AIR WAR ON THE EDGE
A History of the Israel Air Force and its Aircraft since 1947

Bill Norton

An in-depth book on the aircraft, units and exploits of the Israel Air Force. Detailed type-by-type coverage supported by a barrage of photographs follows the IAF from the mixed bag of aircraft of its formative days, through the Suez Campaign, the Six Day War, Yom Kippur and on to today's sophisticated, well-equipped force. Included for the first time are all of the badges and heraldry of the units of the IAF, in full colour.

Hardback, 282 x 213 mm, 432pp, 470 b/w, 60 col photos, 147 unit markings
1 85780 088 5 **£50.00**

VIETNAM AIR LOSSES
USAF, Navy and Marine Corps Fixed-Wing Aircraft Losses in SE Asia 1961-1973

Chris Hobson

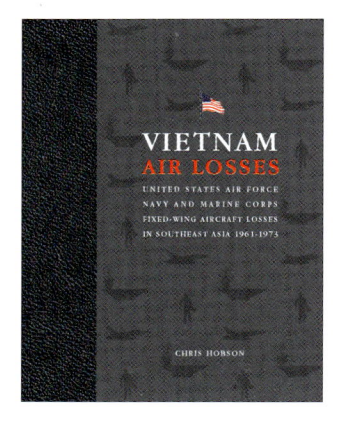

A most thorough and detailed review of all the fixed-wing losses suffered by the USAF, USN and USMC; basically a chronological recording of each aircraft loss including information on unit, personnel, location and cause of loss. Information is also provided on the background or future career of some of the aircrew involved.

Interspersed with the text is background information on campaigns, units, aircraft and weapons etc.

Softback , 280 x 215 mm, 288 pages
133 b/w photographs
1 85780 115 6 **£19.95**